Youth Identities and Social Transformations in Modern Indonesia

Verhandelingen van het Koninklijk Instituut voor Taal-, Land- en Volkenkunde

Edited by

Rosemarijn Hoefte (*KITLV, Leiden*)
Henk Schulte Nordholt (*KITLV, Leiden*)

Editorial Board

Michael Laffan (*Princeton University*)
Adrian Vickers (*Sydney University*)
Anna Tsing (*University of California Santa Cruz*)

VOLUME 302

The titles published in this series are listed at *brill.com/vki*

Youth Identities and Social Transformations in Modern Indonesia

Edited by

Kathryn Robinson

BRILL

LEIDEN | BOSTON

The realization of this publication was made possible by the support of KITLV (Royal Netherlands Institute of Southeast Asian and Caribbean Studies).

Library of Congress Cataloging-in-Publication Data

Names: Robinson, Kathryn May, 1949- editor.
Title: Youth identities and social transformations in modern Indonesia / edited by Kathryn Robinson.
Description: Leiden ; Boston : Brill, 2016. | Series: Verhandelingen van het koninklijk instituut voor taal-, land- en volkenkunde ; volume 302 | Includes bibliographical references and index.
Identifiers: LCCN 2015035169| ISBN 9789004290464 (hardback) | ISBN 9789004307445 (e-book)
Subjects: LCSH: Youth--Indonesia--Social conditions.
Classification: LCC HQ799.I6 Y68 2016 | DDC 305.23509598--dc 3
LC record available at http://lccn.loc.gov/2015035169

This publication has been typeset in the multilingual "Brill" typeface. With over 5,100 characters covering Latin, IPA, Greek, and Cyrillic, this typeface is especially suitable for use in the humanities. For more information, please see www.brill.com/brill-typeface.

ISSN 1572-1892
ISBN 978-90-04-29046-4 (hardback)
ISBN 978-90-04-30744-5 (e-book)

Copyright 2016 by Koninklijke Brill NV, Leiden, The Netherlands.
Koninklijke Brill NV incorporates the imprints Brill, Brill Hes & De Graaf, Brill Nijhoff, Brill Rodopi and Hotei Publishing.
All rights reserved. No part of this publication may be reproduced, translated, stored in a retrieval system, or transmitted in any form or by any means, electronic, mechanical, photocopying, recording or otherwise, without prior written permission from the publisher.
Authorization to photocopy items for internal or personal use is granted by Koninklijke Brill NV provided that the appropriate fees are paid directly to The Copyright Clearance Center, 222 Rosewood Drive, Suite 910, Danvers, MA 01923, USA.
Fees are subject to change.

This book is printed on acid-free paper.

Contents

Preface: Being Young in Indonesia   IX
List of Figures and Tables   XII
Notes on Contributors   XIV

PART 1
Studying Indonesia's Youth: The Big Picture

Introduction to Part 1   2

1   Generation and Social Change: Indonesian Youth in Comparative Perspective   4
    Ben White

2   Contemporary Indonesian Youth Transitions: Trends and Inequalities   23
    Pam Nilan, Lyn Parker, Kathryn Robinson, and Linda Bennett

PART 2
Education—Securing Youth Futures?

Introduction to Part 2   48

3   Teenage Experiences of School, Work, and Life in a Javanese Village   50
    Ben White and C. Ugik Margiyatin

4   Educational Aspirations and Inter-Generational Relations in Sorowako   69
    Kathryn Robinson

PART 3
Friendship, Growing Up, and Peer Surveillance

Introduction to Part 3 92

5   Pouring Out One's Heart: Close Friendships among Minangkabau Young People 94
Lyn Parker

6   Pramuka: Scouting Days of Fun 113
Pujo Semedi

PART 4
Performing Youth in Space and Time

Introduction to Part 4 132

7   Dwindling Space and Expanding Worlds for Youth in Rural and Urban Yogyakarta 134
Patrick Guinness

8   Local Modernities: Young Women Socializing Together 156
Pam Nilan

PART 5
Performing Masculinity, Claiming the Street

Introduction to Part 5 178

9   Streetwise Masculinity and Other Urban Performances of Postwar Ambon: A Photo-Essay 179
Patricia Spyer

10   Violent Activism, Islamist Ideology, and the Conquest of Public Space among Youth in Indonesia 200
Noorhaidi Hasan

PART 6
"Moral Panics" And the Health of the Nation

    Introduction to Part 6   216

11   The Ongoing Culture Debate: Female Youth and *Pergaulan* (*Bebas*) in Yogyakarta, Indonesia   218
      Tracy Wright Webster

12   Young Sasak Mothers—"*Tidak Manja Lagi*": Transitioning from Single Daughter to Young Married Mother in Lombok, Eastern Indonesia   238
      Linda Rae Bennett

    Index   263

Preface: Being Young in Indonesia

Fifty percent of Indonesia's 240 million people are under 30. This, the fourth most populous nation in the world and the country with the world's largest Muslim population, is still in the midst of a messy process of democratization after decades of authoritarian rule. The economy is booming and it is on the verge of becoming a major regional power. Today's youth is key to future prosperity and development. But we know little about the multiple lifeworlds of Indonesian youth or of the varied patterns of transition from youth to adulthood that characterize the socially, economically and politically diverse cultures of the archipelago.

Political actions by Indonesia's young people were a critical catalyst for the dramatic regime change in 1998[1] and today's youth will remain central to Indonesian social, cultural, economic and political development for decades to come. In a popular Indonesian patriotic formulation, youth form the *generasi penerus* ("generation taking the nation forward to the future"). The term *pemuda* (youth) invokes, for Indonesians, the struggle for independence in the 1940s. However, other popular discourses characterize Indonesia's youth as moral hazards. As the Indonesian economy has grown more affluent and open to the world, public "moral panics" are the result of concerns over the deleterious impacts of "globalization" on young people. These include the influences of western popular culture and youth lifestyle, but also its apparent converse: the public displays of piety, street politics, and even political violence, associated with global Islamist movements. In these framings, youths, as they move into adulthood, are caught in the midst of a fraught and uncertain process and, moreover, they present risks to a healthy future national development.

This volume addresses the main question: what are the challenges facing Indonesia's young people as they move into adulthood? It also asks: what does a focus on young people, and particularly their own views of their lives and futures, tell us about contemporary Indonesia and its future? Studies of the political, social, and cultural transformation in the post-Suharto era—the political and administrative changes of democratization and decentralization—have not generally addressed the experience and role of the nation's youth, despite their critical role as agents of change and the architects of Indonesia's future.

---

1   President Suharto was forced to resign as President in 1998 after protests, which included the occupation of the Parliament in Jakarta. He was succeeded by his Vice-President B.J. Habibie who implemented the dramatic political reforms of democratic elections and decentralization.

This volume provides a broad and diversified view of Indonesia's youth, through close-focused studies in a range of locations, from Sumatra in the West to the Moluccas in the east, and which include both rural and urban environments, and large and small cities. The contributors engage with the lifeworlds of Indonesia's young people from a variety of perspectives, including experiences of school and transitions to work; sexuality, masculinity and femininity; class differences and youth experience; gangs, violence and religious radicalism; youth agency; friendship; and cultural expression—all in the context of young people negotiating the dramatic changes of the last few decades.

Authors employ different ways of accessing youth views, from participation in their everyday worlds, seeking their voices, and engaging with their forms of creative expression. The authors are all anthropologists who deploy ethnographic, youth-centered approaches in particular sites, thereby capturing young people's views about their own lives and experience. Some of the papers are by authors who have rich longitudinal historical and intergenerational perspectives on particular communities derived from decades of ethnographic research; others explore hitherto poorly researched areas. The authors engage with a wide range of scholarly research on youth, employing perspectives offered in youth studies and related research in anthropology, sociology and cultural studies, thereby bringing an Indonesian perspective into these bodies of knowledge.

This volume is organized into six sections to bring together chapters that have a particular focus on some of the themes mentioned above. The first section provides the "Big Picture" of the social science approaches to youth, and national snapshots of Indonesian youth experience. Section two asks if education can secure youth futures; the following sections explore friendship; the performance of youth in social spaces; performing masculinity and claiming the street; and the final section addresses moral panics and the health of the nation.

Contributions to this volume originate from research conducted by two major collaborative projects involving leading anthropological researchers on Indonesia. The first was the Dutch-Indonesian project *In Search of Middle Indonesia* (2006–2010)[2] that researched post-Suharto developments in medium-sized towns across the archipelago, and the generational space between child

---

2 This was a joint Netherlands-Indonesia research consortium, funded through a grant from the Royal Netherlands Academy of Sciences (KNAW) under SPIN (Indonesia-Netherlands Cooperation Program). Participating institutions were Gadjah Mada University, Jogjakarta, the Institute of Social Studies in The Hague (ISS), the Amsterdam School for Social Science Research at the University of Amsterdam (ASSR-UvA), the Department of Cultural Anthropology and Development Sociology, Faculty of Social Sciences, Leiden University, and KITLV.

and adult was one of its foci. The project aimed to reframe our understanding of Indonesia by shifting the focus from the commanding heights of central politics and elites to neglected research spaces such as the generational space noted above, as well as the spaces between village and metropolitan city, the upper-middle classes and the urban poor, formal institutions and markets, and between the cultural meeting ground of global fashions and localized practices. These "in-between" spaces, of which medium sized towns have come into sharper focus, have become more critical to Indonesia's future through the political and administrative changes (democratization and decentralization) since 1998. The studies from that project, published in this volume, underscore the significance of youth as a motor of change.

The second contributing project was the Australian Research Council-funded *Ambivalent Adolescents in Indonesia* (2006–2009) (henceforth AAI),[3] which explored the experiences of mainly high-school age students in a range of rural and urban sites across the archipelago. The project addressed the question: In what ways do adolescents in Indonesia embody social transformation? We hypothesized that adolescents are ambivalent agents because they are subjected to conflicting discourses, such as those from their parents and communities, the nation-state, their schools and religious teachers, and globalization. The project explored Indonesian adolescents' experience in seven fields: education; religious, cultural and national identity; the body and sexuality; parents and family; social life; popular culture; and work. These themes all emerge in the contributions to this volume.

The papers were originally presented at the joint workshop *Growing up in Indonesia: Experience and Diversity in Youth Transitions*[4] which was funded by the Australia-Netherlands Research Council and held at the Australian National University in Canberra in 2008.

Kathryn Robinson

---

[3] DP ARC DP0663600. Discovery Project Funded by the Australian Research Council 2006–2009. Chief Investigators: Lynette Parker, Linda Bennett, Pam Nilan, Kathryn Robinson.

[4] 28–30 September 2008. Some of the papers from this workshop have been published in a special issue of *The Asia Pacific Journal of Anthropology*: *Growing up in Indonesia: Experience and Diversity in Youth Transitions*, edited by Patricia Spyer and Ben White, Volume 13, Issue 1, 2012.

List of Figures and Tables

Figures

9.1 to 9.4	Christian billboards and murals in and around Ambon City, 2003–11	182
9.5	Motorbike taxi-stand, Ambon City	184
9.6	Motorbike taxi-stand with Megawati Soekarnoputri, Ambon City, 2003	184
9.7	The fading reputation of a former president, Ambon City, 2005	184
9.8	Motorbike emblem and the 'orange' and lion of the Dutch national soccer team, Ambon City	184
9.9	A spontaneous sidewalk market Ambon City, 2003	186
9.10	Motorbike taxi-stand with text from a Dutch Christmas Card, Ambon City, 2011	186
9.11	Jesus overlooks Ambon Island on a dismantled billboard, Ambon 2006	187
9.12	A 'native Jesus' looks down on refugees fleeing on Seram Island. Soahuku, 2005	187
9.13	Entrance to a Christian neighborhood. Ambon, 2005	189
9.14	Jesus portrait. Ambon, 2003	190
9.15	Jesus portrait. Ambon, 2005	190
9.16	Dokumentasi of a motorbike taxi-stand, Ambon 2006	196
9.17	Motorbiker poses on Christmas morning in front of a Jesus billboard, Ambon 2006	196
11.1	Student responses to brainstorming activity on "what is *pergaulan bebas*"?	224
12.1	Young mothers and their children relaxing after an informal focus group	244
12.2	Young mother Desi proudly presenting her robust son Fatahila	249
12.3	Nuri dressed in her sarong, which she refers to as her "old/bad clothes"	252

Tables

2.1	Surveys collected by location	29
2.2	Snapshot	31
2.3	Job desired as a percentage, compared to fathers' work as a percentage	33
2.4	Elements of the good life: relative importance ranked by means	34

2.5   Main life dreams by sex   37
2.6   Class location by obstacles to dreams   39
2.7   Correlation of class location with obstacle: lack of money, resources, opportunities   40
2.8   Correlation of class location with obstacle: laziness, negative personal traits   40
11.1 Frequency of responses regarding issues confronted by youth in the *Yogyakarta* sample   223

Notes on Contributors

Linda Rae Bennett
is a medical anthropologist based at the Nossal Institute for Global Health at The University of Melbourne. Her research interests include sexual and reproductive health and rights, youth sexuality and gender relations in Indonesian society. She is co-editor of the recent volume: *Sex and Sexualities in Indonesian Society* (with Sharyn Graham).

Noorhaidi Hasan
is Professor of Islam and Politics and currently director of the Graduate Faculty at Sunan Kalijaga State Islamic University of Yogyakarta, Indonesia. Holding a PhD from Utrecht University, the Netherlands, his research interests include Islamic radicalism, youth, and democracy in Southeast Asia.

Patrick Guinness
is Associate Professor at the Australian National University. He previously taught at Universitas Indonesia, Universitas Gadjah Mada, and Universitas Airlangga, and has conducted research in a number of Indonesian provinces, but has a long-term focus on Yogyakarta's urban *kampung* and rural villages.

Catharina Ugik Margiyatin
has a BA in Sociology from Gadjah Mada University, Yogyakarta. She currently works for the Indonesia's Forestry Department, in a mangrove conservation and coastal management project in Bali.

Pam Nilan
is Professor of Sociology at the University of Newcastle, Australia. She has published widely on youth in Indonesia, and also on masculinity and popular culture. Her most recent book is *Adolescents in Contemporary Indonesia*, (Routledge 2013 [with Lyn Parker]).

Kathryn Robinson
is Professor of Anthropology at the Australian National University. Her research on the Sorowako mine has explored the development impact of resource industries, and she has published on gender relations in Indonesia, and Islam in eastern Indonesia.

Pujo Semedi
is an Associate Professor in the Department of Anthropology, Gadjah Mada University. Currently his research is focused on agrarian dynamics and rural social life in Indonesia, based on the case of palm oil cultivation in West Kalimantan.

Patricia Spyer
is Chair of Cultural Anthropology of Contemporary Indonesia at Leiden University. Her most recent book is *Images That Move* (SAR Press 2013) and she is co-editor of the *Handbook of Material Culture* (Sage 2013).

Tracy Wright Webster
is pursuing research interests in gender & environmental issues in Indonesia and is working together with the local community in Jepara (Java, Indonesia) to restore the R.A. Kartini Museum.

Ben White
is Emeritus Professor of Rural Sociology at the International Institute of Social Studies, The Hague. His research has focused mainly on processes of agrarian change and the anthropology and history of childhood and youth, especially in Indonesia.

PART 1

Studying Indonesia's Youth: The Big Picture

Introduction to Part 1

What insights can be derived from an examination of the experience of Indonesia's youth by using social science-based approaches that have been applied in other countries? How can the results of Indonesia's experience be read back into this literature, and impact on its wider ideas? Ben White sets out this juxtaposition in a wide–ranging review of "youth studies" literature. The shifting and variable terminology used in this literature, including "youth" and "adolescence", does not automatically correspond with Indonesian terms such as *pemuda*, *remaja*, and *dewasa*, or more modern terms such as ABG (*anak baru gede*—"newly grown children"). *Remaja* is a relatively new term that implies a period of detachment from one's parents, and the development of an independence now associated with schooling, and which Guinness (in this volume) argues developed in tandem with youth engagement in mass consumption. *Pemuda*, as noted above, is a more global term for the younger generation (encompassing *remaja*), but associated with the period of transition into adulthood (*dewasa*). It continues to carry overtones of a historic vanguard that had a key role in taking the nation forward. *Remaja* (adolescents) begin to create their own social by worlds imitating or engaging with the lifestyles and ideas of their peers and the information they acquire through TV, books and magazines, internet or other media: "They begin to detach themselves from the parental and adult world and to feel the need to be less controlled by it" (White and Margiyatin, this volume).

White argues that scholars (and policy makers) should regard youths as key actors in social change in their own right, and that they should not always be seen in relation to adults. His introduction sets out a position taken up by the authors in this volume that provides a corrective to the tendency of some scholars to write about youth, and hence allows for a challenge to popular stereotypes and the prevailing scholarly wisdom surrounding youth.

The second "Big Picture" chapter (Nilan et al) is a national "snapshot" of high school students, based on the results of a survey conducted by the AAI team, which involved a purposive sample of high school students from nine sites across the archipelago. Most of these sites are explored in further ethnographic chapters in this book (see chapters by Bennett, Parker, Robinson, Wright Webster). Survey results are contextualized in a review of recent research on youth in Indonesia.

The AAI survey compares the views of 16- to 18-year-olds from cities and rural areas, and from Islamic and secular schools, in all the communities where members of the AAI research team conducted their ethnographic studies. So, for example, while the AAI survey found that young people voice some popular assumptions about their peers, in particular anxiety about declining morality, they do not assume these concerns apply to themselves or their friends. The chapter asks what these young people aspire to and how they see themselves in the future, and whether hopes and dreams are shared by youth across the archipelago.

CHAPTER 1

Generation and Social Change: Indonesian Youth in Comparative Perspective

Ben White

Understanding Young People's Lives

One important strength of the modern field of youth studies is its insistence that we study young people in their own right and from their own perspectives, rather than subsuming them under other disciplines; as such, the study of youth is now a more autonomous discipline, with its own frameworks and with youth at the center. This autonomy however, brings with it possible problems and weaknesses, in particular the danger that youth studies may isolate itself from broader studies of social change. Consequently, we need to position young people within larger societal structures, and such a relational dimension has been relatively neglected in recent social studies of youth.

Understanding young people's lives requires us to look at both how youth is "constructed" (imagined and represented as a meaningful social, economic and political category), and also how it is actually experienced by the young. The sometimes wide gap between construction and experience is one key to understanding young people's lives. The study of young people has been approached in many interesting and mostly complementary ways: youth as action, youth as cultural practice, youth as cultural production, youth as identity, and youth as transition (Jones 2009). We can find examples of all of these approaches in studies of Indonesian youth. While all of these are fruitful, this chapter takes a mainly relational approach, seeing youth first and foremost in terms of the dynamics of their relationship with others (adults), in larger structures of social reproduction. The notions of generation, social reproduction, and intersectionality are central to this approach.

---

[1] Emeritus Professor of Rural Sociology, International Institute of Social Studies, The Hague (white@iss.nl). This chapter is based on a paper first presented in Canberra (White 2009). Parts of that paper were expanded into an overview article on Indonesian youth studies (Naafs and White 2012); other parts were further transmogrified for a chapter focusing on rural youth employment and agricultural futures (White 2012a). This chapter includes elements of all three papers, as well as some new material.

The social and scientific construction of youth tends to see it as a period of "transition"—from child to adult, from education to employment, from family of origin to family of destination (for example: Lloyd 2005; Roberts 2009). This is also the case within policy literature; an example of this is the World Bank's report *Development and the Next Generation* (World Bank 2006), which sees youth in terms of these interlinked transitions. But it is important to understand that young people do not necessarily see themselves in this way, or only in this way. Often they are busy developing youth cultures and identities in their own right, as they try to be successful now, as youth, in the eyes of their peers, rather than trying to prepare themselves to be successful future adults. In other words, the "transitionality" that is such a key dimension of conventional categorizations of youth may not be the dominant dimension of youth identity. We can better explore how these two dimensions—"being young" and "growing up"—coexist in dynamic tension, as in Minza's (2014) study of young people in Pontianak.

Another, related dimension of the social construction of youth defines it by what it is not: by the absence of certain adult characteristics, rights, or responsibilities which young people supposedly lack. The problem with both negative and transitional concepts is that, at best, they identify an empty conceptual space by telling us what the thing is not, or what it has not yet become. As research progresses these can become a serious hindrance by imposing an *a priori* assumption of direction, of being on the way to some known future state. We need to fill the empty space by replacing negative and in-between definitions (and the concepts which underpin them) with more positive characterizations of what youth is, and how it is experienced.

Young people are often seen as recipients of socialization into adult norms and behaviors. But, in recent years, youth studies has shifted to a more youth-centered view of young people not just as "learners" but as "makers and breakers" (Honwana and de Boeck 2005), "vandals and vanguards" (Abbink and van Kessel 2005), creators and renewers of culture par excellence, as can be seen, for example, in young people's creation of new language, modes of dress and bodily adornment, and lifestyles. This is paralleled by a view of young people as "agents" rather than "victims". Whether young people are rightly perceived as (passive) victims or (active) agents is a non-question and a non-debate when posed in this limiting either/or form. Young people, like adults, can be both victims (or beneficiaries) of structures, and simultaneously individual or collective agents of resistance and change within those structures.

All age-based boundaries of the categories of "childhood" and "youth", whether established by UN agencies or by national governments, are arbitrary (as we shall see in the next section for Indonesia). As we are all aware, youth (like all life-course stages) is socially constructed, not biologically fixed, and its meaning and boundaries vary: over time, between societies, and within societies. Youth boundaries may also be class-specific, and this is why we need to include the notion of intersectionality in the framing of young people's lives. Intersectionality points to the dynamic links and tensions between different, cross-cutting ("intersecting") axes of identity and difference (for example between gender, ethnicity, class, and generation). In Indonesia, for example, many urban middle-class men and women in their late 20s, who are single, completing an MA degree, and who have not yet entered professional employment, would no doubt consider themselves (and be perceived as) "youth". In contrast, many younger men and women, in their early 20s, having left school at 15 or younger and already working as labourers or market traders for many years, and married with two or three children, would consider themselves (and be perceived as) "adult" in their communities (see Bennet, this volume).

Indonesian Youth, Education, and the Postponement of Adulthood: Two Important Generational Trends

One important change that has been happening to Indonesian youth as in many other countries, is its prolongation. As young people remain enrolled for longer in education, as their average age at first marriage rises, as entry into the labor force is postponed, they remain longer in the state of partial or complete dependency on the parental generation (see Robinson, this volume). Another related but in some ways contradictory trend is that each generation grows up, on the average, better educated (but possibly with reduced everyday livelihood skills) than their parents (White, 2012b). Young people thus experience an extended period in which they are biologically adult, and in formal terms "smarter" than their parents and others of that generation, but with adulthood postponed.

While UN definitions of "youth" usually place it in the age range 15–24 (overlapping awkwardly with "child" which in UN definitions covers age 0–17), recent Indonesian law-making (as in some other Asian, African, and Latin American countries) has now prolonged the formal boundaries of "youth" to the advanced age of 30. In the 2009 Law on Youth (UU Perlindungan Anak), "youth" (the persons, *pemuda*) are defined as "Indonesian citizens who are entering an important period of growth and development and are aged between 16 and 30 years" (UU no 40/2009, article 1.1).[2] The reasons for extending the boundary of "youth" to 30 are not explained in the Law or the academic text

---

2 The same Law on Youth defines "youth" in its other sense (*kepemudaan*, i.e. the state or condition, equivalent to "childhood" or "adulthood") as "various matters relating to the potential,

which accompanied it in its journey through the legislature. In formal definitions of "child", Indonesian law follows the UN Convention on the Rights of the Child (in which childhood stops on the 18th birthday), so that young people aged 16 and 17 are both "child" and "youth".[3]

Many children and young people in Indonesia would not see themselves fitting in these categories and constructions. Many young Indonesians in their middle teens do not consider themselves "children", and defining all people under the age of 18 as "children" risks infantilizing those approaching the upper age limit; the only thing that binds 0 to 17 year olds together is their lack of full legal and political standing. Similarly, extending the boundaries of "youth" to 30 or above—even to age 40 according to the Indonesian National Youth Committee (KNPI 2005)—risks juvenilizing young adults as something less than full members of society, less than full citizens. The extended definition identifies an age group many of whose members have already passed the main markers of "transition to adulthood", such as marriage, the completion of education, and employment in the labor force. This supports the notion that the main basis for the extended definition is political.

In Indonesia, young people's own understandings of youth—as far as can be gleaned from the few studies that have examined this—seem to link the transition from "child" (*anak*) to "youth" (*remaja, pemuda*) with the ability to exercise judgment about right and wrong, and the transition from "youth" to "adult" (*dewasa*) with economic independence from the parental generation.[4]

Young People, Generation and Social Reproduction

The importance of "generation" in processes of social change was highlighted by Mannheim's 1928 essay *The Problem of Generations* (1952), and the notion of

---

responsibility, rights, character, capacity, self actualization and aspirations of youth" (UU no 40/2009, article 1.2).

3   The academic text, like the Draft Law, had originally set the age range as 18–35 years, arguing that the lower boundary of youth should not overlap with "child" (0–17) as defined in the UU Perlindungan Anak, another recent law on child protection. It provides no argument for the proposed 35-year end point, but this is in line with many other Asian governments which define the upper boundary of youth as 35 or even 40 years. While Thailand defines youth as up to age 25 and The Philippines to 30, India, Papua New Guinea and Vietnam have extended the boundary to 35 and Malaysia to 40 (Menpora n.d. 30,36).

4   This tentative generalization is derived from the studies by Sano 2012, White and Margiyatun (this volume), and Naafs 2012 (all from Java), and from Minza's study in urban Pontianak, West Kalimantan (Minza, 2014).

"generation" in this sense has inspired much subsequent work on youth studies in relation to social change. It was one of the ideas guiding Koning's pioneering dissertation on "generations of change" in a Javanese village (Koning 1997 and 2005). There are in fact three important, distinct, but related meanings of "generation". The first is the purely demographic notion of a (chronologically-defined) age cohort; not itself of great practical or theoretical relevance, but perforce the basis for all statistical data and analysis on youth. Second is the notion of generation as relationship; as youth are defined not only by the differences between them and adults, but also by particular forms of youth-adult relationship (Alanen 2001). "Generation" in this second sense, like "gender", is a relational term and a social construction rather than biological fact; thus, "generation" is to (biological or chronological) "age" more or less what "gender" is to [biological] "sex".

"Generation" in this second sense is a fundamental concept for the study of youth, on a par with concepts of class, gender, and ethnicity in the social sciences. This provides a way to capture the structures that set young people apart from other social groups, and constitute them as a social category through relations of division, difference, and inequality between this and other categories.[5] However, unlike gender, class, and ethnicity, "generation" is by definition a moving target: we pass through the generations (or, perhaps, they pass through us), and when we speak of changing generations or generational relations we are not talking of changes happening to a defined group of people, but changes between one generational group and the next. Consider, for example, the fascinating and rapid shifts in the experiences, lifestyles, and identities of urban *kampung* youth which Patrick Guinness observed over three decades (Guinness 2009, Ch. 5; Guinness, this volume). These shifts are not about "young people changing" but about "youth" itself changing as succeeding generations follow each other into, and out of, the "youth" slot.

A third meaning of "generation", and one with great historical relevance and political traction in Indonesia, is Mannheim's notion of a generation that becomes a meaningful social and political category. This occurs when significant numbers of young people develop and express a consciousness of themselves as "youth" by first living through the same historical and social events and experiencing them as significant for themselves and, second, by acting upon this consciousness to cross various lines of division: regional, gender, class, ethnicity, education and so on (Mannheim 1952). This notion is implicit in the Indonesian concept of *"angkatan"* (generation, but with the connotation of a force) as applied to the generations of young people who have been

---

5 Paraphrasing Alanen (2001:13) on childhood as a generational relation.

active in major political upheavals (the national revolution, the downfall of the Sukarno and the Suharto regimes, as well as lesser convulsions like Malari in the early Suharto years): these have been labeled the Angkatan 45, Angkatan 65–66, Angkatan 98, and so on in accord with the year of the relevant convulsion. This is a common theme in research on Indonesian politics, at least since Anderson's classic study of the role of "*pemuda*" in the early Indonesian revolution. The *Angkatan Muda* of 1945, for example, gave "the once innocent word *pemuda*…an exultant consciousness of the sudden emergence of youth as a revolutionary force in those critical times" (Anderson 1972, 1).

Finally, to understand these relations and their dynamics we need the broader notion of "social reproduction", the material and discursive practices which enable the reproduction of a social formation and its members, including the relations between social groups, over time (Wells 2009, 78). "Reproduction" here does not mean the duplication or "cloning" of successive, identical social groups or whole societies; it may equally involve radical transformations. Many consider the contemporary world of youth as reflecting a "crisis of social reproduction", as the global ascendancy of neo-liberal norms and practices brings with it massive public underinvestment in education, health care, social welfare, and employment provision. The work of social reproduction is thus thrown back on individuals, families, and social groups (Katz 2004, 709; Wells 2009, 79). In such situations the young may be forced to improvise their own survival strategies. Parker (this volume) evocatively demonstrates the importance of friendship among youth peers in assisting young people negotiate the new experiences of school and work that differentiate them from their parents' generation.

With meagre possibilities for acquiring adult or senior status, and even more demands from a world which simultaneously includes young people in a global world of consumerism and excludes them from it due to their limited economic means, young people may form a disenchanted generation who see their problems to large degree (and not unreasonably) in terms of generational opposition, and as the result of adult failings. Central to young people's understandings (and often adult understandings) of youth is the idea of "dependence"—relying on others for essentials such as food and shelter—as well as subordination, as both governments and the adult world in general maintain an implicitly hierarchical and patriarchal understanding of how society ought to work, one in which young people are normatively subordinate to adult authority.

Tensions between generations are nothing new, but may well become more accentuated as youth are, on the one hand, romanticized by the adult world as the nation's future, but, at the same time, pathologized and feared when they behave in ways that adults do not like. Youth is seen as both a "dangerous age" and a problem age as young people experiment with drugs, sexuality, dress, and types of recreation of which adults do not approve (Nilan, Parker, Robinson, Bennet, this volume; Wright Webster, this volume). Hence the discourse among policy-makers of "rehabilitation" and "reintegration" of problem youth, street children, and drug users—terms that refer properly to criminals, deviants, and the sick.

Youth and Action

Young people are key actors in most important processes of economic and social change. If we take some simple examples, two important themes in macro-studies of social change in Indonesia and elsewhere are the processes of urbanization (spatial movement of part of the population) and de-agrarianization (sectoral shifts in employment). It is often forgotten that both these shifts are largely made by young people. It is young rather than old who move to towns in search of employment, and young rather than old who decide their future no longer lies in agriculture. The common perception of "peasants giving up farming and moving to cities" is thus doubly inaccurate: it is more a question of the sons and daughters of peasants deciding not to follow their parents' occupations and moving to the city in search of non-farm work. Social change itself is not primarily a process in which people behave in different ways to those they used to; it is much more a process in which new generations of young men and women grow up behaving in different ways from previous generations. This is what the often-heard notion of young people as "makers" rather than "learners" of culture actually means.

Youth are the most active group in urban "street politics" and in movements of major political renewal, in which sometimes, but not always, youth also take leadership roles (Hassan, this volume; Spyer, this volume). Youth have often been at the forefront not only in Indonesia's major national political convulsions, but also in routine national and local election campaigns, including the most recent (2014) parliamentary and presidential elections. When such campaigns and convulsions are over, young activists often face the reality that they have failed to achieve the major social changes desired, such as action against corruption and improvements in the justice system. This highlights a key paradox of young people's involvement in the political process. Ryter notes that "according to their self-representations, the *pemuda* of the generation of 1945…and the nominally civilian *pemuda* of the generation of 1966 were both *pemuda* precisely because they were bold enough to advance the popular will by challenging authority" (2002, 73). But although defined as a group who by their nature challenge authority as the "vanguard of change", once authority has been successfully challenged and a new regime installed, the new authorities consider further change superfluous and see youth as a political vehicle that should no longer challenge but instead legitimize and defend the new regime, and whose critical activism is no longer welcome; the question then becomes how to contain the "excesses" of youth (Ryter 2002, 134; Ryter 1998, 58; Baulch 2007, 19).

Most attempts to steer youth in this direction have produced quite ugly modes of youth organization, such as the Indonesian National Youth Committee (KNPI) established in the early years of the Suharto regime in 1973, or the *Pemuda Pancasila* which, by the 1980s, had become an important political presence throughout Indonesia, with a physical headquarters at every level, each coordinating the level below it (Ryter 2002, 5). In the decentralized, post-Suharto era, young people are regularly recruited into ethnic and religious movements, electoral politics, and urban vigilante groups, by local elites and bosses. *Pemuda Pancasila* and other youth organizations such as Golkar's "Association of Functional Youth Groups" IPK have been active participants in the political gangsterism, extortion, and thuggery of Indonesia's new local democracies (Hadiz, 2011, 88–142).

These two dimensions of Indonesian youth—as the vanguard of political and social change and dangerous threat to social and political stability—coexist uneasily in both popular and academic understandings of youth. Indonesian contemporaries of Anderson writing in the early 1970s also highlighted the importance of generation. Almost 40 years ago, writing in the early Suharto period, Taufik Abdullah observed how notions of "youth" and "the young generation" are often value-laden: "youth as the hope of the nation", "youth are owned by the future", or "youth must be guided", and so on, show how loaded the values attached to *pemuda* are (1974, 1, 3). Noting, in terms reminiscent of Mannheim, that social scientists and historians should define youth not by age but by "social perceptions and shared historical experience", he observes that "social change is characterized by tension in intergenerational relations, which disturbs effective communication between them" (in Abdullah and Yasin 1974, 1, 3). At the same time, Nurcholish Madjid (1973) observed that the "generation gap" (in family relations and broader society) "is not necessarily based in open revolt, but in the perception of the young generation that the previous generation has lost its relevance, is outdated and rigid in its ideas" (1973, 49).

During the period of time between elections, there are still but few channels for the everyday political participation of young people, and they are relatively excluded or marginalized from the institutionalized, mainstream, day-to-day political processes. As a result many lose interest and faith in the capacity of these processes to respond to their interests. For some young people, political pessimism and disillusionment, together with the new consumerism, have promoted a new, non-political cultural identity, as argued by Nilan in the early years of *reformasi*:

> We could argue that since 1998, the generation of young people in Indonesia has lost the definable sense of a generation "for itself" (*pemuda*) and has become more of a generation "in itself" (*remaja*, ABG) linked mainly by temporal similarity rather than by shared political knowledge and purpose.
> NILAN 2004, 190

However, the fact that youth are marginalized from (or themselves tend to shun) the conventional formal circuits of political participation and civic involvement does not necessarily mean that they are passive or apathetic. Political parties and formal youth organizations with links to formal government structures may no longer represent the standard form of youth participation; youth movements may develop new means, often without adult mediation, and follow new strategies (Herrera 2006, 1433; see also Vinken 2006). Youth activism of this kind is seldom welcomed by adults, or by governments.

More generally, youth is also a key life-course period in which identities (including political ones) are shaped. Identities are produced collectively, and in this process class, ethnicity, religion, and sexuality intersect in varying combinations, whether we are talking of organized political, occupational, or religious organizations (such as Ansor, KNPI, HPMI, IPK, Pemuda Pancasila), more underground organizations such as urban street gangs and radical religious sects (see Hasan, this volume), or the various organizations that fall somewhere in between, such as Jakarta's Forum Betawi Rembug (Leksana 2009).

Youth, Gender and Sexuality

Youth is the phase of the life-course in which gender stereotypes tend to harden. The tradition of "youth culture" studies, as developed in Britain and the USA, has been rightly criticized for its tendency to focus on young masculine culture; the same criticism may be made of the tradition of "youth" studies in many countries of the South, which often focus predominantly on male youth, except for certain specific purposes (particularly in studies on sexuality and reproductive health). Several chapters in this volume provide an important corrective, focusing on young women in rural Lombok (Bennet, this volume) and in small cities of Central Java (Nilan, this volume), West Sumatra (Parker, this volume) and Yogyakarta (Wright Webster, this volume). These studies address young women's views and experiences on issues such as friendship, their relationships with their families, and their aspirations for adult lives, including sexuality and marriage.

Youth is also a period of active development of sexuality (and masculinity/femininity); in many social classes, and in some policy circles this is a subject which makes people uneasy, an awkward dimension of youth-adult relations (Manderson and Liamputtong 2002). While juvenile sexuality, and young people's understanding of safe sexuality may have been seen mainly as a matter of morality by early generations, for today's young men and women it has become (because of HIV/AIDS) not only a dimension of normal life but also literally a matter of life and death, in which—like it or not—the young person's right to information should not be compromised.

In Indonesia, important generational shifts have been noted in patterns of courtship and marriage (Smith-Hefner 2005), as well as youthful sexuality both within and outside marriage (Sastramidjaja 2000). The Ambivalent Adolescents (AAI) project, which has generated a number of the chapters in this volume, found that *pergaulan bebas* ("free mixing", a euphemism for youthful sexual activity) is identified by the majority of young people as a great threat, to themselves and the nation, but in fact few of them identify themselves as engaging in such behavior. Reports and rumors about young people's pre-marital sexuality are the subject of increasing concern and moral panic (Djaelani 2006; Sujarwo 2008), evident in the introduction of anti-pornography laws in 2008 and the general dominant discourse about *pergaulan bebas*, as explored by Wright-Webster (this volume).

Bennet's chapter (this volume) neatly decouples the issue of early marriage from youthful sexuality in rural Lombok. Pujo Semedi (this volume) captures the youthful innocence of the scouting troops, and Nilan (this volume) shows that even in the "space of freedom" of the mall, young women in Solo feel that their religious values provide them with a safe framework for "hanging out" with young men.

Youth and Malgovernance: Education, Livelihood Resources and Un(der)employment

Young people are, in many ways, victims of distorted adult governance and state failures to bring about successful transitions in education, in the economy generally, and in employment opportunities in particular. As already noted, in Indonesia and many other regions of the global south, for at least three generations each new young generation is typically better educated than their parents (see Robinson, this volume). This development, however, has not been matched with an expansion of the kinds of employment opportunities for which that formal education is supposed to prepare young people. In Indonesia, as in many countries, secondary and tertiary education continue to progress from "right" and free or heavily subsidized public service to a traded commodity; secondary and tertiary education in both the public and private sector are becoming a "business". Most of the children who do not advance from primary to junior secondary, and from junior to senior secondary school, continue to come from poor families, although the gap has somewhat narrowed over time. There are continuing problems of the poor quality of education, and of unemployment within secondary and tertiary graduates as the economy, even when growing, fails to generate the new modern-sector jobs for which they are formally qualified. (Suryadarma and Jones 2013; Suharti 2013). 24 per cent of Indonesian men and women aged 15–19 and 16 per cent of those aged 20–24 are openly unemployed, and more than half of them have been unemployed for over a year. Contrary to ideas that education can resolve this problem, unemployment is actually positively correlated with educational attainment, at least up to the level of upper secondary graduates (UCW 2012).

As the "Ambivalent Adolescents" study in nine Indonesian regions concludes

> Young people in Indonesia today are deeply concerned with education: they are concerned about the quality of the education they are receiving; they are preoccupied with their own academic performance as individuals; they worry about getting into the appropriate training programme or university; and they worry about getting a job that will be interesting and enable them to become independent. For the most part, they are engaged with the education process, in an active interrogation of the education system.
>
> PARKER and NILAN 2013, 79

Large numbers of graduates, after years of unsuccessful job searches, find a reluctant and frustrated existence in urban informal-sector jobs for which they are overqualified. Meanwhile, the expansion of formal education, and particularly secondary education, into rural areas contributes to a process of de-skilling rural youth, in which farming skills are neglected and farming is downgraded as an occupation. Young people may seem to be uninterested in agricultural futures and aiming to join the movement to the cities (Koning 1997 and 2005;

White 2012a), but this should not be taken for granted. Recent generations of rural youth are often confronted by the narrowing and sometimes complete closure of opportunities to gain access to a plot of land. This may happen under all kinds of land tenure systems, whether land is held in private title, under customary tenure (in which use rights to farm plots are allocated by family or community elders), or as "state lands". This problem is likely only to worsen in the context of new patterns of land grabbing for corporate commercial food (and, recently, biofuel) production, and new pressures on the countryside as economic "refuge" in the face of global recession. Robinson (this volume) recounts the shrinking choices in the mining town of Sorowako where a state-facilitated "land grab" deprived the local people of agricultural land and livelihoods. A recent study in 12 rice-producing villages of West Java, Central Java, and South Sulawesi found that young people, in practice, have no realistic prospect of acquiring a farm while still young. Not surprisingly, they tend to migrate to urban centers, other islands, or overseas in search of non-farm incomes. But the decision to migrate does not necessarily mean a permanent abandonment of the village, and of farming futures; many of them intend to save money and return when there is a prospect of acquiring land through inheritance, purchase, or rental (Herawati and Yogaprasta 2014).

Youth, Trouble, Violence and Victimhood

Robison and Hadiz began their book *Reorganising Power in Indonesia* (2004) with Gramsci's well-known encapsulation of crisis: "the crisis consists precisely in the fact that the old is dying and the new cannot be born: in this interregnum a great variety of morbid symptoms appears". They argued that Indonesia's post-crisis experience of *reformasi* has not amounted to any fundamental political and social renewal, as Indonesia moves from one basically conservative regime to another. This aspect of the post-Suharto years, and its expression in a variety of "morbid symptoms", can be seen as much at local level as in the regional and national manifestations which are the subject of Robison and Hadiz's account.

Among these morbid symptoms at a micro-level, we may include various kinds of fundamentalist identity politics and the proliferation of violence which has taken many forms (Hatib 2012; see Hassan this volume; Spyer, this volume). Another symptom is the explosion of drug use. Observers agree that there has been a spectacular increase in drug abuse and addiction rates among youth in recent years. "Indonesia is in the midst of a full-blown drug abuse and addiction crisis...There is no place in Indonesia that we know of that is free from drugs any more" (Gordon and Gordon 2003, 362). Drug use cuts across class and gender lines,[6] and drugs are easily available in schools and universities (Wright-Webster, this volume); so far, there has been relatively little social science research on this dimension of Indonesia's "chemical youth" (but see Hardon et al 2013).

The enthusiastic new rhetoric of youth agency, empowerment, participation, and citizenship should not obscure the continuing victimhood of many young people, not only at the hands of adults. We may reflect. for example, on the experience of rural teenage girls pressured to leave school and migrate into the domestic service or entertainment sectors (Atsushi 2012), and the many manifestations of abuse and exploitation that young workers are often confronted with:

> (My female employer) often hit me, sometimes she'd pinch me. Sometimes she'd throw water pails at me. Sometimes she would push me to the wall. Slap me. Pinch me.[7]
>
> I felt uncomfortable when (my employer's husband) would be naked outside his bedroom…He'd ask me, 'Do you want to see (my penis)?' He would do this every day that we were left alone.[8]

Young People and the "Right to be Properly Researched"

Finally, one important aspect of generational relationships involving youth is that between young people and the (nearly always) adult professional researchers—like ourselves—who study them. Among the many rights that children and young people should have, one that is not often mentioned (although it could no doubt be derived from existing children's rights or human rights) is "the right to be properly researched". This is another aspect of the generational relationships, often involving power and status differences, between young people and the adults who study them as part of their professional lives.

As researchers we need to ask ourselves: will young people be objects, subjects, or participants in my research? Will information on young people's situation and experiences be obtained directly from them, or by proxy (from

---

6 See for example Beazley (2003).
7 Wani (not her real name), 18 years old, Bekasi, describing her experiences in the job she had from age 13 to 17 (HRW 2009, 14–15).
8 Kartika (not her real name), 17 years old, Yogyakarta, describing her experiences in the job she had when she was 15 years old (HRW 2009, 15).

adults—particularly parents, and teachers—supplying information about them)? Survey research in particular has tended to follow the proxy approach with young people, despite there being plenty of evidence that the best source of information about issues pertinent to young people—even young children—is themselves (Scott 2000).

The ethical protocols of research agencies, sponsors, and professional associations commonly include the principles of "informed consent", privacy, confidentiality, and (sometimes) respect for those we study. "Those interviewed or observed should give their permission in full knowledge of the purpose of the research and the consequences for them of taking part" (Piper and Simons 2005, 56). This sounds very good, but how possible is it to achieve this in real research situations, involving issues that can be sensitive, illegal, or publicly disapproved of (for example, sexuality, drink or drugs, parental violence, or other generational tensions)? And when the social gulf/power relation between researcher and subjects is large—as it often is between adult researchers and young people—how real is the consent given? How important will be pressures from peers and "gatekeepers" (for example, the village officials, community leaders, school teachers, or parents)? Sometimes "privacy" is impossible for purely practical reasons: in crowded rural and urban settlements it is not easy to find a place where a young (male or female) respondent can talk alone to an adult researcher without the presence of others (whether parents, teachers, or peers). "Informed consent", "privacy", and "confidentiality" often have to be contextualized, and the boundaries between what is and is not acceptable are extremely fuzzy.

Consider, for example, the "informed consent" statements currently used in *The Indonesia Young Adult Reproductive Health Survey*, carried out in 2002, 2007, and 2011 with a sample of several thousand unmarried women and men aged 15–24.[9] The interviewers introduce themselves with the following carefully worded "informed consent" formula:

> Hello. My name is _____. I am working with the Central Bureau of Statistics. We are conducting a national survey of unmarried women and men between age 15 and 24. We are interested in your knowledge of, attitudes toward and practice in health care. This information will be used to help the government in developing plans to provide health services tailored specifically to address the needs of young people. We would very much appreciate your participation in the survey. The survey usually

---

9   The example is from Indonesia, but nearly all DHS surveys use the same basic formula in their informed consent statements.

takes about 25 minutes to complete. Whatever information you provide will be kept strictly confidential and will not be shown to other persons. Participation in the survey is voluntary and you can choose not to answer any individual question, or all of the questions. However, we hope that you will participate in this survey since your views are important.

At this time, do you ant to ask me anything about the survey?
During this interview, how should I address you? May I begin the interview now?
In the case of respondents aged 15–17 ("children" in international and Indonesian law), parental or guardian consent must also be obtained, using the same general description of the survey followed by the following:

> We would very much appreciate your permission to have your child(ren) participate in this survey. The survey usually takes about 25 minutes. Whatever information you [sic] provide will be kept strictly confidential and will not be shown to other persons. May we interview [name of children] in private? If you decide not to let your children be interviewed, we will respect your decision. What is your decision?
> BPS ET AL. 2008, Appendix E:175–99

So far so good. The questionnaire then begins with a series of innocuous, standard questions: *"How old were you at your last birthday?"*, *"What is the highest level of school you attended?"* and so on. As the questionnaire reaches section 5 ("Smoking, drinking and drugs") some possibly sensitive areas (particularly if there are others present) are broached: *"Have you ever drunk an alcohol-containing beverage?"*; *"In the last 3 months, on how many days did you drink an alcohol-containing beverage?"*; *"Have you ever gotten 'drunk' from drinking an alcohol-containing beverage?"*; *"Have you ever tried to use drugs (LOCAL TERM)?"*; *"How did you use the drug?"*; *"Did you inject drugs in the last 12 months?"*

Nothing in the "informed consent" protocol, however, suggests to the young respondent that when the interviewer finally reaches question number 701 he or she will be asked (among other questions on sexuality): *"Do you currently have a boy/girl friend?"*; *"When you are alone with your (current/last) boy/girlfriend, to show your love or just because you are curious, have you ever done any of the following: Held hands? Kissed lips? Touched (or being touched) or aroused (being aroused) on your sensitive body parts such as genitals, breast, thigh, etc.?"*; *"Have you ever had sexual intercourse?"*; *"When did you last have sexual intercourse?"* How likely is it that a 15- or 16-year old girl, in either rural or urban Indonesian contexts, will be interviewed by a stranger without the presence of her parents or others? How likely is it that the interviewer will willingly abort the interview at this late stage if signs of unwillingness or discomfort are apparent? Does the young respondent's agreement to answer questions on "various health issues" (in the informed consent statement) constitute sufficiently "informed" consent to questions about his or her sexual activity?

Although there are exceptions, it is probably correct to say that most adult research on youth is characterized by a general "defectologist" approach (identifying things that are "wrong" and need "fixing", or things that are "missing" and that need to be provided in the lives of young people), rather than more general studies of young people in their own right. In this way, the potential of young people is undervalued: "much of the current literature on youth focuses on…the negative consequences of maladaptive behavior and the tremendous costs incurred by society in regulating deviant behavior, rather than on the potential of youth for creative change" (Tienda and Wilson 2002, 8).

Young people are also quite capable of becoming key actors in the process of research itself if we are willing to do research "with" young people, not "about" them (and thus take the notion of "youth-centered" and "participatory" research beyond rhetoric). The research studies collected in this volume have all engaged directly with youth in various ways and many of them exemplify strategies that can be used to engage ethically with young people in the process of research.

References

Abbink, J., and J. van Kessel, eds. 2005. *Vanguard or Vandals: Youth, Politics and Conflict in Africa*. Leiden: Brill.
Abdullah, T., and M. Yasin, eds. 1974. *Pemuda dan Perubahan Sosial*. Jakarta: LP3ES.
Alanen, Leena. 2001. "Explorations in Generational Analysis". In *Conceptualizing Child-Adult Relations*, edited by L. Alanen and B. Mayall, 11–22. London: Routledge.
Anderson, Benedict. 1972. *Java in a Time of Revolution: Occupation and Resistance, 1944–1946*. Ithaca: Cornell University Press.
Baulch, E. 2007. *Making Scenes: Reggae, Punk, and Death Metal in 1990s Bali*. Durham: Duke University Press.
Beazley, Harriot. 2003. "The Construction and Protection of Individual and Collective Identities by Street Children and Youth in Indonesia." *Children, Youth and Environments* 13:105–33.
BPS, BKKBN and Macro International. 2008. *Indonesia Young Adult Reproductive Health Survey 2007*. Jakarta: Biro Pusat Statistik/National Family Planning Coordinating Board/Macro International.

Djaelani, A.Q. 2006. *Pornografi, Pornoaksi dan Prostitusi: Strategi Barat untuk Menghancurkan Generasi Muda Islam: Analisis, Fakta, dan Filosofi*, Bekasi: Rabitha Press.

Gordon, Joyce D., and David D. Gordon. 2003. "Drug Abuse in Indonesia: An Increasing Problem During the Economic Crisis." In *IndonesianThe Crisis: a Human Development Perspective*, edited by Aris Ananta, 362–81. Singapore: ISEAS Press.

Guinness, Patrick. 2009. *Kampung, Islam and State in Urban Java*. Singapore: NUS Press, and Leiden: KITLV Press.

Hadiz, Vedi. 2011. *Localising Power in Post-Authoritarian Indonesia: A Southeast Asia Perspective*. Singapore: ISEAS.

Hardon, A., N.I. Idris, and T.D. Hymans. 2013. "Chemical Sexualities: The Use of Pharmaceutical and Cosmetic Products by Youth in South Sulawesi, Indonesia." *Reproductive Health Matters* 21:214–24.

Herawati, Rina dan Yogaprasta A. Nugraha. 2014. *Menguak Realitas Orang Muda Sektor Pertanian di Perdesaan*. Bandung: Seri Penelitian Akatiga.

Herrera, Linda. 2006. "What's New about Youth?" *Development & Change* 37:1425–34.

Honwana, Alcinda, and Filip de Boeck, eds. 2005. *Makers and Breakers: Children and Youth in Postcolonial Africa*. Oxford: James Currey.

Human Rights Watch. 2009. *Workers in the Shadows: Abuse and Exploitation of Young Workers in Indonesia*. New York: Human Rights Watch.

Jones, Gill. 2009. *Youth*. Cambridge: Polity Press.

Kadir, Hatib A. 2012. "School Gangs of Yogyakarta: Mass Fighting Strategies and Masculine Charisma in the City of Students." *The Asia Pacific Journal of Anthropology* 13:352–65.

Katz, Cindi. 2004. *Growing Up Global: Economic Restructuring and Children's Everyday Lives*. Minneapolis: University of Minnesota Press.

Komite Nasional Pemuda Indonesia (KNPI). 2005. *Anggaran Rumah Tangga Komite Nasional Pemuda Indonesia* Accessed August 3, 2011: http://knpikarangampel.files.wordpress.com/2009/11/anggaran-rumah-tanggal.pdf.

Koning, Juliette. 1997. "Generations of Change: a Javanese Village in the 1990s." PhD diss., University of Amsterdam.

Koning, Juliette. 2005. "The Impossible Return? The Post-migration Narratives of Young Women in Rural Java," *Asian Journal of Social Science* 33:16–185.

Leksana, Grace. 2009. "Struggling to be Young: Brotherhood Among the Poor Urban Youth of Jakarta," *Inside Indonesia* 95.

Lloyd, Cynthia, ed. 2005. *Growing Up Global: The Changing Transitions to Adulthood in Developing Countries*. Washington DC: The National Academies Press.

Madjid, Nurcholish. 1973. "Remaja, Keluarga, & Masyarakat di Kota Besar. 1973. Suatu Usaha Pendahuluan untuk Memahami Persoalan Sekitar 'Generation Gap'," *Prisma* 2:45–51.

Manderson, Lenore, and Pranee Liamputtong, eds.. 2002. *Coming of Age in South and Southeast Asia: Youth, Courtship and Sexuality*. Richmond: Curzon Press.

Mannheim, Karl. 1952. "The Problem of Generations." In *Karl Mannheim: Essays on the Sociology of Knowledge*, edited by P. Kecskemeti, 276–320. London: Routledge. Originally published...(1928).

Mayall, Berry. 2002. *Towards a Sociology for Childhood: Thinking from Children's Lives.* Milton Keynes: Open University Press.

Menpora. n.d. [ca. 2008]. *Naskah Akademik Rancangan Undang-Undang Tentang Kepemudaan.* Jakarta: Kementerian Negara Pemuda dan Olahraga.

Minza, Wenty M., 2014. "Growing Up and Being Young in an Indonesian Provincial Town." PhD diss., University of Amsterdam.

Naafs, Suzanne. 2012. "Navigating School to Work Transitions in an Indonesian Industrial Town: Young Women in Cilegon," *The Asia Pacific Journal of Anthropology* 13:49–63.

Naafs, Suzanne, and Ben White. 2012. "Intermediate Generations: Reflections on Indonesian Youth Studies." *The Asia Pacific Journal of Anthropology* 13:3–20.

Nilan, Pamela. 2004. "The Risky Future of Youth Politics in Indonesia." *Review of Indonesian and Malaysian Affairs* 38:173–94.

Parker, Lyn, and Pamela Nilan. 2013. Adolescents in Contemporary Indonesia. London: Routledge.

Piper, Heather and Helen Simons. 2005. 'Ethical Responsibility in Social Research.' In *Research Methods in the Social Sciences*, edited by Bridget Somekh and Kathy Lewin, 56–64. London: Sage.

Republic of Indonesia UU no 40. 2009. Undang-Undang Republik Indonesia Nomor 40 tahun 2009 Tentang Kepemudaan.

Roberts, Ken. 2009. *Youth in Transition: Eastern Europe and the West.* Basingstoke: Palgrave Macmillan.

Robison, Richard, and Vedi Hadiz. 2004. *Reorganising Power in Indonesia: The Politics of Oligarchy in an Age of Markets.* London: Routledge Curzon.

Ryter, L. 2002. "Youth, Gangs and the State in Indonesia." PhD diss., University of Washington.

Ryter, L. 1998. "Pemuda Pancasila: The Last Loyalist Free Men of Suharto's Order?" *Indonesia* 66:73.

Sano, Atsushi. 2012. "Agency and Resilience in the Sex Trade: Adolescent Girls in Rural Indramayu." *The Asia Pacific Journal of Anthropology* 13:21–35.

Sastramidjaja, Yatun. 2000. *Dromenjagers in Bandung: Twintigers in het Moderne Indonesië.* Amsterdam: Spinhuis.

Scott, Jacqueline. 2000. "Children as Respondents: The Challenge for Quantitative Methods." In *Research with Children: Perspectives and Practices*, edited by Pia Christensen and Allison James, 98–119. London: Routledge Falmer.

Smith-Hefner, Nancy. 2005. "The New Muslim Romance: Changing Patterns of Courtship and Marriage Among Educated Javanese Youth." *Journal of Southeast Asian Studies* 36:441–59.

Suharti. 2013. "Trends in Education in Indonesia." In *Education in Indonesia*, edited by Daniel Suryadarma and Gavin Jones, 1–14. Singapore: ISEAS Press.

Sujarwo, P.J., 2008. *Pontianak "Teenager" Under Cover: Benarkah Perilaku Remaja di Pontianak Sudah Sedemikian Mengerikan?* Pontianak: Pijar Publishing.

Suryadarma, Daniel, and Gavin Jones. 2013. "Meeting the Education Challenge." In *Education in Indonesia*, edited by Daniel Suryadarma and Gavin Jones, 15–52. Singapore: ISEAS Press.

Tienda, Marta, and William J. Wilson. 2002. "Comparative Perspectives of Urban Youth." In *Youth in Cities: A Cross-National Perspective*, edited by Marta Tienda and William J. Wilson, 3–18. Cambridge: Cambridge University Press.

UCW. 2012. *Understanding Children's Work and Unemployment Outcomes in Indonesia: Country Report.* Rome: ILO-UNICEF-World Bank Understanding Children's Work Programme.

Vinken, Henk. 2006. "Young People's Civic Engagement: The Need for New Perspectives." In *YouthContemporary Research: Local Expressions and Global Connections*, edited by Helena Helve and Gunilla Holm, 147–57. Aldershot: Ashgate.

Wells, Karen. 2009. *Childhood in a Global Perspective.* Cambridge: Polity Press.

White, Ben. 2009. "Youth, Generation and Social Change: Indonesian Youth in Comparative Perspective." Paper presented at the workshop *Growing Up in Indonesia: Experience and Diversity in Youth Transitions*, Australian National University, Canberra, September 2009.

White, Ben. 2012a. "Indonesian Rural Youth Transitions: Employment, Mobility and the Future of Agriculture." In *Land, Livelihood, Environment and the Economy in Indonesia. Essays in Honour of Joan Hardjono*, edited by Anne Booth, Chris Manning, and Thee Kian Wie, 243–63. Jakarta: Obor Foundation.

White, Ben. (2012b) "Changing Childhoods: Javanese Village Children in Three Generations." *Journal of Agrarian Change* 12:81–97.

World Bank. *Development and the Next Generation: World Development Report 2007.* Washington, D.C.: The World Bank, 2006.

CHAPTER 2

Contemporary Indonesian Youth Transitions: Trends and Inequalities

Pam Nilan, Lyn Parker, Kathryn Robinson, and Linda Bennett

Introduction

The Ambivalent Adolescents in Indonesia research project (AAI) investigated trends and commonalities in the lives of young Indonesians in the first decade of the new millennium, particularly in the domains of life expectations, social life, popular culture, leisure, sexuality, education, and entry to work. This chapter[1] addresses some but not all of those themes. The main foci below are life expectations, education, and particularly entry to work, in the context of transition to adulthood in the world's largest Muslim nation. The term "transition" here refers to the journey from education to adulthood: work or career, marriage, and parenthood (Furlong and Cartmel 2006, 9; see also White, this volume).

The analysis presented here is based on AAI project survey data collected in 2007 from 3565 Indonesian youth in secondary schools and universities at nine locations between 2006 and 2008. Analyzing this data in the context provided by secondary sources, this chapter offers empirical evidence of some contemporary Indonesian youth transition trends. It identifies some key trends and ongoing inequalities in the lives of young Indonesians who are on the cusp of leaving education and entering the workforce.

It must be acknowledged that contemporary transitions to adulthood in a developing country like Indonesia will not be the same as for western countries in which the concept of youth transitions was first developed (Juárez and Gayet 2014). As those authors point out for developing countries, among other factors, high unemployment rates in certain job markets and modified preferences regarding marriage types, all within a framework of a sharp income gap between rich and poor, "manifest in a world in which fewer certainties result in

---

1 Earlier papers reporting on the project survey data were published as: Nilan, Pam, Parker, Lyn, Bennett, Linda and Robinson, Kathryn. "Indonesian youth looking towards the future." *Journal of Youth Studies* 14 (2011): 709–28; and Chapter 8: "The hopes and dreams of young people." In Lyn Parker and Pam Nilan. *Adolescents in Contemporary Indonesia*, London & New York: Routledge, 2013. This chapter differs from those earlier papers, having been developed and updated specifically for this edited volume.

new ways of experiencing the transition to adulthood" (Juárez and Gayet 2014, 521). Moreover, although globalization has meant a certain homogenization of youth transitions on a global scale, it has also led to "a greater diversification of life paths" (Juárez and Gayet 2014, 522). Thus, various and competing life ideals mean that today transitions may occur at different ages and through different modalities within the same developing country (Gauthier 2007). Yet while transitions are to some extent now decoupled from the education-work-marriage-independent living sequence, and have become much less predictable, they have not de-traditionalized to the same extent as in the West (See White, this volume).

Whereas Indonesian youth transitions in the past were relatively short and direct, now, particularly for the "intermediate classes" (White 2014), they are extended and ever more contingent on education (Naafs 2012; Minza 2014). Young Indonesians are marrying later, having fewer children (and later), and entering the workforce later, than previous generations (see Utomo 2014), with education and employment status affecting dating and choice of marriage partner (Naafs 2012). Yet our survey data demonstrate that young Indonesians pursuing an aspirational path through education towards middle-class prosperity still look forward to a "good life" oriented towards family, religion, and wellbeing, implying some traditional sense of transition to adulthood, despite taking longer (Nilan et al. 2011). Notably, the survey provided evidence that the future transition from education to work was viewed with some uncertainty in the first decade of the new millennium, particularly by young people from less privileged backgrounds. Relative socio-economic advantage and disadvantage was signaled in anticipated obstacles to upward social mobility. Many young people surveyed expressed high expectations and dreams, yet analysis of broader socio-economic trends leads us to assume the likelihood of relatively low outcomes in the transition to work (See Robinson, this volume; White and Margiyatin, this volume).

In *The Jakarta Post* newspaper in January 2010 a number of youth trends were identified, based on a 2009 Roy Morgan nation-wide survey of 14–24 year olds. On a high note, 84 per cent of young Indonesians agreed they were optimistic about the future, even though 90 per cent believed corruption was still the biggest problem for the country. Sixty one per cent had a mobile phone and 39 per cent rode a motorcycle. Finally, whereas, in the same poll in 2004, 70 per cent had reported regularly attending a place of worship, by 2010 this was only 60 per cent (Guharoy 2010).

So what do these 2010 poll figures indicate about trends in the current Indonesian youth generation? Firstly, they indicate the optimistic mindset of young people in a rapidly developing economy. Indonesia's annual GDP growth peaked at 6.5 per cent in 2011, when it was considered one of the world's fastest emerging economies. Even now it is high at over 5 per cent (World Bank 2014). Secondly, they imply the expansion of consumerism and middle-class lifestyles for the contemporary generation of youth (see Luvaas 2013). Finally, they raise questions about the actual impact of the trend for greater public expression of piety and of Islamist politics on the religiosity of Indonesia's youth (see for example Beta 2014).

This chapter is predominantly concerned with urban Indonesian youth from the intermediate classes who engage upwardly mobile aspirations. The argument here is that transitions for that cohort of Indonesian youth are decoupled from the familial and village-based passage to adulthood of the past, but only to a certain extent (see also Guinness, this volume). Although marriages are now principally romantically constituted rather than arranged, marriage and family as a key transition to adulthood is still strongly favored, and taken up by all but a few, despite it happening later than in the past (Nilan 2008; Smith-Hefner 2005). For a newly-married urban middle-class couple, independent living and home ownership has become a priority (Nilan 2008) rather than the sometimes slow transition from post-marital residence in a parental home. Successful marital and housing transitions depend upon a successful education-to-work transition.

Key Aspects of Contemporary Indonesian Youth Transitions

In order to locate the survey and secondary data on youth trends discussed in this chapter, it is necessary to give a brief overview of the major life transition dimensions for Indonesian youth as they move towards adulthood. These are: education, work, marriage and family, and housing.

Education

Completion of education is a key marker of youth transition to adulthood according to the conventional literature. It is presumed this is the sure pathway to paid work. Yet we need to examine it in the Indonesian context to see whether it holds up. The current generation of Indonesian youth is the most educated in history (Naafs 2012), although the quality of that education is often questionable (White, this volume). National gender parity in primary and junior secondary schooling was achieved in 2002 (BPS 2008), and the number of females overall in post-primary education currently exceeds the number of males, although this does vary by province and region (see BPS 2014). Relevant to our 2007 survey, in 2008 64 per cent of young Indonesians aged 13–18 were enrolled in secondary school: 78 per cent at junior secondary level and 51 per cent at senior level, while 17 per cent of older youth were enrolled in tertiary education (UNESCO 2009). In 2013 the Indonesian Statistics Agency (BPS 2014) found that the gross enrolment rate for junior secondary school was 90.48 per cent of the eligible cohort aged 13–15 years and 63.27 per cent of those aged 16–18 years for senior secondary school. According to the World Bank (2014), total participation in higher education is now 26 per cent. Yet, "unemployment rates for educated youth are higher than for non-educated youth. The unemployment rate for 20–29 year olds is almost twice as high for senior secondary and tertiary graduates than for basic education graduates" (World Bank 2014, 101). In other words, while the post-primary education participation rate has been rising, this has not translated into there being more jobs available for senior secondary and tertiary graduates (Suryadarma and Jones 2013). Nevertheless, as the statistics indicate, more and more young Indonesians enroll in senior secondary and tertiary education every year.

Work

As indicated above, according to the literature on transitions, the completion of education is presumed to lead to a job. Yet this is now no longer guaranteed, even in the West. Despite the economic boom, a recent study indicates that in Indonesia youth unemployment is now very high by global standards (Coxhead 2014, 6). Since 2004 Indonesia has experienced "jobless growth" (Manning and Roesad 2007; Aswicahyono, Hill, and Narjoko 2011). Since the passage of the 2003 Manpower Law, employers have been able to offer short-term contracts, outsource some production activities, and employ more than one person in the same job (Manning and Roesad 2007). Thus, fewer new full-time jobs have been created over the last ten years. All labor sectors have remained more or less stable so the number of full-time jobs available to young people entering the labor market has not increased much, relative to the percentage of senior secondary school and university graduates each year.

Over two million new job seekers enter the labor market every year in Indonesia (Winarto-Rogers 2008). This was the context facing the survey cohort. It underscores the risk of not only unemployment but, far more often, underemployment of well-educated youth (Sziraczki and Reerink 2004). This is the situation that faces young people (Naafs and White 2012; Nilan et al. 2011), despite oft-expressed optimism.

Marriage and Family

In the standard transitions literature, the phase of marriage and parenthood represents a further point of independence (after work) in the journey towards being an adult. In Indonesia, the status of spouse/parent is still the essential signifier of adult status (Robinson 2009; Nilan 2008; Utomo 2014; Bennett, this volume). Yet the average age of marriage has increased to the early to mid-twenties, for both sexes (Jones 2005; Utomo 2014). (Although women still tend to marry earlier than men, population statistics indicate the age gap between husband and wife has been diminishing [Utomo 2014]). However, while the urban middle-class is marrying later and later, poor rural people still have a tendency to marry early (Jones and Bina 2008), with some girls marrying in their early teens (Bennett, this volume). In the wider frame, expectations and experiences of marriage are still quite different for male and female Indonesian youth (see Naafs 2012).

The accepted wisdom for contemporary middle-class and upwardly mobile young Indonesians is that education should be completed and a steady job obtained before a couple marry (Nilan 2008). Since this may take some time, long engagements have become common (Smith-Hefner 2005, 442), although cohabitation before marriage is rare. This pattern matches documented youth transitions to marriage in the South Caucasus (Roberts et al. 2009); that of a delayed family formation sequence structurally slowed by a combination of religious restriction, unemployment, and high housing costs. Similarly, a study of youth transitions in Iran found that religious traditions, unfulfilled educational expectations, and high rates of youth unemployment led to a delayed age of first marriage for urban middle-class youth (Egel and Salehi-Isfahani 2010). These studies are indicative of the challenges encountered by young men and women along their contemporary journey to marriage in non-OECD countries. A similar pattern appears to exist in Indonesia (Nilan 2008).

Certainly, the principal signifier of adulthood for Indonesian women is to be married with children (see Naafs 2012). For men, however, legitimate adult status is signified not only by marriage and fatherhood, but also by being *mampu*—able to provide for the family and demonstrate competent status in the public sphere (Robinson 2015). So they may not readily find a girlfriend or a wife unless they can provide for them. For young men on the path of upward social mobility, a secure, well-paid job and the capacity to provide housing ensure their marriageable status in the eyes of young women at the same status level. Moreover, Indonesian middle-class urban families are rarely able to manage their weekly budget and loan repayments on a single salary, which means the double-partner income household is now the urban middle-class norm (Utomo 2004; 2014). This has particular ramifications for female employment expectations and desired family size.

Housing

In the western literature, transition to adulthood is signaled by departure from the family home and the establishment of an autonomous residence. Yet this has been under-researched in developing countries (Juárez and Gayet 2014, 527), and the patterns are very diverse. In Indonesia, for example, departure from the family home by a young person may happen because of studies or work, for example moving into a *kos* or dormitory (Robinson, this volume; McCulloch, Grover, and Suryahadi 2014), labor migration (Elmhirst 2007), or marriage (Nilan 2008). Financial independence is required for the latter. In Iran, one study found a delay in the age of departure of young people from the family home due to increase in years of schooling and fewer employment opportunities, which slowed down the prospect of financial independence (Egel and Salehi-Isfahani 2010). Such extended education and lack of graduate employment opportunities also exist for the contemporary generation of well-educated Indonesian youth (see White, this volume).

In the Indonesian context, an important signifier of middle-class success is home ownership. In the cities, while traditional housing was most often multi-generational and extended, with family members living in the same domestic complex, urbanization has seen the entrenchment of the single-family dwelling. Modern residential estates, multi-storey apartment buildings, and three bedroom houses are now the bywords of urban habitation and mortgage loans. Research indicates an extraordinary expansion of Indonesian urban dwellings occupied by a nuclear family: a couple and 2/3 children (UNDP 2008). This has particular implications for contemporary youth transitions. It is quite common for a young working couple to live with one set of parents until the deposit for a home loan is saved.

In short, we need to acknowledge that contemporary youth transitions in Indonesia, as in many developing countries, are extended and decoupled from the familial and village-based transitions of the past, but we cannot assume that they simply represent what happens in western and developed countries.

Methodology

The primary "evidence" offered here is survey data. In methodological terms it is acknowledged that survey data is always limited in the sense that it can only offer a broad picture of trends for young people without offering a deep sense of the meanings in their attitudes, choices, and expectations. However, the broad view offered by a survey is useful for "mapping" a set of complex phenomena that can be detailed in qualitative data analysis. Reports on the qualitative data collected for the Ambivalent Adolescents project have been published in this volume (chapters by Nilan, Parker, Bennett, Robinson, and Wright Webster) and previously. Our project survey sample was large enough to allow for generalizing claims. It constituted a "purposive sample" (May 1997,

88) of 3565 youth in secondary schools and universities at nine locations between 2006 and 2008. Survey questions aimed to obtain a broad overview of youth experiences, opinions, and expectations in the fields of education and work, social life, and leisure. Descriptive analysis was employed to derive means and percentages, and to indicate the probable strength of variables and correlations (see May 1997, 84). The authors administered the surveys in communities where they have had many years' experience, and this knowledge informed the survey design and the interpretation of survey results.

Locations

The nine locations were largely determined by the prior research experience and contacts of the research team members, which facilitated approaching local educational institutions. While they were not selected to be nationally representative in a statistical sense, they do constitute a relevant range of youth situations and experiences (See Table 2.1).

Bali is an affluent province, deriving revenue primarily from tourism. Data were collected mainly from government secondary schools. More than one-third of respondents in Bali were in vocational high schools. The quality of Balinese schooling is generally high, and there is strong competition for entry into the most prestigious government secondary schools. Over three-quarters of respondents followed Balinese Hinduism.

Banjarnegara is in western Central Java Province which relies on agriculture and related enterprises. The data were collected from Muslim schools.

TABLE 2.1   *Surveys collected by location.*

Region	Number	Percentage
Bali	645	18.1
Banjarnegara	285	8.0
Flores	303	8.5
Jakarta	366	10.3
Lombok	164	4.6
Solo	612	17.2
Sorowako	238	6.7
West Sumatra	454	12.7
Yogyakarta	498	14.0
Total	3565	100

Flores is one of the poorest islands in the East. Data was collected in the capital Ende from one public and one private Christian secondary school; 75.9 per cent of respondents were Catholic.

Jakarta is Indonesia's capital. Data were collected at five government secondary schools, one of which was vocational; 84.2 per cent of respondents were Muslim.

Lombok in eastern Indonesia draws income from agriculture and tourism. Data came from a select Muslim boarding school in a town outside the capital Mataram.

Solo in Central Java is a principal manufacturing center. Data came from government and private secondary schools and universities. 82 per cent were Muslim.

Sorowako is a mining town in South Sulawesi. The main local employer is PT Vale, and it is the largest nickel mine in Indonesia. Data were collected from two private secondary schools, and 71.4 per cent of respondents were Muslim.

West Sumatra is a relatively prosperous area. Data came from Christian, Muslim, and government secondary schools in a major town, and 86.6 per cent were Muslim.

Yogyakarta is a city in Central Java. Administratively, it has been granted Special Autonomy due to the respected position of the traditional ruler. It is a major site for education and tourism. Data came from Christian, Muslim, and government secondary schools and universities, and 87.7 per cent were Muslim.

Similarity Across Locations

Despite minor variation between locations, similarity of response on most attitudinal and aspirational questions was remarkable, and rather unexpected, since striking discrepancies in educational outcomes exist across Indonesia. Furthermore, there were wide variations in local socio-economic circumstances and culture, as well as types of educational institutions attended. Hence, it is remarkable that these young people in different parts of the archipelago who had reached the later stages of secondary education tended to share certain socio-economic and lifestyle ideals and aspirations.

Survey Findings

The Big Picture

Survey respondents were from a variety of educational institutions. 37 per cent were attending government secondary schools, and 14.4 were enrolled in technical high schools. Just under 20 per cent attended Muslim schools and almost the same percentage were at Christian secondary schools. 7.3 per cent were studying at a public university and 2.4 per cent at a private university. Table 2.2 offers a snapshot of key findings.

The typical survey respondent is 16, attends a state high school, lives in the parental home, does not engage in paid work, has a mobile phone, and can use a computer. He or she watches three hours of television a day, and wants to get married at around 25 and have two children. He or she dreams of a professional or para-professional job and identifies a family member as his/her chief role model. These generalizations, while informative, hide some significant variations, such as differences between the sexes and regional distinctions. The transition marker of marriage/parenthood is taken first in our subsequent discussion, in order to frame the later sections on expectations of the good life and perceptions about entry to the labor market.

Marriage and Children

25 was the median desired age of marriage. Male and female responses were clustered on either side of this median: more female respondents wanted to marry at 25 or younger and more males wanted to marry at 25 or older. For example, 44.6 per cent of females wanted to marry earlier than 25, compared to only 21.1 per cent of males. We see here the normative cultural expectation that the man should be older than the woman at the time of marriage. There

TABLE 2.2 *Snapshot N = 3565.*

Males	48.7%
Females	51.3%
Muslim respondents	66.5%
Median age	16 years
Respondents in senior secondary schools	61.7%
Fathers in agriculture	16%
Living at home with parents	75.2%
Working part-time while studying	8.8%
Has a mobile phone	77.3%
Has access to a home computer	50.8%
Median hours of television watched per day	3 hours
Median desired age of marriage	25 years
Median desired number of children	2
Most popular career choice	doctor
Most popular role model	a (named) family member

was higher standard deviation (2.812) and variance (7.909) for males than for females (2.053 and 4.216 respectively), indicating greater female unanimity about the desirability of marrying around the age of 25 (see Jones and Bina 2008, 5). Bennett (2005, 2) reports that if a young woman in Lombok is not married by the age of 25 this could be considered a problem, for example. The ideal then, is for female marriage around the age of 25 and for men, a few years later (see Utomo 2014).

In Indonesia, having a child completes the domestic aspect of the transition to adulthood. Survey responses indicted that the median desired number of children was two, with a mean of 2.51, which was below the national fertility rate of 2.6 in that year (BKKBN 2007). The trend in the following seven years was that the national fertility rate flatlined at 2.4. (However the national target for the fertility rate for 2014 was 2.1, hence the government will re-introduce an intensive family planning program [Kapoor 2014]).

A minor gender difference was identified in our survey data. The mean for males on desired number of children was 2.66, but only 2.38 for females, close to the flatlined figure noted above. Could the young women respondents be contemplating the financial and career impact of having more than two children?

Work and Career Aspirations

Respondents were asked an open question about the job they wanted. Written answers were entered into SPSS as strings then coded as numerics using an adapted version of Erickson and Goldthorpe's (1992) taxonomy of job classifications. The same coding and analysis was applied to fathers' work to see whether a reproduction process (Bourdieu and Passeron 1990) was occurring. In coding, we distinguished between public service work (*pegawai negeri*) and middle-class work in the private sector. A category combining petty trader (*pedagang*) and shopkeeper (*pemilik toko*) was added. Table 2.3 shows that respondents sought jobs of higher status than those of their fathers.

Professional occupations such as doctor, lawyer, teacher, or accountant were desired by 33.3 per cent of respondents, even though only 4.2 per cent of all fathers had a professional job. Of female respondents, 41.1 per cent wanted professional jobs (especially as a doctor), compared to only 25.1 per cent of males. Similarly, although only 4.3 per cent of fathers were in the para-professional sector, almost 20 per cent wanted para-professional jobs. In this category, males mentioned police or military; females most often named nursing. Discrepancies between a father's occupations and the desired occupations of the respondents were one indication of the different kind of transition happening in Indonesia compared to in the West. That is, we do not see generational reproduction of occupation in Bourdieu's terms (1990), but rather a reflection

TABLE 2.3   *Job desired as a percentage, compared to fathers' work as a percentage[2] N = 3565.*

Kind of job desired	All respondents	Male	Female	Fathers' field of work
Professional	33.3	25.1	41.1	4.2
Para-professional	19.7	21.3	18.2	4.3
Public servant	7.6	7.5	7.7	17.9
Private sector	24.0	25.3	22.9	39.0
Trades and technical	5.4	10.1	0.9	0.6
Agriculture	0.4	0.5	0.3	16
Petty trade or shopkeeper	1.5	1.5	1.5	4.7
Semi-skilled or unskilled	0.3	0.3	0.3	5

of the upward credentialing of the Indonesian labor market and aspirations for upward social mobility. We note the substantially greater number of young women aspiring to the professions, even though only 2.7 per cent of their mothers had such occupations; however, the broader trends in youth employment discussed above will probably mean that it will be difficult for them to realize this ideal. However, the overall main pattern in female responses to questions about number of children and desired job was taken to imply that they tended to envisage their future in terms of being part of dual-career and dual-income households with two children.

Aspirations to work in the private sector were common in both sexes at 24 per cent, and the largest percentage (39%) of fathers also worked in this sector. This correlation does indicate some generational reproduction. The young people might perhaps have admired their fathers' salaries, which tend to be higher in private enterprise. Few respondents (7.6%) were interested in the public service as an occupation,[3] even though 17.9 per cent of their fathers were employed there. Less than 1 per cent of respondents were aiming to work in agriculture, whereas 16 per cent of their fathers were employed in that sector.

---

2   Cases of no response, or where a response could not be coded, for example—*gaji* (wages), are not included as percentages.

3   In a technical sense, teachers in Indonesian public schools are part of the civil service. However, in the survey, respondents wrote *guru* when they meant teacher and usually did not mention whether public or private. On the other hand, if they desired to work in the civil service, they wrote PNS (Pegawai Negeri Sipil). We therefore took the term PNS to refer to white collar work in a government office, and coded *guru* (teacher) as a profession.

So few girls wanted to become housewives that it was not separately coded, yet 48 per cent of mothers were reported as housewives. On reflection we decided this might not be strictly accurate since some of those mothers were probably working casually to supplement household income. Our interpretation here recognizes the discourse of women's work in Indonesia where even working women focus primarily on their identity as wives and mothers (see Robinson 2009; Ford and Parker 2008, 9). In reality, middle-class Indonesian households now commonly depend on two incomes (Utomo 2004). Overall, both female and male respondents, regardless of ethnicity, religion, or region, implied a dual-career and dual-income household with two children in the future.

The Good Life

We wanted to know how respondents imagined their lives in the future, so we asked them to rank a number of elements of the "good life" using a Likert preference scale. The list of elements was derived from a prior Australian study on young people's expectations of a future good life (Threadgold and Nilan 2009 (See table 2.4)).

Markers of the School-to-Work Transition in "Good Life" Data

The top ranked elements were: education, a harmonious family, religious faith, good health, and to own a home. There was no gender difference in responses.

TABLE 2.4 *Elements of the good life: relative importance ranked by means N= 3565.*

Element		Mean	Ranking
Good education	pendidikan baik	1.17	1
Harmonious family	keluarga rukun	1.21	2
Religious faith	taat beragama (beribadah)	1.23	3
Good health	kesehatan yang baik	1.27	4
Own a home	punya rumah	1.53	5
Love	kasih cinta	1.56	6
Children	anak-anak	1.77	7
Marriage	Menikah	1.80	8
Close friends	punya teman akrab	1.80	8
Well-paid job	pekerjaan dengan gaji tinggi	1.89	9
Interesting job	pekerjaan yang menarik	1.91	10
Luck	keberuntungan	1.93	11

Of these elements, education (completion of), a harmonious family (attainment of), and to "own a home" are all significant markers for transition to adulthood. Beyond that were elements of work. A "well-paid job" was ranked as extremely important by 43.8 per cent of males but by fewer (36.7%) females. Similarly, 42.2 per cent of males ranked "an interesting job" as extremely important but only 38.3 per cent of females. These differences imply that on the journey to adulthood future paid work still holds more significance for young men. 54.3 per cent of males ranked "marriage" as extremely important, compared to only 42.5 per cent of females. Similarly, 53 per cent of males ranked "having children" as extremely important compared to only 44.7 per cent of females. In ranking these two elements it may be that young men see them as components of a legitimate adult masculinity that has to be achieved, while young women regard them as something that will happen to them. Males also ranked "own a home" more highly than females, presumably as a measure of male provider worth. Indeed, in an earlier study Bennett (2005) found that in Lombok young women identified owning a home as an ideal trait of a potential husband.

In summary, analysis of the question on the "good life" indicates that there was striking unanimity in the importance of education, a harmonious family, religious faith, good health, and home ownership. However, for other elements of the "good life" there were variations according to gender that draw our attention.

A global comparative study of youth well-being that relied on available national statistics Indonesia ranked 19 of 30 countries on the following indices: citizen participation, economic opportunity, education, health, information communication and technology, and safety and security (Goldin, Patel, and Perry 2014, xii). However, when the rankings were adjusted for World Bank Income Classifications, Indonesia was number two of all "lower middle-income" countries in terms of economic opportunity, education, and health as measures of well-being (Goldin, Patel, and Perry 2014, 13–5). We might conclude that compared to many other developing countries, Indonesia provides a reasonable measure of these three elements of well-being in regard to young people as they make their transition to adulthood. However, as White (this volume) indicates, it is economic opportunity, especially access to paid work, that proves the sticking point. Suryadarma, Suryahadi, and Sumarto (2013, 556) report that the "majority of the unemployed in Indonesia are inexperienced young individuals who are relatively highly educated and still live with their parents". Thus, the most crucial transition for young people of both sexes is from education to work, especially given that Indonesia does not have a welfare safety net. In the remainder of this chapter we use survey data to illuminate young people's perceptions of this transition.

Perceptions of Entering the World of Work

Percentages in Table 2.3 above indicate that respondents were moving beyond their father's occupational status in their job and career aspirations. Yet given the high numbers expressing the desire to enter the professions and the difficulty of achieving this, the question must be asked, how realistic are these aspirations.[4]

It is quite unlikely that many survey respondents went on to fulfil the most popular expressed desire of becoming a doctor. Firstly, while over 60 per cent of young Indonesians aged 16–8 years attend senior secondary school, a much smaller percentage continue on to university (World Bank 2014). Secondly, even if young Indonesians do gain university entry, the kind of senior high school they attended will largely determine whether they get a public university place which gives access to professions like medicine. Thus, only respondents attending the best secondary schools in the sample would have been likely to obtain a sufficiently high examination score, and only around 20 per cent of applicants are accepted into government universities annually (Winarto-Rogers 2008). Thirdly, the overwhelming majority of those entering Indonesian public universities to train for the elite professions are the sons and daughters of parents from the prosperous middle-class (Hill and Wie 2013, 174). Our sample consisted of young people from a variety of socio-economic backgrounds, with only a small proportion coming from well-to-do families.

Life Dreams

Respondents showed concern about future paid work when asked about their life dreams.

Table 2.5 shows that for both sexes the largest number of life dreams (over half) referred to: "work, specific job, career, higher education", although girls indicated this kind of ambition more often. The next (smaller) category was "rich, famous, independent" or "making one's mark in the world". Altruistic life dreams were relatively few in number.

Variables of age, religion and location were tested against life dreams but there was no discernable pattern of difference. Once again, this finding seems to bear out the extent to which engagement in post-compulsory education in itself constitutes adherence to the unifying middle-class goal of upward mobility and economic prosperity, and that the school-to-work transition is critical in the transition to adulthood.

---

4   The question asked what job they would like rather than what job they expected to get, so sharply realistic expectations should not have been expected.

TABLE 2.5 *Main life dreams by sex N = 3565.*

Sex	Get a job, career, higher education	Become successful, rich, famous, independent (making one's mark in the world)	Become a good and/or useful person	Make parents and family proud, look after parents
Male	52.3%	17.9%	9.6%	5.8%
Female	61%	18.2%	6.9%	6.3%
Total	56.8%	18%	8.2%	6%

It was the subsequent question on obstacles to the stated life dreams that gave the strongest indication of a respondent's awareness of their own situation of disadvantage or relative advantage relevant to successfully making this transition. A cross-tabulation with the father's occupation signaled that there was a socio-economic pattern here. Testing the relationship between the socio-economic status of respondents and anticipation of future life obstacles required the assembly of a "class" indicator. This was done to allow a determination of the implied correlation between socio-economic class position and perceived obstacles to achieving the life dream.

Devising the "Class" Indicator

Unlike sex, age, and religion, socio-economic status or class is not readily determined through a response to a single question. So a measure of class or socio-economic status in survey analysis often has to be constructed, in this case as a weighted indicator from relevant variables that could be combined to indicate the "class" location of respondents.

Firstly, the father's occupation is the most obvious variable signaling class position, since this points to both household income and resources to support the young person in both education and finding work. Secondly, the number of books in the family home was found to be important. Of 322 survey respondents claiming only 1–10 books at home, more than a third of fathers were in agriculture or semiskilled/unskilled work. Of 717 claiming 51–100 books, over 40 per cent of fathers were in private enterprise. Of 426 claiming 101–200 books, more than half of fathers were in private enterprise or the professions. This pattern supports the notion that the number of books in a student's family home is an indicator of "cultural capital" (Freebody 1993; Bourdieu 1986), important in the process of socio-economic reproduction that constitutes ongoing class divisions. So that was the second variable used to construct the class indicator.

The other variable that pointed to class/socio-economic status was whether there was a computer in the home. Only 6.7 per cent of respondents with fathers in agriculture and 16.9 per cent in semi-skilled or unskilled labor had computers, while 69.5 per cent of respondents with public servant fathers, for example, had one computer at home and sometimes more. Having a computer at home is viewed as a new form of cultural capital, even though it actually acts as an amplifier for existing cultural capital—"the benefits of having a home computer were substantially greater for children from more affluent and educated families" (Attewell 2001, 257).

In summary, a weighted "class" indicator was calculated using the following relevant variables, with father's occupation emphasized,

- father's occupation (0.6)
- number of books in the home (0.2)
- having a computer at home (0.2)

Calculation of this class indicator allowed the identification of five discrete class locations for survey respondents: from lowest [0] to highest [4]. The class location [0] assumes very modest family income and not much cultural capital. For [0] respondents, the possibility of attending a high status school or university leading to a prestigious and well-paid future career is constrained (although not impossible). Class location [4] assumes the father has a prestigious occupation, obtains a high income, and that there is important cultural capital in the home. For [4] respondents, the possibility of attending a high status public school or university leading to a prestigious and well-paid future career is facilitated (although not determined). We acknowledge that these five "class" locations constitute fine distinctions within a broad socio-economic status range of "intermediate classes" (White 2014) in Indonesia rather than a straightforward working-class/middle-class division.

Obstacles to Life Dreams

Using a cross-tabulation, obstacles to life dreams showed a distinct relationship with the weighted class indicator.

Table 2.6 indicates that those in less privileged class locations anticipated encountering financial, resource, and access obstacles, while those in more comfortable economic circumstances were more focused on negative personal traits as possible obstacles to the achievement of their dreams. A calculation

TABLE 2.6 *Class location by obstacles to dreams*[5] *N= 2632.*

			Obstacles to dreams	
			Lack of money, resources, opportunities	Laziness, negative personal traits
Class location	0	Count	302	39
		% within class	64.4%	8.3%
	1	Count	642	95
		% within class	74.8%	11.1%
	2	Count	657	299
		% within class	50%	22.8%
	3	Count	221	302
		% within class	27.1%	37.0%
	4	Count	9	66
		% within class	9.2%	67.3%
	Total	Count	1831	801

using Spearman's rho was undertaken to verify this apparent relationship between the variables of class location and obstacles to dreams.

In Table 2.7 a rho value of −0.342 (p = <0.01, significant at the 0.01 level) indicates a small but definite correlation between class location and the likelihood of writing about lack of money, resources, or opportunities as an obstacle to the achievement of a life dream. This means that youth from more privileged families were less likely to have identified "lack of money, resources, or opportunities" as the primary obstacle. The correlation was notable, given that this was an open question, not one inviting choice from predetermined categories.

When a rho calculation was applied to the other main obstacle, a complementary picture emerged:

In Table 2.8 a rho value of 0.284 (p = <0.01, significant at 0.01)—also a small but definite correlation—indicates that respondents in less privileged circumstances were less likely to write something about laziness or negative personal traits. This implies that those in more privileged circumstances were more likely to nominate non-material factors such as "laziness, negative personal

---

5 Not all respondents answered this question, and some answers could not be coded productively because they were idiosyncratic or referred to fate, for example.

TABLE 2.7 *Correlation of class location with obstacle: lack of money, resources, opportunities.*

			Lack of Money, resources, opportunities	Class
Spearman's rho	Lack of money, resources, opportunities	Correlation Coefficient	1.000	−0.342(**)
		Sig. (2-tailed)	.	0.000
		N	3556	3556
	Class location	Correlation Coefficient	−0.342(**)	1.000
		Sig. (2-tailed)	0.000	.
		N	3556	3556

** CORRELATION IS SIGNIFICANT AT THE 0.01 LEVEL (2-TAILED).

TABLE 2.8 *Correlation of class location with obstacle: laziness, negative personal traits.*

			Class	Laziness, negative personal traits
Spearman's rho	Class location	Correlation Coefficient	1.000	0.284 (**)
		Sig. (2-tailed)	.	0.000
		N	3556	3556
	Laziness, negative personal traits	Correlation Coefficient	0.284 (**)	1.000
		Sig. (2-tailed)	0.000	.
		N	3556	3556

** CORRELATION IS SIGNIFICANT AT THE 0.01 LEVEL (2-TAILED).

traits" as important obstacles to achieving their dreams. These are obstacles that can in theory be diminished by reflexive work on the self, by dedicated application to task, and by a change in attitude, unlike material obstacles that are external to the self and are much less amenable to change through personal action (see Threadgold and Nilan 2009).

From these rho calculations we suggest that, for the young Indonesians we surveyed, those lower on the socio-economic scale perceive, quite accurately, that they do not have a strong chance of realizing their life dreams and, by extension, their career aspirations, due to material and economic obstacles.

Material Obstacles

The major material obstacle to career dreams is presumably the cost to families of education. For example, the per-student cost of secondary schooling is about three times that of primary schooling, while the per-student cost of tertiary schooling is about 13 times as high (Maralani 2008, 713). The families of many survey respondents would have already made considerable sacrifices to keep their child in schooling until the age of 18. The cost of secondary schooling varies greatly across schools. Muslim schools are usually poor and under-resourced, but have the advantage of charging low enrolment fees. Government secondary schools vary greatly in quality and resources, from low quality to very desirable. While all government schools should charge the same enrolment fees in principle, in practice the most popular government schools are able to demand very high enrolment fees and extra-curricular payments. Expensive Christian secondary schools offer pupils an excellent chance of gaining a competitive examination score, but are well beyond the means of most families. Finally, tertiary education is expensive, and scholarships are hard to come by. In short, whether a young person can access tertiary and even secondary education depends primarily on the socio-economic status of his or her family.

Other material "obstacles" in poorer families include the necessity for the young person to provide an income for the household as soon as possible after graduation, and often for the education of younger siblings. Other obstacles are constituted by the difficulties and expenses for young people, especially young women, in relocating for tertiary training and education. Finally, while state and Christian universities offer competitive qualifications for the graduate job market, private tertiary educational institutions do not. It is indeed unfortunate that there are so many unregulated, low-quality training institutes and universities that take the enrolment fees of economically disadvantaged students without delivering the expected outcome of a job-ready qualification.

Conclusion

In this chapter we considered survey data from a purposive sample of 3565 Indonesian youth engaged in education in 2007. Responses depicted young people with upwardly mobile aspirations, yet strong commitment to normative family formation and religious faith. It seems contemporary middle-class youth transitions in Indonesia are not so much fragmented as extended by the necessity to complete schooling and some form of tertiary training before marriage and independent living can occur. The notable work preference in survey responses was for a professional career but we consider that many respondents would not have achieved this.

Our statistical calculations above indicate that they were aware to some extent of the nature of obstacles they faced in achieving their life dreams, with those from poorer backgrounds strongly identifying financial constraint. Moreover, while female respondents were clearly attracted to the idea of becoming a medical doctor, our analysis of responses to other survey questions indicate that this aspiration was unlikely to be realized for all but the few from affluent backgrounds, and even then they would have needed excellent examination results in mathematics and science.

A further finding from the survey data was that both sexes were looking forward to a "good life" in the future, characterized by the foundation of a good education, then a harmonious family, religious faith, good health, and home ownership. Some gender differences were also evident here. For example, male respondents ranked marriage, children, and paid work more highly than female respondents, perhaps indicating that all three constitute important markers of transition to adulthood for Indonesian males.

In conclusion, we propose that moving from education to work was the most important dimension of transition for survey respondents. It is critical for the eventual achievement of adult status, not least because the other key markers of marriage/parenthood and autonomous housing depend on it. Yet many of the original survey respondents would be struggling right now to achieve this as they move through their twenties. While Indonesia has been enjoying economic growth, this has seen a concomitant upward credentialing of the labor market, meaning that employers demand ever higher qualifications from job applicants. However, this trend has not been accompanied by a high rate of full-time job growth. Senior secondary and tertiary graduates still enter a distinctly unfavorable labor market, in which only those lucky few from privileged backgrounds with the best qualifications and family connections can expect to quickly find a well-paid secure job.

References

Aswicahyono, Haryo, Hall Hill, and Dionisius Narjoko. 2011. "Indonesian Industrialization: Jobless Growth?" In *UpdateIndonesia 2011*, edited by Chris Manning and Sudarno Sumarto, 183–226. Singapore: Institute of Southeast Asian Studies.

Attewell, Paul. 2001. "The first and second digital divides." *Sociology of Education* 74:252–59.

Bennett, Linda. 2005. *Women, Islam and Modernity.* London: Routledge.
Beta, Annisa. 2014. "Hijabers: How Young Urban Muslim Women Redefine Themselves in Indonesia." *International Communication Gazette* 76:377–89.
BKKBN. 2007. *Indonesia Country Report,* Jakarta: National Family Planning Coordinating Board – Republic of Indonesia. Accessed May 1, 2009: http://www.itp-bkkbn.org/pulin/004-population_data_information/004_country_report_2009.pdf
Bourdieu, Pierre. 1986. "The Forms of Capital." In *Handbook of Theory and Research for the Sociology of Education,* edited by John G. Richardson, 241–58. New York: Greenwood Press.
Bourdieu, Pierre and Jean-Claude Passeron. 1990. *Reproduction in Education, Society and Culture.* London: Sage.
BPS. 2008. *Perkembangan Beberapa Indikator Utama Sosial-ekonomi Oktober 2008,* BPS katalog 3101015. Jakarta: Badan Pusat Statistik. Accessed March 20, 2009: http://www.bps.go.id/leaflet/booklet_okt08.pdf
BPS. 2014. *Education indicators.* Jakarta: Badan Pusat Statistik, 2014. Accessed August 20, 2014: http://www.bps.go.id/eng/tab_sub/view.php/excel.php?id_subyek=28%20&notab=1
Coxhead, Ian. 2014. "Did Indonesia's Boom Leave its Poor Behind? Adverse Labor Market Trends in the Post-crisis Era." Public Seminar Paper. Jakarta: SMERU, 2014. Accessed August 19, 2014: http://www.aae.wisc.edu/coxhead/papers/CoxheadIndonesia_Boom_Labor_Markets-Feb2104.pdf
Egel, Daniel, and Djavad Salehi-Isfahani. 2010. "Youth Transitions to Employment and Marriage in Iran: Evidence from the School to Work Transition Survey." *Middle East Development Journal* 2:89–120.
Elmhirst, Rebecca. 2007. "Tigers and Gangsters: Masculinities and Feminised Migration in Indonesia." *Population, Space and Place* 13:225–38.
Erikson, Robert, and John H. Goldthorpe. 1992. *The Constant Flux.* Oxford: Clarendon.
Ford, Michele, and Lyn Parker. 2008. "Introduction: Thinking About Indonesian Women and Work." In *Women and Work in Indonesia,* edited by Michele Ford and Lyn Parker, 1–16. London: Routledge, 2008.
Freebody, Peter. 1993. "Social Class and Reading." In *Literacy in Contexts: Australian Perspectives and Issues,* edited by Allan Luke and Pam Gilbert, 68–84. Sydney: Allen & Unwin.
Furlong, Andy, and Fred Cartmel. 2006. *Young People and Social Change: Individualization and Risk in Late Modernity.* 2nd edition. Milton Keynes: Open University Press.
Gauthier, Anne. 2007. "Becoming a Young Adult: An International Perspective on Transition to Adulthood." *European Journal of Population* 23:217–23.
Goldin, Nicole, Payal Patel, and Katherine Perry. 2014. *The Global Youth Wellbeing Index.* London: Centre for Strategic and International Studies. Accessed August 20, 2014: http://www.youthindex.org/reports/globalyouthwellbeingindex.pdf

Guharoy, Debnath. 2010. "Youth Embracing New Decade with Growing Optimism", *The Jakarta Post*, 19 January: http://thejakartapost.com/news/2010/01/19/

Hill, Hal, and Thee Kian Wie. 2013. "Indonesian Universities: Rapid Growth, Major Challenges." In *Education in Indonesia*, edited by Daniel Suryadarma and Gavin Jones, 160–79. Singapore: ISEAS.

Jones, Gavin. 2005. "The 'Flight from Marriage' in South-east and East Asia." *Journal of Comparative Family Studies* 35:1–15.

Jones, Gavin, and Gubhaju Bina. 2008. "Trends in Age at Marriage in the Provinces of Indonesia." Asia Research Institute Working Paper 105. Singapore: National University of Singapore. Accessed March 24, 2009: www.nus.ari.edu.sg/pub/wps.htm

Juárez, Fatima, and Cecilia Gayet. 2014. "Transitions to Adulthood in Developing Countries." *Annual Review of Sociology* 40:521–38.

Kapoor, Kanupriya. 2014. "Indonesia to Face Opportunity, Risk as Population Grows by a Third." *Reuters US Edition,* 30 January. Accessed August 20, 2014: http://www.reuters.com/article/2014/01/30/us-indonesia-population idUSBREA0T0GK20140130

Luvaas, Brent. 2013. "Material Interventions: Indonesian DIY Fashion and the Regime of the Global Brand." *Cultural Anthropology* 28:127–43.

Manning, Chris, and Kurnya Roesad. 2007. "The Manpower Law of 2003 and its Implementing Regulations: Genesis, Key Articles and Potential Impact." *Bulletin of Indonesian Economic Affairs* 43:59–86.

Maralani, Vida. 2008. "The Changing Relationship Between Family Size and Educational Attainment over the Course of Socioeconomic Development: Evidence from Indonesia." *Demography* 45:693–717.

May, Tim. 1997. *Social Research: Issues, Methods and Process*. 2nd edition. Buckingham: Open University Press.

McCulloch, Neil, Amit Grover, Amit and Asep Suryahadi. 2014. "The Labor Market Impact of the 2009 Financial Crisis in Indonesia." In *Working Through the Crisis: Jobs and Policies in Developing Countries During the Great Recession,* edited by Arup Banerji, David Newhouse, Pierella Paci, and David Robalino, 135–62. Washington: The World Bank.

Minza, Wenty Marina. 2014. *Growing Up and Being Young in an Indonesian Provincial Town*. Amsterdam: University of Amsterdam Press.

Naafs, Suzanne. 2012. *Youth, Work and Lifestyles in an Indonesian Industrial Town*. Rotterdam: Institute of Social Studies, Netherlands.

Naafs, Suzanne, and Ben White. 2012. "Intermediate Generations: Reflections on Indonesian Youth Studies." *The Asia Pacific Journal of Anthropology* 13: 3–20.

Nilan, Pam. 2008. "Youth Transitions to Urban, Middle-class Marriage in Indonesia: Faith, Family and Finances." *Journal of Youth Studies* 11:65–82.

Nilan, Pam, Lyn Parker, Linda Bennett, and Kathryn Robinson. 2011. "Indonesian Youth Looking Towards the Future." *Journal of Youth Studies* 14:709–28.

Parker, Lyn, and Pam Nilan. 2013. *Adolescents in Contemporary Indonesia*. London: Routledge.

Roberts, Ken, Gary Pollock, Sabina Rustamova, Zhala Mammadova, and Jochen Tholend. 2009. "Young Adults' Family and Housing Life-stage Transitions during Post-communist Transition in the South Caucasus." *Journal of Youth Studies* 12:151–66.

Robinson, Kathryn. 2015. "Masculinity, Sexuality and Islam: The Gender Politics of Regime Change in Indonesia." In *Sex and Sexualities in Contemporary Indonesia: Sexual Politics, Health, Diversity and Representations*, edited by Linda Rae Bennett and Sharyn Graham Davies, 51–68. London and New York: Routledge.

Smith-Hefner, Nancy. 2005. "The New Muslim Romance: Changing Patterns of Courtship and Marriage Among Educated Javanese Youth." *Journal of Southeast Asian Studies*, 36:441–59.

Suryadarma, Daniel, and Gavin Jones. 2013. "Meeting the Education Challenge." In *Education in Indonesia*, edited by Daniel Suryadarma and Gavin Jones, 1–14. Singapore: ISEAS.

Suryadarma, Daniel, Asep Suryahadi and Sudarno Sumarto. 2013. "Sectoral Growth and Job Creation: Evidence from Indonesia." *Journal of International Development* 25:549–61.

Sziraczki, Gyorgy, and Annemarie Reerink. 2004. *Report of Survey on the School-to-Work Transition in Indonesia*. GENPROM working paper 14. Geneva: International Labour Office.

Threadgold, Steven, and Pam Nilan. 2009. "Reflexivity of Contemporary Youth, Risk and Cultural Capital." *Current Sociology* 57:47–68.

UNDP. 2008. *Human Development Report 2007/2008*. Washington: United Nations Development Program. Accessed May 3, 2009: http://hdr.undp.org/en/reports/global/hdr2007-2008/

UNESCO. 2009. *EFA Global Monitoring Report 2009*: http://unesdoc.unesco.org/images/0017/001776/177683e.pdf

Utomo, Ariane. 2004. "Women as Equal Partners and Secondary Earners: Gendered Expectations on Career and Family Formation in Modern Indonesia." Paper presented at Australian Population Association 12th Biennial Conference, Canberra, 15–17 September. Accessed March 22, 2009: http://www.apa.org.au/upload/2004-3A_Utomo.pdf

Utomo, Ariane. 2014. "Marrying Up? Trends in Age and Education Gaps Among Married Couples in Indonesia." *Journal of Family Issues*. Published online before print June 5, 2014, doi: 10.1177/0192513X14538023

White, Ben. 2014. "Betting on the Middle? Middletown, Modjukoto and 'Middle Indonesia'." In *In search of Middle Indonesia: Middle Classes in Provincial Towns*, edited by Gerry van Klinken and Ward Berenschot, 35–48. Leiden: Brill.

Winarto-Rogers, Isla. 2008. "Unemployment in Indonesia." Paper presented to Australian International Education Conference, Brisbane, 7–10 October. Accessed March 20, 2009: http://www.aiec.idp.com/pdf/winarto_Thurs_1630_M4.pdf

World Bank. 2014. *Indonesia: Avoiding the Gap.* Development Policy Review. Washington: World Bank. Accessed August 19: 2014 http://www.worldbank.org/content/dam/Worldbank/document/EAP/Indonesia/Indonesia-development-policy-review-2014-english.pdf

PART 2

Education—Securing Youth Futures?

Introduction to Part 2

Education has been highlighted by successive Indonesian governments as the key to national development and a pathway out of poverty, and school completion rates in Indonesia seem good. The nation is regarded as on track to meet its 2015 target (which reflects the Millennium Development Goals [MDG]) of universal primary education, and is well on the way to reaching the goal of 9 years compulsory education. The AII survey of high school students (Nilan et al this volume) found that, overall, they embraced education as the best way to secure their future and their transition to adulthood.

However, the education system is poor, and the decentralization of educational management post-2001 has not had the desired effect of improving the quality of education, in regard to infrastructure, teacher quality, or lessening teacher absenteeism. Lack of equality is still a problem, as students in rural areas and those from poor families have fewer opportunities, and hence the school system still perpetuates class differences.

The two chapters in this section address education and transitions to adulthood in two very different communities: rural Java and a mining town in the interior of Sulawesi. In both cases, young people must travel to urban centers to further their education. White and Margiyatin emphasize that de-agrarianization in Java (where it has been especially marked) means there are few jobs in rural areas and so young people need to go to cities to find work. Schooling, coupled with the influence of mass media, has transformed rural youth in Java into people ready for urban, industrial work.

However, the unemployment rate in Indonesia is high among its youth (around 30 per cent), and especially high for university graduates. Youth who have migrated for education face difficulties finding work when they return home, even though there has been an "inflation" of educational prerequisites for many jobs: a junior high school certificate is no longer sufficient for factory employment, for example. Many of the chapters in this book record the disappointment of educated youth at the difficulties they face in finding employment after years of struggle and sacrifice by themselves and their parents.

The extreme case of de-agrarianization is illustrated by the youth of the well-established mining town of Sorowako (Robinson), where industrial development was predicated on the destruction of the agricultural economy. For many young people from the town, "the good life" means being able to return home to work for the mining company and live near their families in their ancestral territories. They have done the self-fashioning necessary to transition to modern adulthood but there are not enough jobs, especially at levels commensurate with their education.

In discussing school-to-work transitions, an important theme that emerges is the impact of the prolongation of childhood and infantilizing of youth due to increasing years of education. In some urban areas children do work part-time which, as in in the West, is associated with better school performance and an easier transition to the labor market. But this is by no means universal.

Ben White has commented that this delayed entry to the labor market has meant a shift from understanding social reproduction through the "value of children" to contemporary experiences of "priceless and useless" children who do not contribute to the household economy but need money to continue schooling.

CHAPTER 3

Teenage Experiences of School, Work, and Life in a Javanese Village

Ben White and C. Ugik Margiyatin[1]

Structure and Action in Young Village Lives

It is now a commonplace to observe that children and young people deserve to be properly researched and understood (see White, this volume). Through listening to young people we gain a better understanding of their experiences and of their capacity to analyze and critically confront situations and problems. This actor focus, however, should not obscure the "structural" fact that children are born and grow up within webs of power, and within larger social economic structures that shape these individual experiences.

These larger structures involve both generational tensions and contestations between young people and the adult world, and the political-economic structures (local, national, and global), that shape the processes of social reproduction in which young people live and grow. Without incorporating these larger structures and the webs of power involved, discourses of youth "agency" and "participation" and development interventions based on them become de-politicized. Reconciling "actor" and "structure" perspectives is an important methodological challenge in childhood and youth studies, and in the social sciences and development studies more generally. There is nothing contradictory in viewing young people—like adults—as simultaneously victims (or beneficiaries) of structural relationships and "constrained agents" maneuvering within those structures and, on occasions, working to change them.

This chapter explores teenagers' experience of school, work, and life in "Kali Loro"[2] village, a relatively typical rural Javanese community marked by entrenched

---

1 This chapter originated in the unpublished report *Teenage Experiences and Views of School, Work and Life in a Javanese Village: Kali Loro, Yogyakarta* by Ben White and C. Ugik Margiyatin. This was part of a comparative project on *Newly Emerging Needs of Children and Youth* in several countries, undertaken by the International Centre for Child and Youth Studies and supported by Plan Netherlands. Research for this study is linked to White's on-going long-term study of "changing childhoods" in Kali Loro, where he first carried out ethnographic research in 1972–73. Thanks to Suzanne Naafs and two anonymous referees for their helpful comments on an earlier version.
2 Pseudonym.

differences in (but not extremes of) poverty and wealth. The study is based on in-depth interviews with four young teenagers in 2006, complemented by interviews with other teenagers and young out-migrants conducted in 2000, 2004, and 2005–06 by Noryanto and Ugik Margiyatin in the same village. The interview process was not always easy, although both Noryanto and Margiyatin were themselves "youth" (in their early 20s) at the time of the interviews and Margiyatin was herself a resident of Kali Loro, thus potentially avoiding some of the power differentials inherent in adults' research on youth, and even approaching "peer research". The respondents clearly felt constrained by the lack of privacy during the interviews, at which one or more adults (parents or others) were usually present. We also experimented with the "PhotoVoice" technique, in which the young respondent is provided with a camera and invited to take a series of photos which s/he feels depicts her/his life and world, and then to caption them.

After a brief introduction to Kali Loro village and some of the changes it has experienced since the early 1970s, we describe the important transformations in education, and in children's division of time between work and school, over the same period. We then present two teenagers' stories in some detail to give readers a feel for the kind of information we were able to obtain. In the rest of this chapter we explore various aspects of teenagers' views on education, work, lifestyles, social life, and futures, bringing in more material from these and the other interviews. The "ethnographic present" refers to the period of the interviews (2000–2006), although we have added one or two details on subsequent developments, particularly on the post-2006 spread of the virtual/digital in young people's lives.

Kali Loro in the 1970s and 2000s

The village of Kali Loro lies in the northern part of Kulon Progo district, in the Special Region of Yogyakarta (southern central Java). It is a large village complex with a population of about 8,000 people in 2,000 households, lying on the fringes of a thin belt of irrigated rice fields (*sawah*) between the Progo river and a low mountain range. At the time of our first study (1972–73) more than one-third of households were landless, while a further 40 per cent owned less than 0.2 hectares; however, six per cent of households owned more than one-half of all the *sawah*. Diversity of livelihoods was already quite striking, with most households earning more than half their income from non-farm sources, particularly petty trade, handicrafts production, and the processing of various foods and snacks for sale.

Since that first field study in the 1970s there are many signs of material improvement.[3] Better roads and a new bridge have cut the travel time to the city of Yogyakarta by about 40 per cent, and the village's main road, on which motor traffic used to be rare, is now a busy thoroughfare for buses, trucks, private cars, and motorcycles. Daily commuting to work or school in Yogyakarta is now possible, though costly, by public transport or motorcycle. The quality of housing is much improved, as nearly all houses have had access to electricity since the mid-1980s, and more than half of all households now have a television set (there were none in the village in 1972–73). Improved irrigation, intensification of inputs, and improved practices have brought rice yields to about twice their former levels; a small plot of only 0.1 ha can now provide about 0.7 tons of milled rice per year, enough to supply the food requirement of a family of four or five persons. Despite fertility well above replacement level, the village's total population has not grown, due to large-scale out-migration of young people.

The pattern of land distribution has become slightly more unequal. The village now produces a surplus of rice above its own requirements; however, because of unequal access to land only one-third of households were self-sufficient in rice in 1999–2000, while one-third had to buy rice for more than half the year. Despite quite marked differences in wealth, lifestyle, and religion[4], of the kind which often give rise to conflict, in Kali Loro life may be described as relatively safe, and open social conflicts are rare.

The Prolongation of Childhood[5]

Excepting a small minority of elite children, the "prolongation of childhood" (or "postponement of adulthood") in rural Java, resulting from more general and longer schooling, increasing age at marriage, and postponed entry into labor markets, is largely a post-colonial phenomenon. In the half-century since Independence, each successive generation in Kali Loro has reached progressively higher education levels. While almost one-third of boys and four-fifths of all girls born in the 1920s and 1930s had no education at all, the numbers of

---

3 Publications on Kali Loro in the 1970s include Stoler (1977a; 1977b; 1978) and White (1976a; 1976b; 1976c). Publications resulting from the 1999–2000 re-study include Abdullah and White (2006) and White (2012).
4 The village has a minority Roman Catholic population of about 15 percent. The major schism however is between traditionalist and modernist Muslims, who are about equally represented.
5 This aspect is analyzed in greater detail, based on the results of time-allocation studies carried out in 1972–73 and 2000, in White (2013).

children not receiving any education among those born in the 1950s were small for girls and insignificant for boys, and by the 1970s—despite widespread poverty—virtually all children attended primary school and many continued to lower secondary school (SMP). More remarkably, among those born in the 1970s (the early years of the Suharto regime) nearly all continued on to lower secondary school and around four-fifths (slightly more for boys, slightly less for girls) entered upper secondary school, thus continuing their education beyond the age of 15 at which compulsory education in Indonesia now ends.

This has had important implications for the involvement of young people in work. Comparison of teenagers' time-use shows important changes between the early 1970s and the next generation in the early 2000s. In the early 1970s the most important activities for teenage boys were the care and feeding of animals, followed by firewood collection, help on the household's own rice farm, and petty trade/crafts. Teenage girls, besides housework and child care, made large inputs to the household economy through trade and handicrafts, followed by agricultural wage-work (mainly rice-planting and harvesting) and non-farm waged work (particularly hand-loom weaving in local workshops). These girls were working hours approaching those of adult women; more than 10 hours daily compared to about 5.5 hours for boys. Most children in landless and land-poor households had experience of wage-work, and/or work such as handicrafts which generated cash income, often used by children to provide for their own needs, such as clothes, school fees, snacks, and tobacco.

By the turn of the 21st century, as already noted, education up to the age of 15 had become virtually universal, with just four per cent of both boys and girls aged 13–15 out of school; more remarkably, four-fifths of boys and 70 per cent of girls in the 16–18 age group were attending upper secondary school. School occupies increasingly more of the time of Kali Loro's children, both boys and girls. As Shiraishi (1997, 123) notes, the education system is now playing a large role in the process by which childhood has become prolonged. Hours spent in school and home-study have increased, as education now occupies close to 40 hours per week for teenagers of both sexes. While teenage girls used to lag behind boys in education, they have now caught up, and girls aged 13–18 actually spend slightly more time in school and home study (37.9 hours) than boys (36.6 hours). Hours of "real" work, both domestic and directly productive, have declined for both groups, but on the whole more for boys than for girls. Girls are still, as in the 1970s, making far greater inputs in domestic work than boys, but the gender differences have now sharpened somewhat. While the hours devoted to non-school work have declined, it certainly is not correct that "children don't work anymore", as some parents told us in 1999–2000. In the 13–18 age group boys are still contributing 2.5 hours per day, and girls almost 4 hours per day, of "real" work, despite the fact that school and study involve them in something close to a 40-hour week which, in the West, is we would regarded as a "full-time" occupation.

Santi's Story[6]

> Since I was a small child, my parents have left me here with my Grandma. They live in Bogor and come to see us once a year, at Lebaran. I communicate with them often, but only by post or telephone

Santi (15 years old when interviewed in 2006) is the youngest of her parents' two children. She was born in Sragen (Central Java), but from the age of three was raised by her paternal grandparents in Kali Loro. In 2006, Santi lived with her grandmother and elder sister. Her grandmother ran a small farm, more to pass the time than as a main source of livelihood. Santi's sister was in class three at upper secondary school (SMU), while Santi had just completed lower secondary school and transferred to the state Vocational High School (SMK) on the outskirts of Yogyakarta city, studying dressmaking.

Santi's parents both work in a plastic factory in Bogor (West Java). They left their two children with the grandparents in Kali Loro at an early age, since their incomes were not sufficient to provide for the whole family in Bogor; the working parents promised that they would eventually come back to live in the village. The children communicate with their parents by telephone from the local public phone kiosk (*wartel*), but not more than once a month. Santi and her sister have both asked for mobile phones but this had not yet been allowed.[7] Their parents usually come home to visit them only twice a year, including the Lebaran holiday.

Santi said that she was unhappy as a child because she had few friends. She spent her time at home. In the PhotoVoice exercise, she took photos of her neighbor's young children with whom she often played in the late afternoon, and wrote as caption "with them, I recover the times [i.e. the childhood] that I once lost".

Living with her grandmother, Santi had to follow both her grandmother's and parents' advice, and discipline in the home was strict. Her grandmother said, "I don't allow her to play or make visits too freely, after school she has to come straight home. A girl must always look after herself, it's different for boys".

---

6 Pseudonym.
7 In the years since 2006 cellphone ownership has spread rapidly all over Indonesia and by the time of the next planned re-study in Kali Loro we expect to find that nearly all teenagers have access to a phone.

In choosing a secondary school and a study path, Santi followed her parents' advice, although this was not what she wanted. She tried to accept her mother's views and arguments that getting a skill like dressmaking would help her to find a job. After graduating, Santi hopes to open her own business in Bogor. Besides being closer to her parents, she thinks it would be easier to earn money there. In the village it is difficult to earn money as a seamstress, due to ever-growing competition,

> Here in the village people hardly ever buy new clothes, only once a year for Lebaran. A clothes maker here would have no business. It's different in the city, people surely buy clothes at other times of year.

Santi feels that life in the village is pleasant because the air is unpolluted, while the city is always busy and crowded. But village people often gossip, and she does not like the way they are always finding fault with each other. Once when a young boy (a neighbor) was trying to approach her, a neighbor spread malicious gossip; "when the neighbors do this, you feel scared and ashamed".

With her parents so far away, if Santi had problems she could only discuss them with her sister. She did not have any close friends to whom she could confide personal matters. Having once had the experience of a friend who could not keep a secret, she was reluctant to confide in others. When there was a problem, Santi wrote it all down and then burned what she had written; this gave some comfort, although it may not have solved the problem.

Santi thinks that men and women should have equal roles, including equal opportunities in education and employment, and she aspires to continue working after marriage to add to her husband's income. When asked if her school matched her expectations, Santi explained, "My present school is good enough for me. The facilities for practical work are quite complete. I hope the school will give me the knowledge I need for my future life. It costs a lot so it shouldn't be a bad school". The entrance fee for this SMK was about Rp. 2 million, and the tuition fees (SPP) were Rp. 45,000 per month (in 2006).

Eko's Story[8]

Eko is the oldest child in a family of moderate means. Both his parents have salaried jobs as civil servants in a secondary school. Eko (14 years old when

---
8 Pseudonym.

interviewed in 2006) has just entered the government vocational secondary school (SMK) on the outskirts of Yogyakarta, specializing as an electrician.

He actually wanted to be a policeman, but considered being able to earn a good living most important. "That", said Eko, "is impossible if you stay in the village". He anticipates that he will have to move to the city. That is why he followed his parents' advice to choose an education that could help him find a job. He had formerly made a plan with his parents, that if he did not get admitted to the police force, he would go to college. By studying for the electrician's diploma he hoped later to work in a factory that produces household appliances like refrigerators, fans, and electric cookers. He has relatives in Tangerang (one of the industrial belts near Jakarta) who he said had a good and pleasant life.

Eko feels pleased with his new school, because he now has many friends from both the Yogyakarta region and further away, although he has not yet made any close friends. Many of them like to use rough language, which shocked him. "I still find it hard to get close to my new schoolmates…trivial things can make them break out in bad language. My friends in SMP weren't like that. I still have to get used to it".

His teachers are mostly okay, but one throws things at the students when he is angry. He thinks the students are quite badly behaved. When they do not obey the teachers, they are punished by being made to do push-ups, and if they still don't listen to the teacher they, or even their parents, would be given a formal warning.

Eko and his school friends have a band. They often go to a studio to practice, and they have given a performance at their school. They like pop music. Eko has been to Malioboro[9] a few times on a motorbike, although he had no license. In the village, Eko participates in mutual-aid work (*gotong-royong*) and the Karang Taruna youth group, although the group is often dormant with no activities. When they go to the Karang Taruna meeting, the youths his age usually just follow the proposals made by the older ones.

Eko's desire for greater freedom, and his frustration at parental regulation of his life, began when he started secondary school.

> When I go out, my parents still ask me where I'm going and tell me when I have to be home. Actually, young people like me can understand where to draw the line between good and bad behavior and should be given more leeway in how we spend our time. Too much control makes us apathetic. I feel resentful and irritated when my parents behave like

---

[9] The city of Yogyakarta's main shopping street.

that…to get over it, usually I turn on the radio full blast, or go to a friend's house.

Eko preferred village life to urban life: in the village, people still support and help each other and the air is clean. But he commented, "What kind of work can I get if I stay here in the village, I'll never make any money…I can't even be a farmer!" He thinks there is no way he can stay in the village unless he gets a salaried job (for example in the civil service, army, or police). His uncle in the police has advised him to apply for the force. He had seen friends and neighbors join the police or armed forces, and they are considered very successful by the community. "If you can get into the police, the work is not too hard…[and] the money is good, your future is assured".

Teenagers' Views on Education, Work and Futures

Teenagers in Kali Loro face a major contradiction. They and their families make great efforts to acquire their upper secondary school diploma, and the escalating costs of secondary education require increasing sacrifices to make this possible, but the "pushdown" effect of widening access to education means that these diplomas are increasingly less likely to open doors to the jobs for which they are qualified. A generation of New-Order rural development (1970s to late 1990s) has provided impressive infrastructural and educational improvement in the village but generated very few new rural employment opportunities for young people, or at least none that are attractive to secondary-school leavers. The futures which teenagers envisage, therefore, nearly always involve leaving the village. Those we interviewed experienced long waiting periods and a need for personal contacts for access to almost any kind of qualified job.

The four teenagers interviewed in 2006 were all in the period of transition from lower to upper secondary school. Already, at this age (around 15 years), teenagers and their parents are confronted with choices. The alternatives to upper secondary school (and the study path [*jurusan*] taken within the school) are limited by financial means and the grades achieved in lower secondary (SMP). Middle and lower income teenagers envisage looking for work directly after completing secondary school, while those whose parents are more financially secure intend to continue to tertiary studies.

Secondary school is not only about learning; it is also about lifestyles, status, and friends. Extended schooling is part of a desirable modern lifestyle which school teaches them to aspire to: a way to avoid the work their parents do; to postpone "real" work; and to prolong the identification of self as student/youth, rather than spending one's days barely covering one's own expenses doing various kinds of manual work while waiting for a chance to leave the village (see also White 2013).

Generally, upper secondary school (particularly when it requires travel outside the village) opens a window onto a greater diversity of lifestyles, and teenagers like to make friends with their age-mates from other districts. Dini, another teenager interviewed, reported that some of her new friends dyed their hair (something forbidden in most schools), "but not in very conspicuous colors". Our interviewees considered themselves somewhat inadequate, ignorant, and awkward in conversation compared to many of their new schoolmates, but try to stay nonchalant and relaxed, and are aware that many others were in the same situation as themselves.

In their new schools, Eko and Santi both found some of the rules quite disturbing. Discipline is enforced with a system of cumulative penalty points; if they reach 100, you are expelled. Another teenager, Dewi, is mainly worried that the upcoming National Exams will be difficult and that she may not pass. Nearly all her friends share these worries; many are taking private lessons after school to prepare for the exams. Shanti explained,

> Competition for jobs is very tight at present. Even in my own class there are so many smart students, and competition for good grades gets heavier all the time…it's this competition that has given me the determination to get ahead…

Dewi, Eko, and Dini made similar comments, finding life tough and competitive, requiring them to work hard in school and take extra lessons outside if possible.

Like Eko and Santi, most young people in Kali Loro imagine themselves leaving the village, and about half of all young people do leave, in search of employment and different lifestyles. The desire to leave the village is shared by both relatively better- and relatively worse-off teenagers, but for different reasons. Wealthier teenagers (including the children of better-off farmers) look forward to the prospect of tertiary education and an urban office job, while others are embarrassed by their relative poverty. Dini described how hurt she feels by gossiping neighbors who feel free to talk about her family's straitened circumstances,

> The neighbors are always gossiping about my family because we are not well off. Maybe if we were rich they would stop talking about us. I really don't like to be treated that way. In the city these things would never happen.

Dini's parents are divorced, and she considers her father irresponsible because he does not provide financial support. They barely have enough to live on, and her mother has no permanent job. She has to support Dini, her younger brother and sister who are still in school, as well as Dini's grandparents. Their poverty and the ways the neighbors treat them increase Dini's desire to leave the village, get a job, and help support her family.

Young people thus see the village as a place that provides no hope of a decent, well-paid job. It is a place to grow up and, later in life, may be a good place to live after retirement, where you can enjoy the fruits of your work in peace (cf. Koning 1997, ch. 6). Farming or farm labor is not regarded as a realistic option, and most teenagers aspire to salaried jobs or at least some urban "indoor" job. Many young people in the 18–30 age group who have completed upper secondary (SMU, SMK) have moved to factory employment and other (mostly manual) work in Jakarta or other parts of West and Central Java, while others join earlier cohorts of migrant relatives now established in commercial farming or small-scale enterprise in Sumatra, Kalimantan, or other islands, while in recent years quite a few have become migrant workers in Saudi Arabia, Hong Kong, or Malaysia.

Male school-leavers or drop-outs who do not leave the village usually work in construction, collecting, and smashing rocks from the river-bed, or as motorcycle taxi drivers (*tukang ojek*); girls who do not leave are more likely to end up helping their parents in domestic and income-generating activities such as farm work, petty trading, or making snacks or handicrafts for sale until, and after, marriage.

Interviews with "older youth"—young men and women who return from Jakarta or other parts of Java for the Lebaran holidays—indicate that school-leavers tend to spend a period of at least one year unemployed or doing various odd jobs in the village, before setting off in search of urban employment. For some this becomes a near-permanent condition: we met a young man who, seven years after graduating from STM (Technical High School), was still unemployed, unmarried, and living with his parents at 25.

Lifestyles, Social Life, and Views on Youth in the Village and Beyond:

Most of our respondents concur that the transition from "child" (*anak*) to "youth" (*remaja, pemuda*) begins at the time of entering secondary school (about 13 years of age); they had varied views on the timing of the transition from "youth" to "adult" (*dewasa*), placing this between 18–21 years, and/or the time one gets married. Those who have started secondary school do not want to be called "child" any more. They feel they now have the right to make decisions for themselves, but they also do not want to call themselves adults, as they still see adult tasks and responsibilities as too heavy for them.

Masa remaja (more or less, adolescence) is seen as a time when one starts to think for oneself. It thus marks the beginning of a period when young people's ideas (about themselves, their use of time, their lifestyles and futures) can differ from those of parents or other adults, and thus a time of potential or actual intergenerational tensions. For one young man (interviewed when he was 23 years old), youth become *"remaja"* when they enter SMP and want to go out at night (if they are boys; as further explained below, greater restrictions are placed on teenage girls' mobility). According to Yanti (18 years old when interviewed and in SMEA Muhammadiyah Class 3), the common term "ABG" *anak baru gede*, literally "a child who's just got big", applies only to the first years of youth (the early teens and lower secondary school years, roughly age 13–15).

Adolescents are often searching for an identity and asking "who am I?" This emerged most clearly in interviews with teenage girls; boys tended not to mention it, although this does not necessarily imply that it is not happening to them. Answers to the "who am I?" question are heavily influenced both by the immediate social environment and interaction with the wider world. For girls, questions about identity and futures are also frequently combined with a need to find a "useful" place in the world. These questions are often hard to talk about with friends. As one of our respondents wrote,

> In fact I'm mixed up about how to face life. On one hand I want to be like my friends, but on the other I want to be myself. I want to find out who I am. Can I be useful to others, or will I only be a burden to them?

The same teenager provided us with 22 captioned photos. Most show friends, family, neighbors, her new school, school-friends, and teachers, all provided with cheerful written commentaries. In contrast, one photo shows an empty stretch of farmland and is captioned,

> *Ini adalah tempat dimana aku sering menyendiri ketika tak ada lagi yang bisa aku harapkan.* (This is a place where I often come to be alone when there's no longer anything to hope for).

Santi and Dewi explained that their schoolmates have very different lifestyles from their former lower-secondary friends. Santi,

> ...Most of my [new] friends have mobile phones. They SMS each other and can easily communicate. I want to have one. Then if anything comes up, like a school homework problem I could discuss it on the phone.[10]

Besides mobile phones, our young respondents noted many other aspects of their new friends' lifestyles. They talk and dress fashionably, and the things they talk about like Sinetron (TV films) and movies are new. Teenagers often go with their friends to town (Yogyakarta), to the shopping malls, just looking and sitting about, and going to see new films. Our respondents had learned to use the internet in lower secondary school. There was no internet cafe in the village at that time, but there was one a few kilometers down the road—but they did not yet see this as important in their lives. On the rare occasions they accessed the internet, they usually chatted with people they have never met.[11] This was the period when mobile phones and the internet were not yet widespread, but already influencing young lives in subtle ways.

This can be seen, for example, in the way Santi's writing style has changed. The first time she wrote something for Margiyatin before starting her new school, Santi used abbreviations in the normal way. But after about one month in her new school this had changed. Compare these two fragments. Before,

> ...sebenarnya aku tuh bingung harus bagaimana menghadapi hidup ini. Di sisi lain aku ingin seperti teman**ku tapi sisi lain aku ingin jadi diriku sendiri...(In fact I'm mixed up about how to face life. On one hand I want to be like my friends, but on the other I want to be myself).

Apart from the idiosyncratic "**" sign for duplication, she is using standard spelling. One month later,

> ...aq merasakan ingin menyendiri, yach tp kita hidup khan tdk bisa sendiri, jd aq lawan aza perasaan itu. Aq coba u/k bersikap biasa** saja, agar dia tdk kecewa atas sikap aq...(I feel I want to be alone, but yeah, we can't be alone in this life, so I fight that feeling. I try to act normally, so he won't be disappointed in my attitude...)

---

10   Santi had more than once asked her parents for a mobile phone, and she was very impatient to get one, the upcoming Lebaran holiday (three months away at the time of our study) was too long for her to wait.
11   These remarks on teenagers' relatively little interest in internet refer to the situation in 2006.

In the second fragment she is using "sms-language", when she still has no mobile phone: *aq* is sms-language for *aku* (I), *tp* is for *tapi* (but), *tdk* is for *tidak* (not), *jd* is for *jadi* (so), *u/k* is for *untuk* (to, for), and so on.

Readers should note that these observations are from 2006, and as might be expected, virtual/digital culture has subsequently become a much more central dimension of teenagers' lives and interactions. By 2014 a young village resident observed—perhaps exaggerating somewhat—"it's not just secondary school, nowadays primary school kids are all busy with Facebook". Teenagers are nearly all in possession of advanced smartphones and active in social media, preferring Facebook to Twitter because is can be used to share photos. Those who do not yet possess a smartphone can open Facebook accounts using their friends' phones. Sharing photos and making new friends are the main uses. When teenagers meet, it's an occasion to show off phones and motorbikes. While only a few years ago a mobile phone itself was a "positional good",[12] now young people differentiate between high-status models (especially the popular Samsung Galaxy), lower-status but still desirable Chinese brands like Lenovo, Advance and Cross, and poor-quality Chinese brands like MITO. Smartphones and the internet are valued for various purposes, including looking for study materials, searching for appropriate verses from the Koran, finding new friends (including boy/girlfriends), watching videos on YouTube, and even campaigning in the recent Presidential election (in which both candidates had significant support in Kali Loro, but with a majority for the losing candidate Prabowo). Even the children of landless and near-landless households, it seems, find a way to buy some kind of mobile phone. If their parents can't afford it, they ask for help from elder siblings or relatives who have jobs outside the village, and some have started keeping their own goats to earn and save enough money. Another impact of the rush to "HP" culture is that many more young people are opting for Information Technology in secondary school and beyond.[13]

Today's *remaja* need money. Not only for school fees, transport and other school costs, but also, for example, *uang jajan* (snack money), money for clothes, going to town, entertainment, cigarettes, the local PlayStation booth, in many cases drugs, and other expensive possessions like radios, mobile phones, or a second-hand motorbike.[14] Paradoxically, as children's needs for education

---

12   Positional goods in economics are "goods whose values derive from the fact that only a small proportion of potential consumers can have them" (Chang, 2014, 223).

13   Many thanks to Henny Lawrensia of Gadjah Mada University for these observations from her current (2014) MA field research in Kali Loro.

14   Young girls are quite clear about the importance and meaning of motorbikes as a symbol of status and freedom: "if a boy has a motorbike he'll certainly find it easier to get a

and a greater variety of consumer goods grows, they are increasingly excluded from the kinds of work which might have earned them money to pay for these needs and they are increasingly dependent on their parents; working to earn money is no longer a significant part of school-going teenagers' experience. This is in sharp contrast to their parents' generation, for whom working, and earning money, outside school hours was part of normal life. In our wider circle of teenage respondents we found only one young man (the son of an agricultural laborer) who spent ten days earning wages as a farm laborer (together with his father) during the school holidays: "not bad at all, I earned enough to buy some new shoes". The general lack of involvement in activities that earn money puts today's teenagers in a condition of strong dependence on parents, elder siblings, or other relatives for access to cash, and this can become a source of tension (see Robinson, this volume).

Young people in the village sometimes form their own organized social groups, both formal and informal, or participate in adult groups. One "official" youth group under the aegis of the village government, the Karang Taruna, is moribund in most neighborhoods. In contrast, religious organizations and other groups based on recreation, sport, and hobbies are quite active. Religious groups that have become more active include the *remaja masjid* (mosque youth), *perjanjen* groups (who aim to spread the Islamic faith by singing spiritual songs accompanied by *tebang/rebana* instruments), the Catholic youth groups, and youth who teach the reading of the Qur'an to younger children. These groups usually become busier as a big religious holiday draws near. There are other active groups based on sport and hobbies, as young people get a feeling of recognition by performing well in football, basketball, volleyball, the *jathilan* (trance-dance), or playing music ("*pekbung*" or pop groups).

Informal circles of friends, both school and neighborhood-based, are common. In 2000, for example, Yanti explained to us how she had been part of a close-knit *geng* in her class, made up of five girls and one boy. The *geng* had one principle, that they would never be restricted by their fellow students—"we all pay the same, so why do they try to boss us about?" The *geng* started because they were sitting close to each other and had the same feelings; they had no conscious plan to establish themselves as a *geng*, but they often went out from school together to buy food at the cross-roads and the group emerged spontaneously. She explained that actually anyone could join the *geng*, on meeting the following conditions, "not shy; not easily offended ("because we all like to make fun of each other"); and not stingy".

girlfriend"; "if you have a motorbike you're free, you can go anywhere you want" (Yanti, age 18).

Teenage boys like to *nongkrong* (gather around together) at night-time at certain spots, for example at the side of the main road, at the junctions where roads lead off into the neighborhoods, on the bridge, in the night watchmen's hut, or *lek-lekan* (staying up all night at a neighbor's ceremony). In these groups young people feel they can more safely do the things they like which adults disapprove of (smoking or drinking), or simply chatting about whatever interests them. They have a sense of friendship, belonging and solidarity. For example, if one of them is treated badly, they respond together as a group (see chapters by Parker and Nilan, this volume).

Some of these (male) groups are known to be quite rough. One group of male school leavers and dropouts, which used to gather around the village's main cross-roads and transport terminal, became known for extorting cash from local shopkeepers. They used the money to spend time in the local "PlayStation" booth, to buy beer or narcotics, or to rent pornographic videos to watch at night in the village office with the help of an obliging official.[15]

Young people make clear distinctions about inter-group differences among the young. One 23 year-old unmarried construction laborer who still hangs out at night-time with friends at the side of the village's main road, pointed to a group of young teenagers watching TV in a nearby house; according to him "they are still *bayi-bayi* (babies)", SMP kids who form their own group, watch TV, and have to be home by about 9 pm, compared to his own group who often get drunk, play cards and don't go home until at least midnight.

Opportunities for *nongkrong* and other spare-time contacts with their peers are much more limited for teenage girls because they are expected to help more with domestic chores, and because of restrictions on their movement after dark. As Yanti explained,

> When I'm watching TV my mother often calls me to help with the cooking or to fetch water from the river. She never asks just once, now she tells me to help with one thing and later another, that makes me lazy...girls are different from boys. Boys have more freedom, they can hang out wherever they want, day or night...but girls have to help their mothers in the daytime, so even if one of us has some time free, our friends will be helping their mothers. It's hard to be a girl. At night we can't go out, it wouldn't look right for a girl to be sitting at the roadside at night.

---

15   The village official's reputation as purveyor of pornography to the village youth made him the target of a protest letter, signed by hundreds of villagers, and was in the end forced to resign in 2000, as Kali Loro's only victim of *reformasi*.

These restrictions are one reason for the popularity of organized religious and social activities among young people, such as the *Taman Pendidikan Al Qur'an* (Koranic reading school for young children) at which Yanti herself teaches, with fifteen other teenagers, three days a week from 3.30—5 pm, and the *arisan remaja* (youth rotating credit association) about which another 18 year old said,

> Young people in the neighbourhood have to get involved in neighborhood activities, because nowadays there aren't many young people left in the village, most of them have gone to the city, so the few of us who are left have to be *kompak* (stick together).

These activities offer a sanctioned form of social interaction for girls, and an opportunity for boys and girls to meet.

They consider the lives of American youth, or those they see in Western films, to be very free; their image of the "free life" of Western youth is often equated with "free sex" and drug use. Young people's views on these matters are ambivalent. On one hand such freedom (as they imagine American youth enjoy) seems appealing as Eko explained,

> They [American or Western youth] have a very free life, without many rules or restrictions, compared to most Indonesian youth, including myself who can still be controlled by their parents. I do feel constrained by all these controls…

On the other hand they think such freedom is not really appropriate for Indonesians: "our culture is different". But they also see that their own culture has undergone many changes, as can be seen from the drinking habits of many young people, and the many extra-marital pregnancies among young girls, and they accept their parents' advice that religion is the main defense against falling into "a life without control". In fact, while today's older generation do not tend to talk about it, juvenile drinking and pre-marital pregnancies were quite common during their own youth, at the time of our first field study in 1972–73 (cf. the observations on adult "moral panic" in several other chapters in this volume).

While all young people in Kali Loro experience quite heavy social controls on their behavior, girls especially feel that people are always watching and criticizing them. Many taboos and restrictions are placed on girls' behavior and attitudes, from dress codes and contacts with boys to evening curfews. Parents are always warning their daughters not to stay out late, to be very careful in their social contacts, to not to get caught up in loose ways, to keep away from situations where they might be harassed or raped, and are very angry if their daughters disobey them.

The social discrimination between boys and girls stands in sharp contrast to the general ideas of gender equality, widely understood in a general or abstract way but matched with continued discrimination in day-to-day life. As we saw earlier, Santi intends to continue earning money after she starts a family and feels that as a woman, she has the same rights to employment as men. But Santi, Dewi and Dini all feel that they are treated and valued differently than men. Although boys and girls now have the same access to education, both girls and boys still think that boys are allowed more freedom. As Eko explained, nowadays men and women have the same rights but:

> A man's life is better. There are many more limits placed on young women. They can't stay out late, they have to be good at cooking, their social contacts are restricted because they're vulnerable to violence such as rape. If you're a man you can chase girls, but it's not thought right for a girl to chase men...

Between Dependence and Autonomy: Ambivalence in Intergenerational Relations

Adolescents, as already noted, distinguish themselves both from children and from adults. They feel that as *remaja* they are able to think for themselves and to make judgements and decisions. For young children, parents and adults are the whole world, trusted and accepted sources of knowledge and values. However, as children begin to enter the "outside" world of broader social contacts and interactions through instruments such as school, community, and media, their view of the world changes. Our respondents see this shift happening at the time of starting lower secondary school. Adolescents begin to create their own social worlds, imitating or engaging with the lifestyles and ideas of their peers and the information they acquire through TV, books and magazines, the internet, or other media. They begin to detach themselves from the parental and adult worlds and to feel the need to be less controlled by it.

Teenage respondents spoke of how they dislike their subjection to parental control, as well as the way neighbors and other adults gossip about subjects such as their boyfriends, clothing, and family situations. Sometimes these pressures, and the harsh or violent forms they may take, are hard to discuss openly. One teenage girl, after a conversation with the researcher (Margiyatin), decided to express her feelings further in a letter,[16] having been unable to express them openly in the interviews which had always taken place in the presence of her grandmother and/or her aunt,

Mbak (elder sister), in fact there are many pressures on young people here. They include:

1. Violence in the home. Adults are often very angry if we do something wrong, when they ought to set a good example, not just get in a rage
2. Conflicts between parents and children are very common
3. Adults often force their will on children
4. Some parents give no attention to their children, so the child feels helpless, some children think their parents don't love them
5. Young people nowadays often fall in love, and when they're rejected or jilted they get frustrated and confused, their hearts are broken

The ambivalence between respect for and dependence on adults on the one hand and the desire for greater autonomy of thought and action on the other are part of coming of age in Kali Loro. Taking a long-term perspective we can see the emergence of a new aspect to inter-generational relations during the last three generations, as each succeeding generation grows up better-educated than the previous. Little is known about the impact of this change on inter-generational relations. Education is a key element in the long-term process of the prolongation of childhood or adolescence, or the postponement of adulthood, through the combination of longer schooling, increasing age at marriage and later entry into labor markets. Each of these processes potentially generates new tensions between generations and new challenges for the transition to adulthood.

Our teenage respondents have shown a high awareness of the larger structures and constraints that limit their future options, both inside and outside the village. It is evident that they have the capacity to articulate their aspirations for a better life and future, to think critically about their situation, and to place problems in broader context. However, none of the formal institutions in their environment offer a vehicle for them to express their opinions and to have them heard. In that sense, despite the widespread acceptance of the public rhetoric of children's and young people's participation rights and active citizenship, at local level these notions remain largely "*omong kosong*" (empty words), as in so many other parts of Indonesia and the world.

---

16 It is interesting to see some young people at least choosing to express themselves through the method—often considered not very youthful—of letter writing.

References

Abdullah, Irwan, and Ben White. 2006. "Harvesting and House Building: Decline and Persistence of Reciprocal Labour in a Javanese Village, 1973–2000." In *Ropewalking and Safety Nets: Local Ways of Managing Insecurities in Indonesia*, edited by Juliette Koning and Frans Hüsken, 55–78. Leiden: Brill.

Chang, Ha-Joon. 2014. *Economics: The User's Guide*. London: Pelican Books.

Koning, Juliet. 1997. "Generations of Change: a Javanese Village in the 1990s." PhD diss., University of Amsterdam.

Shiraishi, Saya S. 1997. *Young Heroes: the Indonesian Family in Politics*. Ithaca: Cornell University Press.

Stoler, A. 1977a. "Class Structure and Female Autonomy in Rural Java." *Signs* 3:74–92.

——— 1977b. "Rice Harvesting in Kali Loro: A Study of Class and Labour in Rural Java." *American Ethnologist* 4:678–98.

——— 1978. "Garden Use and Household Economy in Rural Java." *Bulletin of Indonesian Economic Studies* 14:85–101.

White, B. 1976a. "The Economic Importance of Children in a Javanese Village." In *Changing Identities in Modern Southeast Asia*, edited by D.J. Banks, 269–290. The Hague: Mouton.

——— 1976b. "Population, Involution and Employment in Rural Java." *Development and Change* 7: 267–90.

——— 1976c. "Production and Reproduction in a Javanese Village." PhD. diss., Columbia University.

——— 2012. "Changing Childhoods: Javanese Village Children in Three Generations." *Journal of Agrarian Change* 12: 81–97.

CHAPTER 4

Educational Aspirations and Inter-Generational Relations in Sorowako

Kathryn Robinson

Education figures strongly in imaginings of transitions to modernity in contemporary Indonesia. The colonial lives from the early twentieth century narrated in *Telling Lives Telling History* (Rogers, 1995) prefigure this. For the young male migrants to urban centers who wrote the biographies in that volume, pursuing education meant an embrace of the world outside their villages. Their engagement with modern secular education developed skills which it was believed would equip young people (men in the case of these particular narratives) to participate in the modern world. Education separated the village-born men from the world of their parents and developed in them a modern sensibility of self-fashioning, where achievement (*prestasi*) is validated through the moral frameworks of modern institutions rather than historical frameworks of kinship, piety, and self-reliant livelihoods.

Education leading to modern occupations is now the dominant trope of transition to adulthood in the mining town of Sorowako in South Sulawesi. This enclave of modernity in a remote part of the province is situated in a region which was at the limits of state power prior to the development of the mine in the 1970s (Robinson 1986). The modernity associated with this industrial setting is marked by a commitment to changing ideas, by both parents and children alike, of what competencies are required by adults: it features commitment to goals framed in terms of the modern industrial economy. Some 35 years ago when I first began field research in Sorowako, the indigenous people (who call themselves *orang asli Sorowako*), who had been engulfed by the mine development, did not regard office-based occupations as work (*kerja*), and I knew parents who rejected proposals for their daughters from young men who were office workers on the grounds they "did not know how to *kerja* (work)". Now these white collar occupations are not only desired by young men and women, but valued by their parents and by prospective parents-in-law.

Inter-generational relations relating to social reproduction pivoted around marriage, which was ritually marked by a communal feast where the community recognized the new status of bride and groom. Parenthood was signified by the adoption of teknonymous terms of address which indexed a sharp transition from childhood to full adulthood (Robinson 1998). This has now given way to an extended period of youth in which children pursue education as the path to adulthood (see White, this volume). Thus, in the critical years of adolescence, young people are exposed to strong influences outside the sphere of family and kin, a break with past practice. In the period prior to the mining project, kinship-based power of families (especially parents) was exercised in arranging young people's marriages (Robinson 1998), but nowadays parents by and large leave significant choices in matters marking the transition to adulthood in the hands of their children. This begins with educational choices, and parents accept the responsibility to support them financially as best they can for the years it takes them to succeed in education. Poorly educated parents make economic sacrifices to support their children in paths which they often barely understand. Thus, education figures strongly as a factor in the reconfiguration of relations between parents and children, and of notions of inter-generational responsibility (see White, this volume).[1]

The reconfiguration of parent–child relations in transitions to adulthood includes the children's free choice of marriage partner, now commonly someone met while studying. The high value placed on education, and the necessity and /or choice to study away from home means that young people are away from their families in the critical years of transition to adulthood. Prior to Sorowako's immersion in the industrial economy, parental control of the resources that a young man needed to provide to the bride's family for a wedding party gave elders leverage over their children's choices at this threshold of adulthood (Robinson 1998). The changed social and economic context is associated with the apparent weakening of an individual's ties to "traditional social collectivities" (Buchmann 1989, 21). However, I will argue below that the expanded forms of individual choice are still framed by parents and children alike within a morality of proper conduct for parent–child relations that has arisen within those "traditional" social collectivities.

This chapter examines a cohort of high school and university students' experiences of this education-led transition to adulthood and the manner in which their aspirations are formed. New forms of inter-generational relations in social reproduction, and associated subjectivities, are critical aspects of the industrialization-led modernity of contemporary Sorowako. While the life-course patterns of young people are diversified relative to those available to their parents (in regard to education, work and marriage), the specific historical context of Sorowakan social transformation means there are commonalities in

---

[1] I am using generation here to mean a "principle of descent relationship" (Kertzer 1983, 142) in relation to social reproduction. I am also drawing out differences in experience between young educated people and their parents' generation.

the life-course experience of the cohorts of young people in the early 21st century (c.f. Buchman 1989).[2]

Introducing Sorowako

PT International Nickel (Inco) established a nickel mine and processing plant in Sorowako in the 1970s. Since 2006 the mine has been owned and operated by Brazilian company Vale. Sorowako is located in the mountainous interior of the island of Sulawesi, on the shores of lake Matano, some 660 kilometers from the provincial capital, in what was then Nuha sub-district in the district of Luwu. The indigenous inhabitants experienced a dramatic transformation of their agricultural-based livelihoods as their agricultural lands were forcibly acquired for the mine and a total transformation of their social landscape, as many thousands of migrants came to the region seeking work. The 2004 census put the population of the Nuha sub-district at around 42,000, and about one quarter live in the suburbs of the company town-site and contiguous the area of the original village, where most of the indigenous Sorowakan population live alongside migrants. The population of the town overwhelmingly comprises migrants who have come from all over Indonesia, and the world, although the proportion of expatriate employees has gradually declined to just a handful (32 in 2004).

The mine has transformed the basis of the local economy. The company, supported by the distant district government, forcibly converted the Sorowakan's prime agricultural land to the site for the company townsite including a golf course (Robinson 1986). However, those indigenous households in which members have had continuing employment with the mining company (almost all of them men) have fared well, as have a small group of local entrepreneurs, while those who have remained in the agricultural sector have had restricted opportunities to benefit from the development. The households still reliant on farming are the poorest in this community.

The overwhelming physical presence of the mine and its associated facilities, and the significance of the mining company as the principal local employer, permeate the organization of daily life in Sorowako. The mining town is a modern enclave dominated by educated middle-class Indonesians. Local people

---

[2] This study was a component of a larger project on the social experience of adolescents in Indonesia, the Ambivalent Adolescents in Indonesia Project (henceforth AAI) ARC Discovery project DP00663600, Chief Investigators Lynette Parker, Linda Rae Bennett, Pamela Nilan, and Kathryn Robinson.

embraced the industrial modernity of the mining project, and most desired the new opportunities and life styles: the indigenous Sorowakans are now increasingly joining that middle-class, with education and professional employment as principal vectors of change. But Sorowako is different from similar middle-class enclaves in urban agglomerates elsewhere in Indonesia because of its relatively small population. There is no urban commercial center with a mall, only several markets and numerous small shops, more characteristic of a village. Unlike a small town, there is no cinema. Sorowako is also characterized by relative geographical isolation[3]; students have to go away to pursue education, sometimes in secondary school and almost universally for tertiary studies.[4] But the survey of senior high school students conducted by the Ambivalent Adolescents Project (of which this study formed a part) showed patterns of consumption similar to the samples within cities. For example, there is a high rate of motorcycle (30%) and mobile phone ownership among students at the secondary school established by the mining company (see Nilan et al., this volume)

The Study

This research focuses on transitions to adulthood in Sorowako for a cohort of young people whose life-course has been dramatically different from that of their parents. New paths for passage to adulthood shed light on the fundamental social transformation occurring with the development of the mine.

Individual and group interviews were conducted in 2008 and 2009 with tertiary students who had returned home for Idul Fitri (Islamic "new year"), and with young graduates who had returned to Sorowako. Two samples of senior high school students aged 16–18 were surveyed using the common instrument from the AA survey (see Nilan et al, this volume): one drawn from the school established by the mining company; and another from the other senior high school, STM Budi Utomo, a private vocational school run by the Yapman Foundation. I also had discussions with parents and teachers. The students,

---

3 It is around 14 hours by express bus (overnight) to Makassar, and 4–5 hours by road from Palopo, formerly the district capital. There is a daily plane service run by Vale, and people can buy tickets if there is capacity. Employee's children can use the facility of this plane when returning home for holidays.

4 The exception to this are the increasing numbers who are able to pursue studies at the tertiary institution (Akademi Teknik Sorowako, ATS) that the mining company has now established in Sorowako to provide professional training.

teachers, and parents interviewed were from the village (where most of the indigenous population live) and also the company townsite; residents of both areas are represented in the sample of school children surveyed. There was little difference between the village and townsite in regard to aspirations and practice for furthering children's education. The analysis of interviews and the survey data has been contextualized and interpreted through the knowledge I have developed from over 30 years of engagement and observation of historical changes in Sorowako.

Schooling in Sorowako

Sending children away to pursue secular education has a relatively long history in this remote region, and has apparently been a custom in other parts of Indonesia as well. Hildred Geertz (1961, 116–17) reported that Javanese parents were desirous of sending their children away from home as part of their upbringing and Heneveld (1978, 75) speculates that this customary practice may have influenced the concentration of secondary education in urban areas, in addition to consideration of demographic factors (the pool of potential students in the catchment area). While in Sorowako in the late colonial and early independence periods this practice was mainly associated with a village elite—already connected to the outside through trade in dammar and rattan[5] via the port at Malili—it was firmly fixed in the social imagination prior to the Darul Islam (DITI) era between 1950 and 1965. This was an armed revolt prosecuting the ideal of Indonesia as an Islamic state (Robinson 1983). In this period, the rebels burned the village and the people moved to rebel territory, the jungle accessed by way of the opposite shore of Lake Matano. DITI cut off rural areas under their control from the city and residents were blocked from trade and communication with the outside. Several young Sorowakan men from elite families who had left the village to pursue secondary education were caught in the provincial capital Ujung Pandang (now Makassar), and they had to survive on their own. Several were successful in achieving education, in at least one case to tertiary level, while their younger siblings never realized education beyond basic primary level. (One of the tertiary graduate's younger brothers became the teacher in the school that was established in the jungle [Robinson 1983].) The people returned from their refugee locations in the mid-1960s, just

---

5   There was also some mining of iron ore in the latter years of Dutch colonial rule (Robinson 1986).

a few years prior to the exploration that resulted in the establishment of the mine and processing plant (Robinson 1986).

Since the development of the mining project, parents in Sorowako have made considerable sacrifices to educate their children. They have a clear understanding of the link between education and employment: the indigenous population assumed education was the only factor that differentiated them from the higher paid, higher status immigrant managers, who they saw as reaping the benefits of this development on their land (Robinson 1989). Indeed, the quick uptake of modern contraceptives offered through the company clinic was linked to the understanding that parents needed to limit fertility so they would be able to provide education for their children; education was (and still is) regarded as the provisioning (*bekal*) that parents provide for their children's future, and framed in terms of ideas of proper conduct for inter-generational relations. This is commonly expressed through an analogy with the way that that, formerly, parents had gifted adult children with all the elements required for production in the agricultural economy. Land, tree crops, and buffalo were the basis of the livelihoods of independent households formed after marriage (Robinson 1989; 1998). This conceptually defined the responsibilities of intergenerational social reproduction.

Agricultural livelihoods were all but destroyed by the mining company's monopolization of land (Robinson 1986) and parents had limited resources. In the 1970s, they were already teaching children Indonesian as their first language as a foundation for their success in the education system, and the modern world of industrial employment.[6] The indigenous Sorowakans quickly began to valorize competencies for industrial work rather than the skills of agriculture. In this emerging industrial town there was a convergence between the company's interests and the government's development agenda for nation building: to limit population growth and to use the education system to produce "quality human resources" (see Munro 2009).[7]

Inco established a modern school system teaching children of employees to high school level in the early 1970s. The schools run through a company-funded foundation, the Sorowako Education Foundation (Yayasan Pendidikan Soroako, henceforth YPS). YPS provides schooling from kindergarten to senior high school, including special education for children with disabilities. Children of

---

6   I found a similar preference for teaching Indonesian as first language in the Southeast Sulawesi sub-district of Rauta which borders on Nuha, and which is the site of a new mine currently in exploration phase.

7   Kipnis (2011, 162–63) describes a similar link between link of education, "human resources" and nation building for China.

non-employees mostly attended the single primary school in the village, where there was at that time no post-primary education.

The remote location has meant young people have to move far away from home for all tertiary education and, for many children of non-employees, quality secondary education. When I first went to Sorowako in 1977, just as the Inco nickel processing plant was coming into production, cash was short, and parents utilized their networks of kin and/or business associates in order to find accommodation for their children in town so they could pursue education. Choices included the sub-district capital Wasuponda, Malili (at that time the capital of the neighboring sub district), the then-district capital, Palopo, and occasionally the provincial capital Ujung Pandang (now Makassar). The "billeting" of children commonly involved an exchange of services—the children would be required to do household chores or assist in a small business in return for their lodgings and food, perhaps some small assistance with school fees. This practice is known in some parts of Indonesia as the *pengampu* system (Jones and Nagib 1999). Parents would also support the children with provisions (*bekal*-usually sacks of rice) sent from the village.

Patterns of educational opportunities and outmigration for education have shifted over the years. There are now more schools in the local area, including a state junior high school in Sumasang, a new suburb of Sorowako, and the aforementioned private secondary vocational college (stm Budi Utomo), as well as Inco's yps school. But large numbers of young people migrate from this locality to major towns in Indonesia to pursue education, especially senior high school and tertiary studies. In an area where public education is amongst the poorest quality in the province,[8] graduates of yps have high rates of success in achieving university entrance. Success (*prestasi*) at the company school translates into direct entry to some of Indonesia's prestigious universities.

Education as a Hope/Entitlement from Industrial Development

Good education is desired by parents and children alike, appreciated as a benefit of modernity and of living in the company enclave. The indigenous population has, from the beginning of the development, demanded that their children be given access to the quality education provided by the mining company as a component of the compensation they feel they are owed for giving

---

8   Overall, the performance of students from Luwu Timur district was 23rd of 24 districts in South Sulawesi in 2008 (personal communication, Maryanto, Head of yps, citing government data).

up their land to the mine. There is a strongly-held common view that the education provided at YPS is superior to state education. The large amount of homework and longer school hours (compared to the state schools) for YPS students are regarded by parents as concrete evidence of this higher quality. Desire for better education for children is linked to their hopes that "locals" will benefit from the mine though employment (Robinson 1986). They have continuously expressed the demand that indigenous Sorowakan people have privileged access to company employment as well as the company-funded education system that provides the pathway to employment. On numerous occasions, this right has been granted in at least a limited form (and for a limited time), but access has been by no means universal for children of indigenous non-employees.

On numerous occasions indigenous Sorowakans have demonstrated against the perceived failure of the company to live up to its undertakings to them, including promises about access to schools. Since Reformasi (the period following the fall of the Suharto regime in 1998), they have on several occasions adopted the tactic of blockading the road between the worksites and the elite residential areas. Managers have been held hostage in the comfort of the golf club and courteously provided with take-away meals (*nasi bungkus*) by local women. The negotiated settlement of one of these disputes, in 2004, included an undertaking that children from indigenous families would be able to attend the quality schools established by the company, even if they do not have a parent in the company's employ. This privilege has been extended to children who pass an entrance exam, and is subject to places being available.

In 2008, the YPS High School had 397 students enrolled at junior (SMP) level, 111 of whom were non-employees' children. At senior level (SMA) there were 360 students, 126 of whom were children of non-employees.[9] Overall, including enrollments in primary school, 20% of YPS students were children of non-employees. Among the student respondents in the survey conducted as part of the Ambivalent Adolescents research project[10] (all final year students at the YPS and all the senior high school students at Budi Utomo), 24% of the YPS respondents reported that their fathers were indigenous, whereas none of the Budi Utomo students can be identified as having indigenous Sorowakan parents.

---

9   SMA had 25 teachers; SMP 26.
10 A survey conducted as part of the Ambivalent Adolescents project (see note 1; Chapter 3 in this volume), the Sorowako sample revealed that there were no indigenous (OAS) children at the Budi Utomo vocational school, whereas there were a significant number at the YPS school. Some indigenous children attend the recently opened state SMP in the new suburb of Sumasang.

On the other hand, YPS statistics showed that only 50% of school-age children of Inco employees were enrolled in YPS schools. Some Inco employees chose to send their children away to school, especially to senior high school. Reasons included a desire for children to attend particular high prestige schools in Java; concern that opportunities for extra-curricular activities like music or dance lessons are limited in Sorowako; or, in a few cases, family reasons such as the need for teenage children helping in the care of elderly parents otherwise living alone. However, the usual reason for employees' children not attending YPS schools was that they lived in settlements other than Sorowako located some distance from there, especially the new settlement of Wawandula. Hence these children do not enjoy the company-provided education that is an entitlement in employment contracts (Maryanto, Head of YPS, personal communication 2008)

Warouw (2004) has illuminated the manner in which exposure to the Indonesian educational system and mass media creates subjects ready for industrial employment, even among rural children in Java. The government educational agenda emphasizes the development of "quality human resources" for national development. The experience of living in a world dominated by the rhythms of industrial work means that children in Sorowako grow up understanding what competencies are required for modern industrial employment. These competencies are performed in the village: men dressed in overalls, wearing steel-cap boots and hard hats, and carrying lunch pails, catch company buses to report for shifts. In former times, the sound of the shift siren would be heard three times a day all over the town—now it is used to signal with precision the time for breaking the fast in Ramadan (*buka puasa*). Material rewards and social status in Sorowako are linked to one's place in the labor market. which in turn depends upon education and skills. Achievement in rising up the company hierarchy is rewarded with good salaries that support a middle-class lifestyle, and a modern house in the occupationally-stratified company town site (Robinson 1986) where the managers live.

The AAI survey showed that Indonesian rural children in particular aspired to become civil servants, an occupation offering job security and status, but low pay. In Sorowako, however, this was not a common aspiration (see Nilan et al, this volume). Rather, they aspired to professional middle-class occupations. While for many years local people struggled for all but the most menial jobs in the mine, now increasing numbers of young "locals" with university degrees have professional jobs in the company. There is now a whole generation of young people with higher educational qualifications. Sorowako has an apparently high number of university graduates, especially in technical subjects and accounting.

A local organization, the Association of Sorowako Graduates (Ikatan Sarjana Sorowako), listed 191 members with tertiary education, including diplomas and degrees in 2008, and 41 of them were working for Vale.[11] The desire for employment with the mining company is an important driver of educational aspirations: engineering and accountancy are popular choices in the cohort I met (see below). Both boys and girls have been given opportunities for education (Robinson 1989) and there has been a recent change in the company culture, resulting in an increase in the number of women in the workforce, including on the mine site. Young professional women in smart clothes and high heels confidently driving company cars are now a common sight. However, the situation in Sorowako mirrors that of Indonesia as a whole (and indeed most developing countries) in that there is a "mismatch between schooling and the job market" and "job opportunities are not increasing rapidly enough to absorb all young labor force entrants into the kind of work they expect to obtain" (Jones 1998, 59–84).[12]

Family Adaptation to New Forms of Intergenerational Social Reproduction

Family life and family relations in Sorowako have adapted to pursuing the now universally-valued goal of education for children. Even if children gain access to the YPS school, there are higher fees to be paid than at government schools, but parents report that they are happy to make the necessary sacrifices to raise the additional fees due to the aforementioned perception that YPS grants a superior education. Even greater financial effort is required to send the children away to school or university. Apart from the fact that in most cases the students are totally supported by parents or other family members—although in the few cases of permanent Vale employees, the children get some company support—the families have to forgo their children's labor in supporting household income; for example, if the household has a small business or engages in agricultural activities. In one unusual case, a young man who is now an NGO activist told me he chose NOT to go on to higher education once he graduated from YPS, as he had younger siblings and did not want to burden his farmer

---

11 Only five were civil servants, most of them teachers.
12 While there has been a resurgence of the local agricultural economy in recent years, as more land is made available by the mining company and there has been a surge in cultivation of cash crops, young people who have spent years away in education have neither the skills nor aspiration to take this up.

parents (farming families being among the most disadvantaged in this increasingly stratified society). He chose to *merantau* (sojourn) in Makassar and Java to work with NGO s and has returned to establish an organization representing indigenous rights.

Indigenous Sorowakan parents (and many of the migrant workers) by and large have only primary or at best junior high school-level education. They do not have a strong basis for understanding what is required to develop the competencies for success in higher education. But they have great faith in their children's ability to make good choices and to succeed. Young people in Sorowako rely on information from their teachers about which tertiary options to pursue. In this cosmopolitan environment where many company employees have higher education qualifications and knowledge of opportunities in Java (from where many of them come), students also report getting advice from neighbors in the company townsite. The fathers of children at YPS are almost all private sector employees (that is, almost none are civil servants), which marks this group as different from the samples of adolescents surveyed in other parts of Indonesia (see Nilan et al., this volume). Mothers of YPS students are most likely to be reported as housewives, which is a reflection of company employment policies, and it clearly does not translate into a lack of aspiration on the part of girls (or their parents) to pursue a profession.

Assistance from Parents

While Vale employees receive an allowance for their children in tertiary studies, non-employee parents also manage to find the necessary educational fees, and transport and living costs (which usually include *kos* [boarding house] fees and a monthly allowance). I asked one man, a farmer, how he had supported four of his children to go to university in Java. He expressed surprise at my question: "You can always make money". He had become a rattan trader in order to support his children and commented that he was fortunate in that his last child was just about to graduate when a national government ban on exporting unprocessed rattan came into effect. I saw his attitude as reflecting the commonly expressed belief, in the face of economic difficulty for example, that "*Tuhan yang menetukan semua*—Our lives proceed according to God's will." "*Kita manusia harus berusaha*—as human beings we are required to make an effort".

Support for their children's education is regarded as a fundamental responsibility of parents. A man with no fixed employment educated four of his nine children to tertiary level: "*memang orang tua*" (indeed that's what you do as a parent), he remarked. Another couple—a junior high school (SMP) graduate who retired in 2008 after 30 years working for Inco, and his wife who has only primary school education (SD)—supported all of their four children to go to university. Two of the four of them had dropped out, but the parents were philosophical, not angry. "We gave them the chance so they cannot come back at us later", the wife said with a calm smile. Another indigenous Sorowakan friend, whose children are all educated and two of whom married university friends and settled in Jakarta, expressed a common moral framework articulated through a religious idiom: "We are only given them to care for (*dijagai*), for a while". Parents express a respect for the children as autonomous beings as an aspect of their religiosity. But they also accept the responsibility to help them prepare for adult life.

How Successful is the Strategy of Pursuing Education to Realize Goals?

There is a small cohort of indigenous Sorowakan men with only primary or junior secondary education who have worked for the mining company for several decades, most of whom are now approaching retirement. Some of them advanced to foreman or, in a handful of cases, management level. This would not be possible today for people with limited education and no prior work experience. As it stands, educational qualifications alone are not a sufficient "passport" to employment with Vale; recruits are tested for specific skills and work experience. This is sometimes regarded by young indigenous graduates who aspire to industrial employment as the company "shifting the goalposts".[13] It is also regarded as an area where there is room for corrupt practices by the bosses making the selection, to give preference to their "own" (meaning co-ethnics or people with personal connections) (see Robinson 1986). Some of the students I interviewed commented that they would seek employment elsewhere once they had graduated as Inco was perceived as too difficult (*sangat susah*).

A young indigenous woman, daughter of a company employee, said that her parents had advised her "*jangan terpaku mau kerja* Inco [now Vale]" ("Don't

---

13　Prospective employees have to sit tests and many young graduates fail these. I was asked by one indigenous Sorowakan friend to intercede with a Canadian manager that I knew who had interviewed his son, a graduate with many years work experience in Java. I did not want to do this as I knew this would not be effective with this man. By chance, he commented in conversation on the process of recruitment in his section and said that the people he interviewed were not skilled enough.

just hang your hopes on employment with Inco/Vale"). Her situation was unusual in that her parents were encouraging her to think of employment elsewhere. I met many young female graduates who had come back to Sorowako on graduation, at their parents' request. Boys moving on to seek employment elsewhere after graduation is more readily accepted than it was for girls: for young women, marriage is accepted as a reason to not return home, but employment generally is not. Many of the graduates I interviewed were working in jobs not directly related to their field of education, for example one young engineer was working in Guest Relations, hoping he would eventually get a job in his field, and an IT specialist was working as a kindergarten teacher.

Children Achieving

Parents with poor education may, however, have some knowledge of which are prestigious universities, expressing pride if their children graduate from "top tier" institutions like University of Indonesia (UI) or Bandung Institute of Technology (ITB) for example. (Like the Chinese students in Kipnis [2011] study, educational achievement brings prestige for children and parents alike.) While parents pay the bills, they have enormous faith in their children's capacity to make the right choices and do not interfere. One mother described her feelings when she attended her daughter's graduation and she and her husband were called to the podium to accompany their daughter when she received a prize. "We felt all our efforts [supporting her] were repaid".

Both parents and children emphasized the positive value of children leaving home. Students studying away would typically respond, when asked what was good about being away from home, "*bisa lebih mandiri*" (you can be more independent.) And are your parents proud if you are independent? "*Otomatis* (of course)" one boy replied, with his friends agreeing. Parents "*mau lepaskan*" (want to let go of) their children. In the words of another boy: "*Mandiri, itu pendidikan baik bagi anak* (independence, that is good education [from parents] for children)". In contrast, the students agreed that if you stayed in Sorowako you were "*sangat dimanjakan*" (spoiled, in the sense of infantile). Another common statement is that leaving home allowed them to "seek experience" (*cari pengalaman*), expressed by one young woman in terms of "learning to seek other people's culture (*belajar cari budaya yang lain*)".

Others spoke of enjoying making friends, in the *kos* (boarding house) and at university, with students from elsewhere in Indonesia. Of course, for students from Sorowako their school experience has already been quite "cosmopolitan" because of the mix of socio-cultural backgrounds (at least 14 different identified cultural-linguistic groups at YPS for example) of fellow students. However, several of the townsite mothers expressed the view that children from remote mining towns like Sorowako were at a social disadvantage in that they were "too naïve", as they had only experience of "nice people" so did not know how to deal with "bad people". Indeed, public conduct in Sorowako is surveilled by company security and the main complaint of "bad behavior" by adolescents is related to the number of youths congregating with motorcycles. The head of YPS expressed the view that the children from such an affluent environment sometimes had difficulties adapting to poorer living conditions; in their urban *kos* in Java, for example, the adjustment to cold water splash baths, when they are used to hot showers, is difficult (for those who live in the townsite).

Students do report feeling homesick and lonely when they first move away. Some say they return home frequently in the first few months, but they soon settle into a pattern where they return home once a year at the end of the fasting month of Ramadan for Idul Fitri. This is a time to be "spoiled", to "eat whatever you want". "No Indomie (instant noodles)" one of them joked, this being the food students turn to if money is running out. One young man hinted at other benefits in living away from parents: "During Ramadan (the Islamic fasting month) it is very peaceful, no conflict". By going away to university and even to high school, the students are able to avoid potential conflicts with their parents as they move from childhood to adulthood and seek autonomy as independent adults.

What did their parents do to prepare them for independence? This question seemed to flummox students home on holidays, and they came up with responses like "*selalu didik*" (always given instruction) but in regards to what? "Keep your room tidy", was one response as they struggled for an answer. But it seems that the main message they received that prepared them to leave home was the importance of higher education, a message that would be reinforced every day in Sorowako by the social environment where education translates into well paid jobs and prestige, and as the YPS school provides an academic environment that valorizes tertiary studies and demands high performance standards from teachers.

This willingness to let children leave home, and giving them the freedom to choose the educational path that the parents pay for, is in strong contrast to the inter-generational relations of the transition to adulthood that I encountered in the 1970s. Then, marriage marked transition to adulthood and I found that most parents were still active in arranging marriages (Robinson 1998). Whereas the parental control of resources enabled them to control their children's choice of spouse, now they do not want to control choice of education, which is the significant marker of transition to adulthood. What remains constant in regard to parent–child relations is the idea of proper parental conduct, the moral obligation of parents to ensure their children have the basic "wherewithal" to form independent households. This was once factors of production, now it is qualifications, skills, and work experience.

High Level of Support for Children's Education as Parental Duty

As noted above, while children are reliant on parental support to continue secondary and tertiary education, parents leave choices in these matters to their children. This extends to children choosing to leave Sorowako to attend Senior High School elsewhere, in some cases. My neighbor, for example, is a widow with four children, three of whom have tertiary education and live at home and work at the company offices. Her youngest child (aged around 21 in 2008) was studying at university in Bandung, where he had attended senior high school and then university. At the time of our conversation, he had not been home for two years. She and his older siblings were supporting him. She reported that he chose to go away to High School saying that he wanted to learn to be independent (*mandiri*). She commented "if that is their choice, you have to support them". One mother asked rhetorically: "*tergantung anaknya mau kemana?*" ("Children dependent on parents, where would that lead?"). Another woman, whose children went to high school in Malaysia, said she "wasn't ready in her heart" for them to leave, but she understood that if they graduated from the International School in Kuala Lumpur they could choose any university that they wanted, anywhere in the world.

Students express an awareness and appreciation of the parents' efforts on their behalf. A young woman described how her widowed mother had sold cakes in order to pay for her university education. They were aware of the rising costs of public universities and the way in which their education was a burden to their parents. They acknowledged a moral framework for conduct by dependent children: one young woman (who had a diploma but was not yet able to continue to achieve her desire of a degree) commented (in English) "You have to try don't waste time because your parents not forever working for you".

Young people also rely on support from kin other than their parents, most usually siblings. There is an expectation that unmarried children who have found employment will help parents to support younger siblings until they have their own family responsibilities. For example, my widowed neighbor, mentioned above, reported that her eldest son helped support his brother at school in Bandung because he realized he was "*penganti bapak*" (replacing the deceased father). One young woman had lived with an expatriate family, assisting with household chores in a manner similar to the model pursued several decades ago. They had supported her education, including tertiary education in Yogyakarta—but this is an unusual case. Uncles and other kin outside the nuclear family are not perceived as reliable: some students found that promised funds may never be forthcoming, as the relative who had made an undertaking responded first to needs closer to home. (This is a consequence of the cash economy where money can be exchanged against a wide range of goods and services, unlike the agricultural commodities that were the basis of the pre-mining economy [Robinson 1986]).

Living Independently

Unlike 30 years ago when students were placed with family or friends when they went away to study, parents now prefer their children to stay in a boarding house (*rumah kos*), even if they are still school-age. Parents say that if the children stay with a family, even relatives, there can be too many demands on their time. One mother said: "I paid for *katering* (meals provided) so my student daughter could be free to pursue her studies". Twin girls, daughters of a Javanese man working for the mining company, chose to finish high school in the parents' home town in Java, but lived in a *kos*. Why? They "*pingin pengalaman*" (wanted experience). They had contact with their relatives but chose not to live with them. Another view expressed was that parents did not want to bother relatives (*bila repot*). One young woman initially stayed with a friend of her father's in Bandung, "so I had a *wali* (guardian), so I wasn't alone"; and he assisted her to find a *kos*. The preference for *kos* involves an element of status as well as autonomy—parents do not want their children to be beholden and hence vulnerable to being ordered about, so they prefer the formal link of paying cash to the *ibu kos* (female proprietor of the boarding house).

Parents do not normally have any contact with *ibu kos*—although some had traveled with their children to help choose lodgings. One mother had regular phone conversations with the *ibu kos,* but this was not common. Many of the students talked about the warm relations they developed with *ibu kos* and the other residents. This was especially marked for girls, who face more restrictive house rules (curfews, restrictions on visitors), than boys: of the students I interviewed, almost all the girls were living in *kos*, but several of the boys had other living arrangements, such as living in a house owned by their parents. One indigenous family had contracted a house in Makassar for all of their children, three boys and a girl studying at high school and university, and the mother visited from time to time.

The *rumah kos* as an institution allows students independence—studying away from home and developing life skills.[14] But at the same time it replicates inter-generational familial power that is gendered, in the person of the *ibu kos* and the stricter house rules for girls than boys. The institution of the *kos* allows parents to feel that someone is standing in for them in terms of moral guardianship and discipline. For many students, the *kos* is a "home from home", and it is not uncommon for them to live in the same establishment with the same housemates for all of their time at university.

Education and Proper Conduct

As noted above, young people mention the value of being able to *mandiri* (become independent, "stand on their own two feet"). Children as young as 16 leave Sorowako and travel, most usually to Java (Semarang, Bandung, Jakarta, Jogjakarta, Bogor), to complete high school or to undertake tertiary education. Most go on their own to live in *kos* and they find this challenging. Even those with siblings or friends in the same city often do not stay in the same *kos* as they prefer to choose to live close to their school. Parents and children alike narrate the experience of sojourning for educational achievement in the same terms: the student aims to *mandiri* and the parents support this as a goal. This narrative of transition may appear to hold a contradiction, as the independence of living and studying away from home is achieved through, in most cases, total financial support from parents. I only met a few students who worked while studying: one reported that she worked as a lab assistant on campus, and another boy had begun working in a pyramid selling scheme. (These jobs earned only supplementary income). But the nexus between these apparently contradictory facts is through the moral framing of expectations of proper conduct by both parents and children. There is a high level of parent belief (*kepercayaan*) and trust in their children. Parents reported that they expressed to their children the hope that they would respect the sacrifices they make and the opportunity they are being given. In a discussion of this matter, one boy threw in the comment: "our parents say 'don't embarrass us'" and his friends agreed that if children do fail, parents are disappointed (*kecewa*) rather than angry. When I asked students if they weren't tempted to just "skive off" they invoked notions of conduct: "our parents believe/have faith in us". Overall, they express an understanding of the sacrifices made by the parents to support

---

14 Parker (this volume) discusses the importance of teenage girls' friendships in educational institutions and in *kos*, for developing life skills.

them at school. (Most of the university students I interviewed were progressing smoothly through their degrees). A father remarked that if the children want to succeed at university they have to be "very ambitious" and not engage in "ABG" behavior (Anak Baru Gede, an acronym sometimes used to imply young people who indulge in inappropriate behavior) like smoking and drinking. Because they know this, he feels parents believe children will be responsible. The twin girls mentioned above, who left home to finish high school, commented that, living in the *kos*, they had more freedom (*lebih bebas*) but they were also more responsible (*lebih bertangunjawab*). A few parents mentioned that their children had begun but not completed tertiary education; however, when I asked the young woman who was assisting me to locate some "drop-outs" for interview she told me quite sternly "There are no drop-outs here, only people who give up because they can't afford the fees".

The Role of Schooling in Forging a New Community

The leisure activities reported by the young people in Sorowako in the AAI survey (Nilan et al., this volume) differ from those of adolescents in other urban centers, and look more like the children in rural sites. High school students in Sorowako are more likely to report spending time "hanging out" and chatting with friends than do students in large urban centers, and this often happens in each others' homes (rather than in malls, as in the cities). Computers are increasingly common in homes, including in the village, and children surveyed in Sorowako are more likely to access the internet at home than in most other sites surveyed, except Jakarta and Bali. School (in this case, YPS) is an important site of leisure activity and the children report many activities in afterschool clubs. The YPS students surveyed reported "spending time with friends" as the most important spare time activity, whereas the small sample of students from Budi Utomo were more likely to report spending time with their families. Sorowako has a local FM radio station that plays music located near the YPS school, and it is run by school students. There are some new "drop in" places that have developed in recent times, for example the cultural center built by the Luwu Timur district government that houses the Measa Aseroa ("We are One Heart") performance group, and has other activities like English conversation clubs. An art teacher from YPS and his dancer/choreographer wife are leading figures in this center. Another recent addition is the internet café, established at the privately run vocational school (STM Budi Utomo), where activities are watched over by headmaster Pak Anwar Idi or his wife. Patrons can choose booths where you sit on chairs, or set up to sit on the floor.

The latter mode is popular with students who come in groups to hang out. The YPS students also like to come there as they can play games and do homework simultaneously.[15]

Emerging Modern Identities

School is an important site for forging a new locality-based identity, attached to the institutional presence of the mine and smelter. Students feel proud of their school—when asked why they chose the school many YPS students replied "Because it's the best school in Sorowako" (in terms of facilities and academic standards). They strongly identify with the school, and feel proud of the activities it provides and the manner in which it provides a stepping stone to further education. Budi Utomo students also expressed pride in their school, and this also reflected modern values: they were most likely to comment that they valued the manner in which it provided work experience and a clear school-to-work transition.

The two schools seem to reflect some emerging occupational class differences: Budi Utomo students are oriented to trades but YPS fosters academic aspirations. In the AA survey, YPS students had a high rate of motorcycle (30%) and mobile phone ownership. When I reviewed the survey with the YPS teachers, prior to them distributing the survey to students, when we came to the question about mode of transport to school, one of the teachers pointed out we did not include the option "driving a car", a choice exercised by some YPS students but not in the other sites surveyed.

The students, both at the local high schools and in the cities where they pursue their education, have a presentation of self that conforms to the middle-class norms of the city, not those of a small town. The AAI survey found that patterns of phone and internet use of Sorowako high school students were almost the same as those of students in the cities of Jakarta and Solo, rather than those of a small town like Mataram. The YPS school, with its academic culture, high quality facilities, and abundance of extra curricular activities, provides a foundation for developing social personhood which follows middle-class norms. However, the AAI survey showed this embrace of a modern consumer culture (TV and DVD viewing, mobile phones) to be common to high-school students across Indonesia.

School is an important place for hanging out and developing friendships. Students form strong relationships within their cohorts; indeed, the groups of

---

15   Nilan (this volume) describes internet cafes as sites of leisure and also peer surveillance.

vacationing university students I interviewed had long-standing school-based friendships, although were now studying at different institutions, and in different cities. I asked one group of vacationing students about their "ethnic" identity and the students replied that they were *"penduduk Sorowako"* (population of Sorowako) a term that distinguishes them from the *orang asli Sorowako* or indigenous Sorowakans, but also does not assert an identity based on parents' linguistic/cultural group (Robinson 2012). School experience forges a modern place-based identity as well as developing new forms of self-fashioning suited to industrial modernity and employment. The educational experience in major towns in Sulawesi and Java exposes them to the trends in lifestyle and expectations of Indonesian urban residents, however, and they also become vectors of new ideas and cultural practices, some of which are adopted by their parents (in another reversal of the customary forms of knowledge transmission, from parent to child).

Conclusion

Education is a central aspiration of Sorowakan people, parents and children alike. It is considered the most significant adaptation they can make to the social and economic environment of the mining town. In accommodating the changes in their social and economic environment, there have been significant shifts in inter-generational relations in regard to social reproduction and the ways to enact the morality of proper conduct that encompass parental responsibilities. The gap in social experience between the parents and youth cohorts has meant that parents express a great deal of faith in their children's abilities to make the right choices and to responsibly pursue their goals when they move away from home, sometimes at a young age. This contrasts markedly with the forms of inter-generational power that regulated transitions to adulthood in pre-Inco times, when marriage followed by parenthood was the marker of transition to adulthood, and in which parents took a strong role in choice of spouse (Robinson 2009, Ch. 6). Parental control of the resources necessary to transition to adulthood in some ways replicates the generational power of previous generations, but the rapid pace of change in this community means that parents have to rely on their children's knowledge and judgment on the ways parental resources are expended. They do not vest as much in the educational success of their children, as the Chinese parents in Kipnis' (2011) study, but rather encourage their children to succeed in this modern mode, and accept their responsibility to provide the opportunities. The commitment to tertiary education (and the associated idea that this should be completed and should lead to employment) before marriage means young people in Sorowako experience an extended period of financial dependence on their parents. But because of the necessity of leaving home to study, this dependence is under conditions of personal autonomy. Education has provided a path for many young people to leave their families in Sorowako, through marriage and through employment, but parents embrace their children's success in the rapidly changing world and encompass their parental responsibilities in terms of an enduring moral framework forged under different economic conditions.

References

Buchmann, Marlis. 1989. *The Script of Life in Modern Society*. Chicago: University of Chicago Press.

Geertz, Hildred. 1961. *The Javanese Family: A Study of Kinship and Socialization*. New York: The Free Press of Glencoe.

Heneveld, Ward. 1978. "The distribution of development funds: new school building in East Java", *The Bulletin of Indonesian Economic Studies* 14:63–79.

Jones, Gavin W. and Laila Nagib. 1999. "Education and labour market issues in East Nusatenggara", *Development Bulletin* 48:13–16.

Kertzner, David I. 1983. "Generation as a Sociological Problem." *Annual Review of Sociology* 9:125–49.

Kipnis, Andrew B. 2011. *Governing Educational Desire: Culture, Politics and Schooling in China*. Chicago and London: Chicago University Press.

Munro, Jenny. 2009. "Dreams Made Small: Humiliation and Education in a Dani Modernity." PhD diss., Australian National University.

Robinson, Kathryn. 1983. "Living in the *hutan*: jungle village life under the Darul Islam", *Review of Indonesian and Malaysian Affairs*. 17:208–229.

Robinson, Kathryn. 1986. *Stepchildren of Progress: The Political Economy of Development in an Indonesian Mining Town*. Albany NY: State University of New York Press.

Robinson, Kathryn. 1989. "Choosing Contraception: Cultural Change and the Indonesian Family Planning Program." In *Creating Indonesian Culture*, edited by P. Alexander, 21–38. Sydney: Oceania Publications.

Robinson, Kathryn. 1998. "Love and Sex in an Indonesian Mining Town." In *Gender and Power in Affluent Asia,* edited by Krishna Sen and Maila Stivens, 63–86. London: Routledge.

Robinson, Kathryn. 2009. *Gender, Islam and Democracy in Indonesia*. London and New York: Routledge.

Robinson, Kathryn. 2012. "Indigeneity, Locality and Recognition: Young People's Shifting Engagements with Modernity in an Indonesian Mining Town (Sorowako South

Sulawesi)." (8–9 June 2011) In: *Online proceedings of the symposium "Young Lives, Changing Times: Perspectives on Social Reproduction"*, edited by Ute Eickelkamp. Sydney: University of Sydney, 2012; http://youngliveschangingtimes.wordpress.com/

Rodgers, Susan. 1995. *Telling Lives, Telling History: Autobiography and Historical Imagination in Modern Indonesia*. Berkeley: University of California Press.

Warouw, N. 2004. "Assuming Modernity: Migrant Industrial Workers in Tangerang, Indonesia." PhD diss., Australian National University.

PART 3

Friendship, Growing Up, and Peer Surveillance

Introduction to Part 3

School experience is not only about building for successful future through becoming employable: school is also a particular kind of social world, different from home, where friendship and lifestyle are immediate daily concerns. Friendship plays a critical role in assisting young people in their transition to adulthood, and this is a key focus of the chapters in this section (papers by Parker and Semedi), and it emerges as significant in many other chapters. Parker emphasizes that friendships fill an important gap at a time of rapid change when young people experience aspects of transitions to adulthood that are unfamiliar to their parents.

Parker identifies friendship as a lacunae in anthropological studies of young people in non-Western societies, despite recent academic interest in intimacy. Against the backdrop of an examination of the scholarly interrogation of friendship, she presents a subtle and poignant account of the friendships of young women in a small town in West Sumatra. She points to the significant role of these peer relationships in facilitating the transition to adulthood, as peers support each other with knowledge and in seeking new experiences

The crucial importance of these intimate relationships (expressed through the idiom of *curhat* [to share intimacies]) for these young women, living away from their families, emerges in Parker's conversations with them. While in many parts of Indonesia there is a long tradition of young people leaving home for education (as discussed in the previous section), the current scale of this movement seems unprecedented, following the expansion in school participation and de-agrarianization (White and Margiayatin this volume).

Semedi investigates The Scouts (Pramuka) organization as a pleasurable site of peer relationships. Branded as a corporatist organization of the New Order, it might seem to be somewhat out of date; it is regarded as "uncool" by many young people who choose to join new and flourishing independent environmental groups, for example. But Semedi's ethnographic study shows the Scouts as a "morally righteous" organization (approved of by parents) that provides a venue where enthusiastic young people enjoy peer companionship while learning some of the skills they will need in their transition to adulthood. For instance, he describes some quite complex activities where adults are largely absent and young people have fun while also learning skills such as organization, management, leadership, playing roles, taking charge, teamwork, and problem solving. It is also a space of gender equality where girls and boys can both take leadership positions.

Both papers in this section show the importance of peer relationships for moral development outside the sphere of kin relations. The Scout troop activities and the informal socializing of the young women in Parker's study both provide contexts for cross-sex mixing, including romance. In both these papers, and in many other chapters in this volume, we see the important role of youth as each other's "moral guardians", as peer pressure keeps young people safe from some of the moral hazard that popular discourse associates with youth socializing (see papers by Nilan, White, and Margiyatin, as well as section six of this volume). Thus, friendship and peer group activities emerge as providing critical spaces for the transition to adulthood.

CHAPTER 5

Pouring Out One's Heart: Close Friendships among Minangkabau Young People

Lyn Parker

Introduction

This chapter examines the meaning and significance of close friendships to Minangkabau young people. Although the literature on adolescence in Western societies stresses the importance of "peer groups" for young people, there are very few anthropological studies of friendship that explore friendships among young people in non-Western societies, and barely a hint of the importance of friends in the literature on young people in Indonesia (though see Bennett 2005 and Jennaway 2002 for passing references). Through the experience of fieldwork in West Sumatra, and analysis of field notes and interview transcripts, I realized not only the importance of friends for teenagers but also the significance of friendship as a medium for the transition from child to adult.

The chapter draws upon nine months of fieldwork conducted in a highland town in West Sumatra, which I call by the pseudonym Kota Sejuk, between 2004 and 2008. It focuses upon young people who can be called *remaja*—that is, young people of high school age. In this study, I focused on senior high school students, aged 16–18 years (see also Parker and Nilan 2013), while I also included a small group of young working women whose friendships are discussed towards the end of this chapter.

I begin with a brief survey of some of the anthropological and social science literature on friendship. The neglect of friendship in anthropology stands in striking contrast to the dominance of kinship studies in the discipline; kinship and friendship seem opposed, and, interestingly, the contrast between friends and family was often mentioned by my teenage research participants. One could reasonably have expected that with the post-structural turn and heightened interest in social process, emotion and the "many voices" in society, not to mention the rise of practice theory, friendship would have become more common in the anthropological corpus. Furthermore, as Giddens (1992) and others have noted, in Western and in many postcolonial societies, the old patterns and certainties of social relations based on the family and community are being transformed with and by globalization. In 1999 Giddens proposed that new forms of intimacy are replacing older connections in three key areas of our lives: sex and love, parent–child relations, and friendship (Giddens 1999). Interestingly, he elaborated upon the first two and neglected to expand upon friendship. Is friendship, then, a "given", something that is assumed to be so obvious, so common and universal, that there is no need for analysis? *Au contraire*, Brain (1976, 13) seems to comment: anthropologists, "having made a ritual obeisance to the importance of emotional ties outside structured kin groups, have apparently despaired of describing them in detail—most probably due to their delicate and non-articulate nature". This chapter aims to describe how friendship is meaningful for Minangkabau young people, and some of the features of their friendships. It shows that these friendships are neither delicate nor non-articulate, and that they do a lot of social "work".

It is not just anthropology that has neglected the analysis of friendships. Roseneil and Budgeon commented in 2004 that "little has changed since Beth Hess pointed out in 1979 that there is "no large corpus called the 'sociology of friendship' to provide an alternative archive for the study of intimacy and care beyond the family". (Roseneil and Budgeon 2004, 138). They note the many new forms of intimate relationships, and the blurring of the lines and movement between sexual and friend relationships in Western societies (especially among the gay communities, but also friends with benefits, those who are living apart together, partners who do not have sex together, and so on).

The tenor of the few studies of friendship in non-Western societies is quite different. Strangely, there seem to be more studies of friendship among street children than of friendship among children who live at home (e.g. Mizen and Ofosu-Kusi [2010] for Accra, Hecht [1998] in northeast Brazil, Kovats-Bernat [2006] in Port-au-Prince, and, most useful for my purposes, work by Beazley on street children in Yogyakarta [e.g. 1999; 2000; and 2002]). Perhaps the visibility and availability of street children, combined with their stark living conditions, piques the interest of researchers. Pervasive themes in this literature are the need to survive, precariousness, desperation, and the ever-present threat of violence. We are also coming to see the importance of trust and loyalty among bands of street children for help in times of trouble, which is often seen as an extended system of mutual exchange or reciprocity, protection, and companionship (see especially Mizen and Ofosu-Kusi [2010] and Beazley [2002] for street girls in Yogyakarta).

Friendship is by definition personal and inter-personal, and un-institutionalized. Friendship is based on emotion, the emotions of liking, love or affection, and often involves loyalty. Commonly, anthropologists comment on friendship as a relationship based on reciprocity, as was noted for street children. Friendship among children who work can also be economically productive and cooperative (Dyson 2010). Although often functionally important in social relations, and of great significance to the people involved, friendship is usually voluntary and informal. A striking feature of friendship is that it commonly occurs between social equals, of the same age, gender, and class, not to mention race and ethnicity. Although anthropologists and sociologists have noted this, it is also often noted that friendships are autonomous and not embedded in social networks constructed according to other criteria. This apparent contradiction—that people choose friends who are "like them" but friendship is perceived to be a voluntary, unique and autonomous relationship—is intriguing, and one to which I will return at the end.

The Western ideal of friendship is often said to be traceable to the Aristotelian ideal. Aristotle's ideal of civic virtue occurred when good men (sic) with purity of purpose make good, friendly alliances for the benefit of the community. This ideal of pure and noble friendship between men is common in Western literature and popular culture, and is accompanied by the stereotype that "women are incapable of such attachments" (Griffiths 1995, 2). In the sociological literature on Western countries, there is a common idea that young women are bitchy, competitive and disloyal to each other, and that because they are in competition for males, they cannot sustain long friendships with female peers. However, there are a growing number of studies that provide positive representations of friendships among young women, and Robert Bell (1981) has suggested that gender is probably the most significant of all social classifiers in shaping friendship. I will mention three ethnographies in the Western corpus that raise issues relevant to the Minangkabau context.

Angela McRobbie's (1977) study *Working Class Girls and the Culture of Femininity* in England stresses a "culture of femininity", a supportive interior "bedroom culture" of sleep-overs and support for friends as they agonized over their relationships and worked at their appearance. In short, she described "a real sense of solidarity" (1977, 143) among girls. Vivienne Griffiths (1995), in her work *Adolescent Girls and Their Friends: A Feminist Ethnography*, found that English girls' friendships provide them with confirmation and affirmation of their developing identities. Friendships between girls in rural north England are deep, intense, and long-lived. Graham Allan's book *Kinship and Friendship in Modern Britain* shows different patterns of friendship for men and women, shaped by their "quite distinct social and economic positions" (1996, 92). These different positions provide different opportunities for making friendships. Men usually develop more "public" friends – in work places, in social, sporting and interest clubs and pubs – while women's friends are elicited from a smaller catchment area and are more private. Men's friendships tend to be shallower than women's. Men share interests that are generally external to their personal selves: it might be a hobby held in common, a shared workplace or common participation in a sport. Women's friendships, on the other hand, are consistent with their "responsibility for the management of relationships within the home (and elsewhere)" (Allan 1996, 94). "Confiding in one another about their different personal relationships, seeking advice, and discussing problems is, in other words, as consonant with their personal and social identity as it is discrepant with men's. It is important that the dominant construction of femininity does encourage closeness, empathy, and the expression of feelings" (Allan 1996, 94). I posit that there is a similar gender difference in close friendships among young people in West Sumatra.

Sociologists have also been interested in the ways friendship is different according to class location. Again, Allan provides a convenient starting-point, with his description of friendships among middle-class and working-class adults in Britain. The middle-class "model" of friendship is the dominant and definitive one in society. Allan begins by differentiating the relationship from the context in which it was begun and is developed. When someone meets and likes a person, for instance, at work or at the pub, the relationship can continue and develop in that context, or it can transcend that context and "overflow" into other contexts. Allan says that the middle-class friendship typically extends beyond or transcends the initial context, say the workplace, particularly into the home context. The use of the home (and family) for entertaining is particularly significant, because this is the individual's private zone. Allan notes that this "symbolizes the independence of the relationship from the initial context which defined it. It clearly gives priority to the relationship over its context" (1996, 87). In contrast, the working class friendship rarely extends beyond the initial context in which it was begun. The context defines the relationship, and "what matters is the shared participation in the activity, not the commitment to the relationship for its own sake. [..T]he relationships are often viewed as more collective than middle class friendships are. [..T]hese ties are rarely seen as exclusive. Rather, they tend to be conceived as more open, often occurring in group contexts" (Allan 1996, 87–88).

The important and more general point Allan makes is that "the patterns of people's friendships reflect and are built around their social locations and social identities" (1996, 94). The data from Sumatra confirm this finding, though from the point of view of young people's experience of friendship, this is not what is important about friendship. I propose that gender identity, class location, and age are all formative of friendships among Minang adolescents. Most importantly, schools provide the "catchment area" for friends: young people find their friends at school. Choice of school depends upon gender, class, geographical proximity, religiosity of parents, and academic performance of the adolescent student (see Parker 2009). Most young people find friends among their classmates, so friends are usually the same age. Schools also provide the fuel and "props" of friendship: the day-to-day activities that friends talk about, the people that they both know, the pressures that they share.

The large majority of high school students in Kota Sejuk commute to school each day from home; some are from out-of-town and board with family; some board in houses and boarding-houses (*kos*) in the town; the rest live in dormitories (*asrama*) associated with the boarding schools. I had expected that those living in *kos* would be quite free and easy and mobile, especially when compared with those living at home and in Islamic boarding schools (*pesantren*), but *kos* in this town are always single-sex; they always have an *ibu kos* and a night-time curfew (*jam malam*), usually the sunset prayer time of Magrib; and none allow opposite-sex visitors, so young people living in *kos* are in fact quite strictly supervised.

Apart from schools, the main contexts in which friendships develop and are nourished are *les* (private after-hours tuition), *kos*, *warnet* (internet cafés) and *rental* (computer rental kiosks), shopping, sports and *nongkrong* or "hanging out" in parks, cafés and street corners, and travelling to and from home to these sites of socializing. For boys it is common to "hang out" on street corners or outside snooker halls, or to gather around a motor-bike or *bengkel* (bike repair shop)—not least to "*cari cewek*" (look for girls). The situation is quite different for girls: social surveillance of girls is strong, and their mobility quite tightly restricted (Parker 2009). However, there is not a strong bedroom culture, such as McRobbie described for English girls: there is not a culture of sleep-overs, and, with the exception of the fasting month, girls do not go out at night.

The Meaning of Close Friendships for Young People

Indonesian words for friend, such as *teman* or *kawan*, gloss a very large catchment group—people who are actually related in a very shallow way. For instance, school teachers always assume that all the students in the class are "friends": a student will be directed to bring along his or her friends—and that means everyone. I have been in classrooms of 60 students where everyone is considered a "friend", and they would be shocked to know that it is typical in Australian schools to only have a small group of friends within any one class. Similarly, it is common to do things in groups of friends—even if it means going out of one's way or making a much longer journey and less efficient use of time, in order to do things "together". In these and other ways, "friend" in Indonesian society has different meanings to "friend" in Australian society.

Here I want to divert slightly to examine close friendships, mainly, but not always, between two friends. I begin with some examples of *teman akrab*, or close friends, then move on to the relationship between *teman curhat*. The word *curhat* in *teman curhat* is *bahasa gaul* (youthful, cool slang) and consists of an amalgam of two shortened words that together mean to pour out the contents of one's heart (*curahan* is an outpouring, outflow or expression; *hati*, the metaphoric heart). This expression was only used by females in my study. Boys who are best friends are more likely to use the expression *teman akrab*, intimate or close friend, which has a rather different quality, but the *akrab* relationship can be between boys or between girls. I did not find any boys or girls who described an opposite sex friendship with these terms, but young people said that *curhat* happens between the sexes (*pacar*) in romantic relationships.

Friends and Openness to New Experiences

Almost all of the participants in my study identified positive things about having friends: friends could share your joys and sorrows, provide new information, and introduce you to new people and new ideas. This open attitude to the world was very often associated with friends, as were new experiences; many young people noted that friends introduced them to new people, new homes, new places, pastimes and practices, and new opinions. An enthusiastic female student at a vocation school was fulsome in her identification of the value of school for increasing the number of friends she could collect, which was seen as a good thing: friends are "social capital" and an assumed social good.

> I really like school because, first, we can get more knowledge. And secondly, we can increase the number of friends we have. If we are chatting with someone else, then Insya Allah we will be able to continue the conversation if we have education. Then we will be able to have many friends, friends from anywhere, from our village, and from [she lists surrounding towns and a couple of towns in other provinces.] That means we'll have many friends and enhance our life experience.

As noted above, school is an important source and platform for close friendships among "like" young people. One exception to the pattern that I identified above occurs when students attend a very small school. If a school is very small, students of different ages and genders usually mix freely together, and students socialize across a relatively large age range. Widya was a young man, 18 years old, who had gone back to school after "dropping out". He went to a very small, low-grade private tourism school. He was two years older than his classmates, and this meant that he was mixing with students up to five years younger than himself. Given that his same-age best friend (*teman akrab*) from his original time at school was already employed at an international hotel, and that, in his words, they were like *aur dan tebing* (bamboo and riverbank—thus, inseparable), he was worldly-wise and experienced in comparison with his classmates. He worked on his grandmother's farm on weekends, planting tomatoes, chillies and beans, but he was unusual in that he sometimes hung out with his friends in town till one o'clock in the morning, sleeping at his friend's *kos*. His long-standing and close friendship with his former class-mate brought him many stories of foreigners as well as new experiences. He was the only school student I knew who admitted he had seen a condom, for instance. This example shows, first, the strength of school-based bonds of friendship. It is common in Indonesia for people to meet their former class-mates or school-mates decades later, and for that apparently tenuous link to become the basis of a renewed friendship. The example of Widya also shows how, in this society, at this particular juncture, friendship plays a significant role as a carriage from childhood to adulthood, by introducing young people to outside and novel knowledge and experience.

The "*Geng*"

At one highly desirable (*favorit*) state senior high school, seven middle-class girls had formed a "*geng*" (gang), which they had named, in typical Indonesian fashion, by devising an acronym from the first letters of their names. The girls described the gang members as *teman akrab* (close friends), rather than *teman curhat* (best friends). Most of the members were very positive about the gang, and found their easy socializing lots of fun. Although there is some literature that portrays violent Indonesian gangs of school boys (for example, Kristiansen 2003), this gang was just a group of friends, who said their relationships were "*normal*" (!) and that they "just enjoyed" ("*enjoy aja*") doing things together. The *geng* was just a symbol of a group identity, an egalitarian sharing-and-caring for each other. Sometimes they all wore pink if they went out together, for example to the market or to a pop concert. Since they were all in the same class, and did most of their *les* after school together, they were together virtually six days of the week. There was often an hour or two between school and *les*, or between two *les*, and the friends often went to their favorite café or to the market to shop or hang out. Apart from that, they took it in turns to visit one another's houses, though only occasionally as they were very busy with their schoolwork. They liked to swap glossy magazines from Jakarta such as "*AnekaYess*". The gang appeared very egalitarian, and there was no leader. Within the gang most girls also had one or two *teman curhat*—best friends.

Interestingly, the gang members all mentioned that they had discussed menstruation before many of them had had their first period, and they cited this as a strong point that demonstrated the advantages of having a group of friends. Since almost all girls are ignorant about menstruation until they first get their period, this information was highly prized and considered helpful. Again, we can see friends carrying the adolescent from the world of childhood to the world of adulthood—particularly in the absence of sex or reproductive health education from parents and school.

The gang usually gets together for the birthdays of their members, usually, but not always, at the home of the one celebrating the birthday. The celebration of birthdays is a recent phenomenon, imported via magazines and American TV shows. Most older people do not celebrate birthdays, and many young people still do not, as their families do not mark the birthday in any way. The celebration of birthdays requires a group of people who all consider it a worthwhile event to celebrate. Parents usually do not remember, and many do not even remark upon the fact when a family birthday rolls around on the calendar. If young people are heavily socialized into "Western"-style behavior (for example, from television shows and magazines), they might feel hurt by this forgetting, interpreting it as their parents failing to consider them important enough to commemorate their birthday. Others, like the gang members, keep their friends' birth dates in their diaries and phones, and might send SMS messages on the day, or organize a get-together at a café or at the home of the "birthday girl" or other gang member. Other occasions that are celebrated with get-togethers include Idul Fitri and the end of exams, or the friends will set aside a day in the school holidays when they will have a "picnic".

However, two members, Rini and Fitri, had strong reservations about the gang. (This will be discussed later: Rini in the section on *Peer Pressure?* and Fitri in the section on *Girlfriends and Boyfriends*.) Nevertheless, the gang is innocent and friendly, without a high level of group coercion: if someone cannot afford to go out or is not allowed to go out, for example, to a café, the group either decides not to go, or the person concerned does not go, but everything returns to normal immediately after.

Girl Talk, Shopping, and "The Good Path"

Shopping, or window-shopping, is a common activity for groups of girl friends, and boys sometimes go to the market too, "*cari cewek*" (to look for girls). Shopping in such cases should not be dismissed as "just shopping", as though it is empty time: it is a key activity for friendships between young people. Shopping is a field of practice that enables young people to develop their own sense of self-presentation—that is, their personal appearance and style, and, more broadly, their sense of self as moral beings. I will discuss it here only as a girls' activity, because I have not been shopping with boys.

Girls who are out shopping may or may not be actually looking for something to buy. Often they are "just looking"—at the merchandise, and prices, but also at the people. They might be with their mothers or sisters, or with their friends. If shopping with their mothers, they might be buying food for the family, or clothes for themselves. I will talk about going shopping with friends, because that is what I have done with teenage girls. Usually girls are shopping for clothes or for small trinkets such as hair ornaments, pins, and brooches for their *jilbab* (headscarves). Although there are some shops in town, these are usually patronized by tourists and wealthier locals, so usually young women go shopping in the market. The market in this town is outstanding: it has a remarkable array of shops and stalls, and the goods and merchandise range from live eels and ducks to computers. And the smells! It is a wonderful place to go shopping—not only for the wide variety of goods but also for the good humor and politeness of sellers. Apart from the food market, there are coffee shops and cafés, a large noodle drop-in center, and shops and stalls selling gold and gold jewelry, mobile phones, CDs, tapes and VCDs, all manner of small and large electrical goods, furniture and foam rubber, stationery, magazines, comics and books, calendars, and posters; there are tailors and shoe-repairers, and hundreds of stalls selling clothes, underwear, textiles, shoes, bags, *jilbab* and hats, bridal costumes, trinkets, and hair ornaments.

Most girls love to go shopping with their friends. They prefer to go to the market than to the shops and two small malls that opened in 2007. After a quick stroll through the new mall with two young women, we sampled the fast food chicken outlet and announced ourselves disappointed with the new mall: several of the shops were just duplications of the stalls at the market, and the department store was staffed with snooty young women from out of town who seemed to have no interest in serving us. My companions quickly realized that the malls had higher prices and less variety than the market.

They would often only go for less than an hour, between school and *les*, or on the way home from school. They keep up a running commentary on the fashions they see, mentally "trying them on" not so much for size as for "look": they are looking for clothes that will go with their existing wardrobe, but, more importantly, they are trying to work out what image the clothes would project about themselves. They comment on the tightness and clinginess of the fabric and the fit of the design, the extent to which it would reveal their body shape and hide what they see as their faults in appearance, the degree of transparency of the material, the color and the message that the color would portray, the length of the hem, neck-line, or sleeve, and so on. I was amazed at the length of time they would discuss all these details (and I have teenage daughters of my own!), and the meanings of the details: would people think, if they wore a green *jilbab*, that they were "for" an Islamic party? Would a lacy trim around a *jilbab* be interpreted as indicating that one had a flippant attitude towards religion? Would this skirt stick to one's legs too much because it easily retained static electricity? They would often reference their mothers and fathers in these considerations: "No, Dad wouldn't let me out in this" or that, or "No, Mum would say it was too tight". The girls use their friends as a mirror against which they can measure the "look", and generally the friends provide feedback that is conservative and "safe". A girl might be attracted by a tight, red top and ask her friends what they thought of it: one might start by acclaiming it, "*Cool*", or "*Seksi!*"—but then another would check them with, "Your Dad might not like it", or "But would your Mum let you out wearing that?" After a couple more comments on the negative side, they might all join in the hilarity with exaggerated, ridiculous scenarios, like "Imagine if Mrs X [school teacher] saw you in that!" or "What if you came back to school after graduating and wore that!" There is always a reference point, a respectable standard, against which the imagined look is compared, and friends actively mediate between the potential transgressor and the respectable standard. The important point is not just that friends accurately mirror one's self-presentation: they actually bring one towards "the right path" (*jalan yang baik*)—they are an external conscience.

If there is one feature of Minang girls' friendships that seems to stand out from those in the scant literature on non-Western friendships, it is this function of friends as moral guardians. Such informal, and intimate, conversations as the one above in the market reinforce discursive norms of morality for young women. Their friends guide them as to what constitutes a moral "good girl" appearance: they must not wear revealing clothes—that would show that they were not good girls; they would shame their parents and teachers (and bring down their wrath) if they were seen in public immodestly dressed; they will need to negotiate a path through courtship to marriage very carefully indeed to secure a husband who will do honor to their family and lineage (Parker 2009).

Friends Like Family

For students who board in an Islamic boarding school, friends become like family. They form the most intimate human environment of the teenager's life, and in many ways become a substitute for family. Here the term *teman akrab* is commonly used, and not just to describe the relationship between two friends. Often these boarders do not return home for months on end; they often lose touch with their families, because they have no means of communication. Something of the qualities of these relationships is conveyed by Aisyah, a most articulate boarder:

> At the beginning I was very homesick (*sangat rindu*) for my family, that's for sure. Indeed, in this dorm...we are ordered (*disuruh*) to live together, helping each other, but the difficulty here is, with friends, for me personally, I feel I have yet to adapt properly to my friends' different personalities. I still don't know much about my friends' characters. So sometimes we feel heart sick, we have a conflict of understanding (*sakit hati, selisih paham*), but, Insya Allah, we will adapt ourselves to fit in here (*bisa beradaptasi menyesuaikan diri disini*).
>
> [... later] We are all close here, all intimate (*akrab*), probably because Allah allows us three years for us all to be together here from class one to class three, so the intimacy (*keakrabatan*) among us is extraordinarily tight (*erat*). The feeling among us friends is very tight. The proof will come in three years' time when we'll be separated and very sad. So we are all intimate friends, special friends, we'll be very sad when later we are separated, but although we will be separate, our hearts will remain as one.

Aisyah noted how they all support one another to choose goodness and not be led astray; in talking about peer pressure, she said that anyone who was tempted to go "in the wrong direction" ("*ke arah yang tidak baik*") would be automatically corrected by the majority in the boarding school who are committed to the good path.

Peer Pressure?

The discussion about friends was often highly moral in tone. We have seen that friends serve to keep one on "the good path" (*jalan yang baik*), and prevent one from going astray, down "the wrong path". In discussions about friendship, and in analyzing their friendships, no-one admitted the opposite: that friends can also lead one down "the wrong path". I found this something of a contradiction: friends could open one up to new experiences, but this was never perceived as leading one into trouble. It was always positively valued. Young people did not seem to see their friends in terms of "peer pressure" or as "a bad influence".

When I would construct scenarios of negative "peer pressure", where friends would pressure one into doing something they didn't feel happy out, and ask young people if they experienced this, a typical answer was this from a male youth:

> I don't really experience peer pressure: if my friends have some activity that they want to load me up with, I don't have to join in. It's just up to me whether or not I follow.

Rini, from the previously mentioned girls' gang (see above, *The "Geng"*), was not so happy in it. Rini was one of the few young people interviewed who identified friends as a problem. In an informal (recorded) interview, she said of her gang members, "They are buckets!" With this comment, she meant that they were leaky buckets: she had treated them as *teman curhat*—friends to whom one can pour out one's heart—but they had not kept the trust she had implicitly placed in them and had revealed her secrets outside the group. Trust is an essential element in the *teman curhat* relationship. Not only did she no longer trust them, she also thought that friends could be a potential source of trouble. On this point she was rather contradictory. On the one hand, she said that she did not personally experience peer pressure – she said, if she didn't go along with something her friends had planned for everyone, they might get angry with her temporarily, but she would just not do it, and it would all be all right the next day. On the other hand, in answering impersonal, theoretical questions, such as "What do you think is the most important problem that young people face nowadays?" she said: "The problem of socializing, making mistakes in choice of friends and in the end doing forbidden things". ("*Masalah pergaulan, salah memilih kawan dan akhirnya masuk ke hal-hal terlarang*".) It seems that choice of friends, and perhaps judgment of character, were problems that she had identified for herself. In this, Rini was typically self-reflexive: these young women were actively creating their own self-identity, and interacting with friends was an important element in this self-construction. Her reply seemed to imply that peer pressure had been a problem for her, and it was probably something she had experienced to her detriment. However, it was not negative peer pressure in the sense that is usual in the sociological literature: it seems that she did not like the way that friends tell you about yourself.

I found the occasional young person who was able to talk in a more considered and profound way about her friendships. Suzi, for instance, a student at a top senior high school (SMA, Sekolah Menengah Atas), talked about her friends within a framework of her career dream: she wants to become a psychiatrist. She said:

If I want to become a psychiatrist, I should start now, I should become someone's best friend (*teman curhat yang baik*), and be able to mix with all people (*bisa bergaul dengan semua orang*). [...] I practice this at SMA, how to socialize with my friends, and I invite friends to pour out their heart (*curhat*) to me and so I become the solver (actually *pemecah* = breaker) of their problems. [... Later: I have three close friends.] They each have their own personalities. [...] These three really are the perfect friends for me, even though they have some bad qualities, for instance, one is too egotistical, another has a great sense of humour and the last one is great as a repository for my thoughts. They really are very grown-up (*dewasa*).

Suzi is also very close to her younger sister, and "pours out her heart" to her, but she notes that her sister cannot give advice like her *teman curhat*. According to Suzi, her friends allow her to analyze their characters, and to develop her inter-personal skills. They give her advice about daily problems, and they teach her about themselves and thus about herself. Again, we see how friends act as a mirror, while also engendering self-development and self-awareness, and strengthening a growing sense of personal identity. In Suzi's self-conscious evaluation of her inter-personal relationships it is tempting to see friendship as contributing to the individualism identified by writers such as Giddens (1991) as characteristic of late modernity.

Girlfriends and Boyfriends

One small group of two girls and one boy, whom I met occasionally in a town park, finally owned up to the fact that their threesome consisted of two different types of relationship. Kiki (girl) and Toni (boy) were *pacar* (boy-friend and girl-friend), and Kiki and Eni (both girls) had a *teman curhat* relationship. In this case, the friendship between the two girls was a convenient cover for the romantic *pacar* liaison, and made the public *pacar* fraternizing more respectable. This was one of very few cases I found of a schoolgirl friend aiding and abetting a *pacar* relationship. Generally it was thought that students at school were too young to have a serious *pacar*, and that teenagers should concentrate on getting good marks at school above all. This is not to say that girl friends did not talk about boys or *pacar*: boys were one of the main topics of conversation among girls. However, often the *pacar* relationship was more of a *frisson* than a reality. The two might exchange innocent SMS messages, such as "Hello! What are you doing?" and "Have you eaten?" Many *pacar* relationships consisted of little more than an exchange of passport photos and SMS; actual conversation and socializing was usually done within groups. During senior high school, formerly large single-sex groups gradually became more heterogeneous, with sometimes two groups joining together and sometimes just a large mixed-sex group forming.

However, among an older age-group (for instance among university students), arrangements wherein girlfriends would help one another to further a serious romantic relationship between *pacar* were much more common. One in which I inadvertently became embroiled enacted a rather complicated plot: university student girlfriends deceived parents via mobile phones, while the two young lovers stole away for a weekend of illicit love.

Fitri (from above, *The "Geng"*) was one of the few girls in senior high school who had a boyfriend. He was a university student in Padang. Her parents knew about him by the time I interviewed her. They had wanted to meet him as soon as they heard about it—indeed, they had insisted on meeting him; having subsequently met him, they had given their permission. But he caused Fitri huge problems with her friends: they did not approve of him, or rather, they did not approve of the fact that she had a boyfriend who would distract her from her studies. Their disapproval and constant teasing caused her stress. This she identified as her "Number One Problem"—that is, having a boyfriend was not a problem in itself: the problem was the conflict with her girlfriends over the boyfriend. Again, we see the pattern wherein friends helped to reproduce dominant ideas about what constituted a "good girl", this time with regard to having a boyfriend. The dangers were twofold: having a boyfriend would potentially damage both her educational attainment, and her reputation as a modest young woman and therefore her marriageability.

Another girl, Filma, who attended the small private tourism school, also had problems with her friends, who did not approve of her two (concurrent) boyfriends. She was an unusual and precocious young woman, the youngest of four siblings, and was used to going to Padang and socializing with older and more cosmopolitan young adults than was usual in my field site. She said that the main problem she was experiencing was "trying to explain to her friends that she wasn't as bad as they suspected"!

In the literature (for example Leonard 1980), it is common to observe that as girls get older and more involved in romantic/sexual relationships with boys, their female friends fall away and female friendships fade. This is usually noted as a problem of jealousy: that is, girlfriends resent the time and attention that their friend lavishes on a boyfriend. In West Sumatra, the few cases I have of girlfriends' disapproval of their friend's boyfriend is couched in moral tones: it's not the identity of the boy or jealousy that is the problem (at least it's not framed that way); rather, the friends advise against having a boyfriend at all, because at school age girls are supposed to be studying, not having boyfriends. Some take a more explicitly moral line: that having a boyfriend is "approaching *zina*" (that is, approaching sex outside marriage, a major sin in Islam), and is therefore wrong and sinful. I cannot say that jealousy is a point that I would care to identify as a theme for the West Sumatra case, though it is definitely a theme in the literature for youth in the West. My sample of girls with boyfriends was so small that I could not identify jealousy as a theme, and I would hesitate to generalize.

Living-Away from Home Friendships

Another context in which close friendships develop is the *kos* and student dormitory. I visited many *kos* and interviewed many young *kos* residents, as well as *ibu kos*. Two girls who stayed in my memory were renting a very cheap (hot and leaky) room of makeshift construction on the roof of a family home. They were sleeping on two single mattresses jammed together, and there was no other furniture in the room. They said they were 19 years old (though they looked younger) and were living away from home for the first time. Both had only been away from home a month at the time of interview; one had come on her own from her village and had found the place to live on her own. In my field notes I noted they

> seemed so young: they were terribly homesick and clung to each other for support; they had chosen this place because of the *ibu kos* and low price. They were not seeking freedom—*au contraire*, they sought the tight control of an *ibu kos* in a rather terrifying new world. They were fresh from the village, and were struggling with the new life.

They came from completely different places and had not known each other before becoming room-mates. Both were taking a one-year computer course at a private college. For now, at least, they were *teman curhat*, a relationship that developed not only because of a common study program and college, but importantly in the crucible of shared social isolation. They described how they would go to sleep each night, in each other's arms, sobbing with homesickness and loneliness.

Working Girls' Friendships—a World of Limited Opportunities

We have seen the importance of school as the catchment area for sourcing friends, exemplifying Allan's point that friendships develop according to social opportunity (1996, 92ff). In the limited literature on friendships and work among children in the Global South, work, like school, can provide that social opportunity (e.g. Dyson 2010). However, the picture from my data is different. Here I briefly present some vignettes of "working girls" of senior high school age who sadly contrast the intimate friendships they experienced at school, a friend-rich environment, with the much more limited friend opportunities they experienced at work.

The main industries in Kota Sejuk are tourism, education, and textile production. Most young women who were working are either employed in sales, in shops and in the market, or are employed as *anak jahit* (literally, sewing children). Educational attainment rates are very high in this town, and I struggled to find young people who were school aged but not in school.

Young single women in workplaces usually work because their families cannot afford to support them through senior high school or further. They are, by definition, working class. Often their free time is very limited, and when they do have a day off it is spent quietly at home, sleeping, or in washing clothes, ironing, cooking, and caring for young siblings. They do not talk of excursions to the city, renting movies, or reading expensive glossy magazines; they do not use the internet and do not go to pop concerts. At most they wander the market and shops, perhaps buying nothing or a simple hair trinket. Their lives are dull and unexciting. Their social world is extremely circumscribed, and opportunities to meet new people extremely restricted. This is particularly the case for "sewing girls", who work in closed workshops and sometimes have no days off, or are only allowed a day off once a fortnight.

Sri is a young woman who sells children's clothes in the market. Sri comes from a poor family: her father trundled a mobile cart around the streets and the market, selling ice-blocks, for a living. When I asked Sri about her friends, she said, rather disconsolately, "I don't have any, only my friends at my workplace. When I was at school I had friends, but they're all working in factories now or at uni".

Rosi is a "sewing girl" who lives in the *asrama* attached to a textile workshop, making shawls and other "traditional" garments. Rosi described how they almost never had time to "*nongkrong*" (hang out): they were there just to sew, and at most they could exchange confidences at meal-times or when they were resting. Consequently she had no close friends (*teman curhat*) at her place of work and living, and she contrasted her current situation with her group of friends at school. She said,

> the five of us were best friends (*teman curhat*)...we could talk about our families, our friends and our boyfriends with each other, we told each other everything and we were all girls—classmates.

Although they still communicate occasionally by phone and SMS, she noted sadly that they were all separated (*pisah-pisah*) now.

Nur was another sewing girl, who lived and worked at her workplace. She used to have a *teman curhat* there, but that girl had moved away. I asked her, "So now, to whom can you pour out your heart?" to which she answered sadly, "I just bury it inside myself".

The Significance of Close Friendships for Young People

I promised in the Introduction to return to the apparent paradox that people believe that they choose their friends freely and that friendships are autonomous relationships between individuals, and yet they actually take friends from very circumscribed social groups so that friends are usually "just like them". I submit that the trust and intimacy deep friendship entails is difficult to find and nurture with others who are too different, and that deep friendship is rare between two people who are socially very different. This is not to say it is impossible, or that it does not happen, but we have seen, in the comparison between school and work situations for young women in Minangkabau, that friendships do indeed develop according to opportunity: schools provide a socially friendly climate in which individuals have a good chance of finding and recognizing like individuals as friends, and a much more fertile and pliable soil in which friendships can grow, than do many work-places for young people. But friendships are not the same as structured, prescribed relationships such as family relationships, against which friendships are invariably contrasted. Those relationships that are pre-determined have to be maintained, and any breach or rift has major social implications—divorce is the best example. Break-ups of friendships, on the other hand, do not usually cause major social upheavals—though of course they can be deeply distressing to the individuals concerned.

The phrase *teman curhat*—the friend to whom one can pour out the contents of one's heart—captures the idea of the best kind of friends, according to girls: those to whom one can disclose and unburden oneself of all one's problems, fears and worries, without fear of gossip, betrayal, or ridicule. All friends are a sort of carriage for adolescents, conveying the young person from childhood to adulthood, but *teman curhat* are also mediators that enable the young person to engage intimately, intersubjectively, with a socially-sanctioned other who is not too other.

Teman curhat function as a mirror, a safety valve and a moral barometer and guide. They steer the young woman through the ever-lengthening years of "youth" towards respectable adulthood, helping her to guard her modesty and virginity, and hence enhance her marriageability. *Teman curhat* provide support and comfort, intimate sharing, and the opportunity for self-expression. Trust is an essential element in the *teman curhat* relationship. Once trust is lost, the friendship dies.

Through these examples I suggest that for young women at school in West Sumatra, and perhaps to a lesser extent for young men, friends are an important and positive force for emotional and moral self-development. Friends aid in self-awareness, and in the crafting of self-identity. The combined features of the *teman curhat* relationship lead me to conclude that the intimacy of the *teman curhat* relationship allows young women to transcend the disparity between the self and the other, and helps them to straddle the gap between dependence and independence. *Teman curhat* are highly valued by girls and young women, and constitute one of the most emotionally important and formative relationships that adolescent girls experience.

References

Allan, Graham. 1996. *Kinship and Friendship in Modern Britain*. Oxford: Oxford University Press.
Beazley, Harriot. 1999. "'A Little But Enough', Street Children's Subcultures in Yogyakarta, Indonesia." PhD diss., Australian National University.
―――― 2000. "Street Boys in Yogyakarta: Social and Spatial Exclusion in the Public Spaces of the City." In *Companion to the City*, edited by S. Watson and G. Bridge, 472–88. London: Blackwell.
―――― 2002. "'Vagrants Wearing Make-up': Negotiating Spaces on the Streets of Yogyakarta, Indonesia." *Urban Studies* 39: 1665–83.
Bell, Robert. 1981. *Worlds of Friendship*. Beverly Hills: Sage.
Bell, Sandra, and Simon Coleman, eds. 1999. *The Anthropology of Friendship*. Oxford and New York: Berg.
Bennett, Linda. 2005. *Women, Islam and Modernity; Single Women, Sexuality and Reproductive Health in Contemporary Indonesia.* London and New York: Routledge.
Brain, Robert. 1976. *Friends and Lovers*. London: Hart-Davis, MacGibbon.
Dyson, Jane. 2010. "Friendship in Practice: Girls' work in the Indian Himalayas." *American Ethnologist* 37: 482–98.
Giddens, Anthony. 1991. *Modernity and Self-Identity: Self and Society in the Late Modern Age*. Oxford: Polity Press.
―――― 1992. *The Transformation of Intimacy. Sexuality, Love and Eroticism in Modern Societies.* Cambridge: Polity Press.

———1999. "Runaway World." Lecture 4 of the Reith Lectures, delivered in Washington DC through BBC Radio 4. Accessed September 24 2008 http://www.bbc.co.uk/radio4/reith1999/lecture4.shtml.

Griffiths, Vivienne. 1995. *Adolescent Girls and Their Friends; A Feminist Ethnography*. Aldershot: Avebury.

Hecht, T. 1998. *At Home in the Street: Street Children of Northeast Brazil*. Cambridge: Cambridge University Press.

Jennaway, Megan. 2002. *Sisters and Lovers; Women and Desire in Bali*. Lanham: Rowman and Littlefield.

Kovats-Bernat, C. 2006. *Sleeping Rough in Port-au-Prince: An Ethnography of Street Children and Violence in Haiti*. Gainesville: University Press of Florida.

Kristiansen, Stein. 2003. "Violent Youth Groups in Indonesia. The Cases of Yogyakarta and Nusa Tenggara Barat." *Sojourn* 18: 110–38.

Leonard, Diana. 1980. *Sex and Generation: A Study of Courtship and Weddings*. London: Tavistock.

McRobbie, Angela. 1977. *Working Class Girls and the Culture of Femininity*. MA thesis, University of Birmingham.

Mizen, Philip and Yaw Ofosu-Kusi. 2010. "Asking, Giving, Receiving: Friendship as Survival Strategy among Accra's Street Children." *Childhood* 17: 441–54.

Parker, Lyn. 2009. "Religion, Class and Schooled Sexuality Among Minangkabau Teenage Girls." *Bijdragen tot de Taal-, Land- en Volkenkunde* 165: 62–94.

Parker, Lyn, and Pam Nilan. 2013. *Adolescents in Contemporary Indonesia*. London: Routledge.

Roseneil, Sasha, and Shelley Budgeon. 2004. "Cultures of Intimacy and Care beyond 'the Family': Personal Life and Social Change in the Early 21st Century." *Current Sociology* 52: 135–59.

CHAPTER 6

Pramuka: Scouting Days of Fun[1]

Pujo Semedi[2]

Introduction

This chapter explores structural factors and subjective motives behind the participation of Indonesian youth in the scout and guide movements, a tight social arena squeezed between the patriotic morality of scouting movement founder Baden-Powell and the political interests of the Indonesian state. It gives insights into the scouting movement in Indonesia by looking at the "fun" element, through focusing on scouts and guides (termed "Pramuka" in contemporary Indonesia) as social actors.

Since its introduction in 1912, scouting has been very popular among Indonesians. In 2002 there were approximately 16 million Indonesian young people, from third grade primary school age to university students, registered as Pramuka (Gerbang 2005). The popularity of the scouting movement for contemporary Indonesian young people can be partly explained by examining the ideal role of scouts. Scouting has been described as a "character factory", a third domain of socialization after the family and the school. It is believed that through the scouts and guides, children and youth develop good character. They can learn the qualities of trustworthiness and discipline, develop their intelligence, gain skills and make handicrafts, improve their physical health, and learn self-care for the good of the community (Baden-Powell 2004, 44–46; Rosenthal 1986, 4–6; Pramuka 1969, 10).

However, these descriptions are general ideals of scouts and guides worldwide. In Indonesia, the popularity of Pramuka is also explained by the movement's historical attachment to larger social institutions, whether they were royal courts, nationalistic movement organizations, religious organizations, political parties, or government agencies. In return for the lavish support provided by these institutions, through funding and the provision of facilities, the Pramuka movement has served them by helping to increase the popularity and loyalty of constituents. The scouting movement in Indonesia has acted as a kind of seedbed to raise loyal cadres and to win popular support (Muecke 1980, 408).

---

1 This chapter is produced through my participation in the KITLV's In Search of Middle Indonesia Project. I am grateful for the generous academic support from the project.
2 Department of Anthropology, Gadjah Mada University.

Yet neither of these explanations tells us much about why joining Pramuka troops is popular with children and young people themselves. One direction of explanation looks at macro-level ideals and influences. The other looks at the phenomenon from the point of view of the social actor. On the one hand, explanations that rely heavily on Baden-Powell's rhetoric and state influence factors will provide a misleading picture of scouts as merely the puppets of ideology or of state policies for the production of ideal docile citizens. On the other, a purely actor-oriented approach to understanding the Pramuka movement denies the structural framework in which the movement takes place. It is necessary to find a framework which provides the actors with moving space while also acknowledging the symbolic references that make their actions meaningful.

The Interpretive Approach

The approach of understanding the Pramuka movement through the experience of the scouts and guides themselves is a fruitful place to start. As a popular scouting song proclaims, "Fun anywhere. Fun here. Fun there. Since I've been a scout. I can have fun any time, anywhere".[3] The song implies that scouts are active agents, keen to fill their days with fun. Yet their movement and capacity as active agents to have fun is facilitated—made possible and yet constrained—by existing structures, both the moral rhetoric structure of Baden-Powell that informs the scouting movement worldwide, and the political structures of the Indonesian state enshrined in the mother institutions that have supported Pramuka troops in the past and present. This chapter asks the following questions: What do youth gain from their participation in the scout movement? And how do they maneuver themselves in such a tight social arena in order to achieve their own goals? Primary data for this chapter mainly came from my participation observation among *penegak*, scouts aged 15–18 years of age, in Pekalongan Public High School 1 (PHS 1 hereafter) in 2007–2008, during their weekly training and outdoor activities, sometimes with troops from other schools. Secondary data was obtained from written sources such as scouting manuals, weekly newsletters, and magazines maintained by the library of KITLV in Leiden, as well as by some scoutmasters in Indonesia. During field observations I focused mainly on obtaining data on what the scouts really do rather than what they say they do, to avoid bias between those two different levels of data. In a way, data resulting from this process is fragmented, as they are nothing but the recorded events themselves. Considering the constant process of

---

3 A liberal translation of the Indonesian scout song *"Di sini senang, di sana senang"*.

dialectic between humans and their surroundings we can expect to get a proper picture of the motives and intentions of Indonesian youth in joining Pramuka, as well as their maneuvers within the movement, when the ethnographic data are put within relevant cultural, social, political, and historical contexts.

The Structure of the Indonesian Scouting Movement

From the time it was established in Indonesia during the Dutch colonial period, scouting has always been attached to political or mass organizations with strong support either from the ruling class, or politicians, or both. Initially it was the colonial elite, the Dutch, who were attracted by the idea of bringing Lord Baden-Powell's youth movement to the Dutch East Indies. A year or so prior to the outbreak of the First World War the scout movement, which was naively supposed to be "free from any religious denomination and political orientation", was established with aim of molding the colony's youth into good citizens who would be loyal to the Dutch Monarch, loved their country, obeyed and respected legitimate authority, took responsibility for their duties, were well-mannered, benevolent and helpful, and loved nature (ENI VI 1927, 311).

It did not take long for native Indonesian nationalist movement leaders to discover the great potential of the scout movement for their organization and political struggle. First of all, the scouts' patriotic credo "country first, self second" (Baden-Powell 2004, 28) fitted nicely with the spirit of the nationalist movement. Secondly, the scout movement did not appear to be a subversive force. Almost without delay, Indonesian nationalist movements across the country and from different ideological backgrounds established their scout troops. Baden-Powell's scouting law of "loyalty to the King, and to his officers, and to his country" was soon subjected to a very liberal interpretation (Sedia 1938, 16–17, 253; Pryke 1998, 323). The fire was started by Prince Mangkunegara VII in Surakarta who, in September 1916, established in his principality the scout troop *Javaansche Padvinders Organisatie* (JPO) (Suharini 2000, 18). Just as their name suggested and their oath stated, the JPO scouts were loyal to the "Prince and the beloved Motherland". Troop membership was exclusively for citizens of the principality. Around the same time, the Moslem Muhammadiyah movement, and then Boedi Oetomo, the first nationalistic political movement, fell into step, establishing their own linked scout troops (Pandu Rakjat Indonesia 1951, 134; Raharjendra 1990, 40). Not wanting to lag behind, the majority of political, religious, and mass organizations in the country established their own scout troops as a way to train cadres, who would be loyal to the mother organization's cause, for militant action, following the credo: "*Bidji jang baik dan koewat betoel itoe ditanem moelai misi ketjil*"—good and strong seedlings must be nurtured from the time they were small (Politiek, 1 1982, 152)—and "*In de jeugd ligt de toekomst*"—in the youth lies the future (Kwartir Besar SIAP 1938, 35).

The trend continued until the outbreak of the Pacific War when in 1942 the Japanese Occupation authority banned the scout movement and sent the youth to join the auxiliary army instead (Anderson 1961, 48; Mertoprawiro 1992, 26). At the conclusion of the independence war in 1949, the old practice of mass organizations raising their own scout troops returned, but with even stronger enthusiasm because it was perceived that scouts could be useful as political party tools. Scouts were deployed as ceremonial guards in political party meetings, as flag bearers in the party's street campaigns, and were engaged in conflicts that reflected the parties' antagonism towards each other. Since the scouts rendered their loyalty primarily to their mother organization rather than to God, country, and humanity, the ultimate values of the scouting brotherhood stood merely as rhetoric. Scouts linked to nationalist parties perceived other troops linked to socialist and religious parties as "enemies" rather than as brother scouts, and the feeling was reciprocated.

From Scouts to Pramuka

Tired of this situation, in 1961 President Sukarno took a bold step by uniting Indonesian scouts and guides into a single body called *Praja Muda Karana* (Pramuka), literally meaning Young Cadres of the Nation (Pramuka House Rules 1961). From then on, Pramuka were under total government control. Apparently for Sukarno, youth was too precious a national asset to be left in the hands of political parties and mass organizations.

When General Suharto assumed the country's political leadership in 1966, he happily accepted Sukarno's legacy of Pramuka. He attached the centralized structure of Pramuka as a corporatist body of the Indonesian New Order government and intensified scouting activities with regular national, provincial, and municipal jamborees, giving lavish government financial support. Different from other authoritarian governments—China and Vietnam for instance—Suharto's regime regulated the youth movement through facilitation and political protection rather than blatant indoctrination (cf. Marr and Rosen, 1998, 146). National Jamboree and *Wirakarya* Community Development Camps were the apex of scouting activities as a nation-building movement, where scouts from all over the country, of different mother tongues and cultural backgrounds met, played and worked together in well-organized programs.

In 1971, through Presidential Decree No. 12/1971, Suharto revised the Pramuka 1961 House Rules to make the Indonesian President the Head of the Pramuka National Advisory Council, now consisting of cabinet members and other high ranking state functionaries. At the next level down, provincial governors were appointed as Heads of Regional Advisory Councils that consisted of the heads of every branch of governmental services and commanders of the regional armed forces. This pattern was replicated at municipality and district levels, where mayors and district heads were appointed as Heads of Branch Advisory Councils. Implementation of the 1971 house rules thus placed Pramuka under the direct control of the government.

For decades it has been a tradition for Indonesian scouts and guides to base their troops within schools (Gugus Depan Bandung 2006), although the troops "belonged" to the community—in the form of political parties and mass organizations. Schools were "borrowed" for the purpose because they had the facilities needed for training, such as class rooms and school yards. Pramuka troops were also attracted to schools because these were the best places to recruit entry-level cubs and brownies. In 1965 the National Chief of Pramuka issued a decree in collaboration with the Minister of Education (Decree No. 165/Kab/1965) that suggested primary and high school students join the Pramuka troop adjacent to their homes. This practice was further sanctioned in 1978 by the Minister of Education. Every public and private school was obliged to become a Pramuka base and have its own troop. From that time on Pramuka have been attached to schools and people often perceive the local troop as a school's extra-curricular activity. However, in spite of the Ministry of Education policy, Pramuka remained a voluntary organization. It may be noted that, to save parents spending money on school uniforms—among other reasons—until the mid-1990s every Friday and Saturday primary and secondary school students were obliged to attend school wearing the brown Pramuka uniform, but the students were not obliged to become scouts or guides.

Attachment to government structures and to schools benefited the Pramuka movement during the New Order. During the early period of the New Order, for many Indonesians the 1965 slaughter was still vivid in their minds. They knew the fate of the members of Pemuda Rakjat (Youth of the People) Group of the Communist Party following the coup, a large number of whom had lost their lives in the bloodbath. Indonesians were aware that before they joined Pemuda Rakjat many of the ill-fated youth had been active in Kepanduan Putra Indonesia, the Communist Party's scout movement. During the New Order, Indonesians also witnessed the brutal activities of political party youth, the Satgas Partai (Party Task Force), who proudly presented themselves as thugs doing the work of the government party, Golkar. Satgas Partai youth might have received praise from functionaries in their own party, but their activities aroused hatred or at least antipathy from the wider population. By comparison, in the eyes of Indonesian parents, joining Pramuka was obviously much better for their children than joining Satgas Partai: scouting was politically safe and correct because it was not about practicing politics, yet it was legitimately attached to the main structure of the society, that is, to the state.

Pledges and Working Committees

In a very real sense Pramuka is a moral movement. Members are bound by the promise to become exemplary citizens who believe in God, are loyal to the Motherland, are well-behaved and responsible, and care for the environment (Abbas et al. 1990). Institutionalization of this promise is carried out by reading the pledge aloud during the flag-raising ceremony which is performed regularly at the opening of each weekly gathering. The scout or guide is idealized as a gentle patriot who is willing to help others. Scout masters like to tell the story of how, in their youth, they were obliged to carry three marble-sized stones in their pocket every day. Each was to be thrown away once a virtuous deed—such as picking up a shard of glass on a path, or helping a sick neighbor to see a paramedic—was accomplished. At the end of the day no stone should be left in the pocket.

Scouts and guides are trained not just to recite their promises of thrift, resourcefulness, responsibility, and so on, but also to live accordingly. They are required to plan their self-development program, deal with any problem they face during its implementation, and finally to evaluate the whole process, all on their own. Scouting is well known for its game-playing and outdoor survival skills training. Some of the training that continues today may seem absurd. We might ask who is going to use semaphore flags and Morse code to communicate when everybody now has a mobile phone? Yet despite the anachronistic flavor, it is a joy for Pramuka to learn such rare skills.

Moreover, the training provides young people with an arena for playing autonomous roles. Some of them—because of expertise or election—will act as trainers while others act as trainees, even though both are in the same age group. Role-playing takes place in almost all activities since Pramuka are quite independent in organizing their own troop and training programs. To a great extent they have the field to themselves, because the scoutmaster or guide mistress generally watches from a distance to give advice and help only if needed (Takijoeddin 1968, 15). Pramuka raise funds to finance their troop's programs by selling home-made snacks, soft drinks, scout emblems and pins, and collecting second-hand goods.

In short, Pramuka is based on a principle of group education. Individuals are organized into a squad of around ten members, and around four squads form a troop. Each squad has a leader, and each troop has a board consisting of the troop leader, a deputy-leader, a secretary, and a treasurer (Kwartir Nasional Pramuka 1987, 231). The leaders of the squad and the troop are expected to behave as role models. They provide mentoring and are bestowed with the right to command in their respective units. A squad leader provides training to increase the members' skills and to consolidate squad unity, and a troop leader can socially discipline squad members and leaders who fail to adequately perform their obligations as troop members. In summary, Pramuka are trained to learn the idea and practice of teamwork, to cooperate with their friends to solve common problems, and to achieve common goals.

Regularly, perhaps twice in a semester, Pramuka troops organize a program that extends their weekly training. This might be hiking, camping, inter-troop competition, a leadership course, or a regional jamboree. Since these occasions involve a larger number of participants than usual they need a longer period of planning, a greater amount of funds and equipment, and more complicated management. They cannot be run by the squad and troop leaders acting alone. So a working committee, a *panitia*, is usually formed. Working committee members are recruited from senior troop members to provide the administrative, material and technical support required by the program. If it is a hiking trip then the working committee plans, prepares the trek, appoints checkpoint masters, arranges emergency help on stand by, and chooses the location. If it is a camp the working committee will set up the site, and prepare and run the program. A troop outing may require less than ten scouts on a working committee, but the 1981 National Pramuka Jamboree in Jakarta, with some 26,000 participants, was run by a working committee more than 2,800 strong (Kwartir Nasional Pramuka 1981, 23). When a scout or guide is elected or appointed as part of a working committee this means taking responsibility for real work. Only if the committee is working well will a troop activity run well. If something goes wrong in the program, usually it is the working committee that is blamed first (Kincir 1973, 10). That is partly why *pramuka* take their working committee tasks seriously. Responsibility on a working committee comes with a meaningful reward of control over the implementation of a program or component activity. They are not merely playing the role of leaders but are bestowed with real authority, power, and responsibility. Oddly enough, there are rarely any articles or reports about working committees in Pramuka magazines or bulletins. The Pramuka working committee is like a car engine which makes the whole thing roll and produces the result, yet is hidden from view.

A Day of Rites: Joint Training in Pekalongan

Early in April 2007, scouts and guides of PHS 1, PHS 3, and Moslem High School of Pekalongan staged a one day joint-training exercise. For that purpose a working committee of 20 *pramuka* was formed from those troops. All were second-year students because first-year students were considered too junior, while the third-year students were no longer active, since they were supposed to be studying hard for their final exam. A week before the training took place, the committee held several meetings to discuss the committee structure, the training program, and personnel in charge of each component. The committee was efficiently divided into an executive board consisting of a leader and deputy, two secretaries, and two treasurers, with three section leaders for general affairs. They decided the training would be held in the PHS 3 school premises and that each troop should send at least 20 scouts and 20 guides. In this way each *pramuka* would get the opportunity to know and cooperate with *pramuka* from other high schools. After some calculation the treasurer confirmed that the training would cost Rp 1,400,000 (around US $150), mainly for lunch, snacks and beverages. Contributions were drawn to cover this cost, Rp 100,000 from each troop and Rp 7,000 from each participant. The budget planning was prepared by the committee without any intervention from scoutmasters or guide leaders.

On the day, an hour before the training participants arrived, the working committee arrived at SHS 3. The previous day the consumption section had ordered snacks, lunch, and beverages from a restaurant, and settled the bill with money from the treasurer. Very little spoken direction was given to arriving scouts, who relied on a large hand-written training schedule attached to a wall. Others prepared five flag standards; for the national, Pramuka, and troop flags. By 07.30 most participants had arrived, and again without many words one of the scouts called for attention. He ordered the joint training participants into seventeen lines and then staged a rehearsal for the opening ceremony. Under his command one hundred and twenty *pramuka* were transformed into a single compact body that dutifully moved in unison, came to attention and at ease, faced left and right, opened and closed ranks, and stepped back and forth. Some thirty minutes later the opening ceremony was held. A scoutmaster from PHS 1 troop stepped up on a podium to act as the ceremony inspector. After the general salutation, the recitation of the Pramuka Oath and Promise, and a report from the working committee leader about the joint training day, the inspector made a short speech closed by a wish for successful training. The ceremony leader then put the ranks at ease. Next, another working committee member, a guide, came up and addressed the participants telling them that after the ranks were broken they were to form squads of twelve scouts according to a list she had prepared. "You get five minutes to form squads and elect your squad leader", she commanded. She distributed the list to several *pramuka*, stepped back, and the ceremony leader broke up the ranks.

Like marbles spilled out of a box the *pramuka* noisily moved around in confusion, looking for their squad. The ones holding lists stood separately and loudly called out names of squad members. Before long the confusion diminished and everyone gathered in circles of ten persons on the basketball court floor to elect the squad leaders. With only seconds to go before the allocated five minutes lapsed, the working committee guide came up to the basketball court again and barked a countdown: "Five, four, three, two, one, zero. Form ranks!" Dutifully twelve lines of squads formed up. The working committee guide announced that the following activity was marching drill: "Every squad is to practice basic drill and there will be working committee members to evaluate and improve your marching technique. And now break ranks!" For an hour, under the bright tropical morning sun every squad practiced marching drill. Sweating heavily, they kept moving back and forth in marching steps, facing right and left, opening and closing lines on the squad leader's command, trying to achieve perfect neat marching formation. Working committee members were serious in giving their evaluations: "Your line is not straight enough… this way". "Chin up…!" "Keep the sight lines…!". Without uttering a word the squad did their best to comply with the criticisms.

The marching drill was followed by knot-tying, which was to be demonstrated through tripod construction. Each squad was ordered to create a tied tripod of bamboo poles in fifteen minutes. Seconds before the allocated fifteen minutes lapsed a working committee member barked out a countdown. Before reaching zero, all twelve tripods were standing in the center of the basketball court, while the participants sat down in shady spots around the court to avoid the glaring sun. Five members of the working committee carefully examined the knot-tying on the tripods and called upon a representative from each squad to be quizzed. They were asked what is a tripod, how can it be used, ways to make it, knots to use and so on. The best tripod was awarded praise and the squad danced merrily amidst applause. The squad with the worst tripod was chastised then entertained the other participants with singing and dancing which they conducted no less merrily than the winning squad. Having finished with knot-tying, participants were ushered into the hall for morning break. Sitting in circles, the working committee flocked together on the carpeted area while the participants sat on the bare floor. Five working committee members from the consumption section swiftly distributed packs of snacks and iced tea. For fifteen minutes the hall was noisy, with almost everybody talking. The floor was littered with snack packs and plastic bags. Two members of the consumption section came up with large bags and cleaned up the mess. On their own initiative some participants got up to help them.

All in all the one-day joint training ran well. The later activities of discussion, artistic performance, lunch, and group exercises were carried out smoothly. The closing ceremony was held at 16:15, with leader of PHS 3 troop acting as the ceremony inspector, since all scoutmasters and guide leaders had left the training at 11.00 that morning. He told the ranks that the joint training had been very satisfying, that it had given them the opportunity to get to know each other and work together, and that he was looking forward to the next joint training. Upon barking his closing command to break ranks, the ceremony leader positioned himself next to the line of the working committee. Almost automatically the front-most working committee member stepped out of the line, shook the ceremony leader's hand, bade him farewell, and stood next to him as he received handshakes from the others. Without comment everybody in the ranks followed suit and the line expanded to form a circle on the basketball court. When the circle was completed and everybody had shaken hands with everybody else, the ceremony leader spoke loudly; "Once again brothers, sisters, I bid you farewell. Till we meet again. *Salam pramuka!*" In unison they replied "*Salam!*" Then everybody left, except the working committee members, who collected equipment and materials and did a final check to ensure nothing was left behind. The following week they would meet again to write up their technical and financial report on the joint training day.

The April 8th joint training consisted of rites and games, and perhaps some of the participants perceived it as that—a playful activity to occupy a weekend. For the working committee however, it was real and demanding work that needed to be planned and implemented. Indeed, it was serious work. Without good planning and efficient management it would have been impossible to keep 120 *pramuka* in one place, not going astray, and doing what they were told to do for the whole day. Perhaps because of the history of ideological rhetoric from government or other sponsoring bodies, somewhere in their minds the working committee members believe that all those Pramuka rites and games are good for the nation and society. When asked about benefit of joining Pramuka, most scouts and guides gave a standardized answer along the lines of: "It is good to have positive activities (*kegiatan*) and nice to be with friends". Yet what they got personally from Pramuka involvement was not merely a strong sense of nationalism or comradeship, but also experience of team work. They gained skills for organizing programs, they took on leadership roles, and they had the opportunity to sample the right to order other people around, the sweet taste of power—perhaps just a little dose, but enough to let them know how sweet it is, and probably sufficient to motivate them to taste more.

Variation in the level of adherence to scouting values among individual scouts certainly exists, from the lowest to the most highly committed. There is similar variation in the collective performance of scouts over time. In general, however, because of their oaths and good deeds, *pramuka* are praised by the Indonesian community as morally correct youth. They represent the kind of resourceful, disciplined, skilled, learned, and well-behaved young people that parents are happy to see. For some young people, though, the Pramuka movement seems anachronistic, old-fashioned. Since the late 1970s there has been a spread of nature-lover youth groups, along with expansion of the range of extra-curricular (*ekskul*) activities in high schools. The new groups and activities have provided young Indonesians with alternatives for filling their leisure hours, releasing their energies, and constructing their identities (Tsing 2005, 122; Semedi 2006, 140). As signified by their "hippie" looks, including baggy pants, army shirts, and long hair for boys, the nature-lover groups were notorious for their adherence to freedom, endorsing a loose organizational structure, and—to a degree—anti-establishment attitudes. Soon, Indonesian youth in their thousands joined them or established their own groups. At the same time, extra-curricular activities in science, the arts, sports, publication, and religious learning which are not necessarily less fun, but are less strict than Pramuka—they do not demand uniforms, official ceremonies, and regular weekly training—gained the attention of high school students. Both the nature lovers and *ekskul* enthusiasts tend to share a similar view of *pramuka*, that they are definitely out of fashion, and uncool. This view, however, has in effect strengthened the good image of scouting for the older generation and for *pramuka* themselves, that scouts and guides are well behaved, and that the national Pramuka movement is, in short, a well-organized, positively-oriented, morally credible youth institution.

Days of Fun

State regulation and patriotic moral codes set strong limits on scouting social space. *Pramuka* are forbidden to engage in activities against either the interests of the state or established moral codes. For formally observing this limitation, however, scouts and guides receive substantial compensation in the form of social warranty and trust from wider society to run their programs on their own. For example, Indonesian *pramuka* are officially gender separated, the boy scouts and girl guides have their own troops and squads. When *pramuka* go camping or join for a jamboree, the guides have their own "village" and to some extent their own program. In a typical camping program, the ground is divided into three main sections: girls' village, boys' village, and public ground where scouts and guides can mix. Above troop base level, however, gender separation is often blurred and most activities are gender-mixed. In the above case of the Pekalongan joint-training, the working committee was a mixture of genders. Furthermore, when they go for hiking, they will often reorganize their gender-separated squads into temporary mixed-gender ones; for reasons of safety along the trek, squads consist of both scouts and guides.

Indonesian parents are sensitive to male–female relations among youth. They consider it the most worrying moral issue. The utmost care is taken to limit the chances for a girl to go out with a boy unless there is a sure sign that they will proceed to matrimony. Oddly enough, this moral concern over female virtue does not seem to be applied in the case of scouts and guides mixing. It must seem to wider society that nothing will go wrong between girls and boys as long as they are under the umbrella of Pramuka.

It is Sunday April 27th 2007. The Pramuka of PHS 1 are getting ready for a beach trek. According to the schedule, they are due to leave at 08:30, but since 07:00 the school yard has been noisy with chatter as each participant arrives and moves around here and there in some excitement. Some have walked in on their own, some have come on motorcycles, or in cars driven by parents who have left as soon as their child runs to join their friends. The atmosphere is relaxed and pleasant. The young people talk about things the way youth usually communicate, describing their recent experiences, their difficulties in understanding lessons, telling stories about the idiosyncrasies of teachers and so on. Only the working committee members look serious. They are gathered in front of the teachers' office discussing the program. Rani, the committee chairwoman—a second year student wearing the Moslem head cover—is carrying out a last check on transport, meals, and the program of activities along the trek. "Dul, is the truck ready?", "Sure Ran!", comes the response. "How about drinking water, snacks, breakfast, and lunch Wid?", "They are ready Madame Leader", Widya answers. "Checkpoints, emergency squad, equipment?", and so on. "Today we will go on our own, because Scoutmaster Chisnun cannot join us. This is okay, we can handle the program", Rani tells her team and nobody looks surprised or worried at the announcement. "Tell the members to change uniforms. It is almost eight fifteen, we should start soon". The order is given and soon everybody changes their brown Pramuka shirt for a light blue, long sleeved, T-shirt.

After a quick opening ceremony, where Scoutmaster Chisnun delivers his speech on the positive value of outdoor activity and advises them to behave well, all 58 participants, bearing light backpacks, climb into a large truck bound for Sigandu beach, some eight kilometers away. Along the way they talk to each other. Arriving at the beach they are lined up and the original squads are reshuffled to form five gender mixed groups, each consisting of nine guides and scouts. "Well done guys", Rani says, addressing the troop, "our finishing point is Ujung Negara beach. There will be several checkpoints along our ten kilometer track. Just follow the coastline and you won't get lost. Don't litter the beach. If you come across plastic garbage please collect it, we will dispose of it at the checkpoints. Get your drinking water and breakfast. Have a nice walk". Squad One begins the trek. The other squads follow at fifteen minute intervals.

Under the intense morning sun, Squad One walks slowly. Someone starts to sing but no one joins him. It looks like the heat has absorbed their will to sing and while away their lazy pace with small talk instead. After two kilometers, Squad One comes to the first checkpoint, in the shade of a large tree. They line up and the squad leader, a guide, orders a salute to the checkpoint master. Sloppily the squad gives a military salute. After the checkpoint master has returned the salute, the squad leader reports that her squad is in good shape, and ready for further orders. "OK. Your order is to…but first a song and dance please…", replies the checkpoint master. Perhaps because of the shade and the cool beach wind, Squad One regain their earlier exuberance. Merrily they sing a Papuan song, swaying their hands and walk-dancing in a circle. "Thanks for the great performance. Your task is to collect ten different types of shell around here and if possible identify their names", orders the checkpoint master. Upon completing their task, Squad One continues the trek, walking in the heat again. Somewhere before the second checkpoint they came across a large beached jellyfish. "Hey-hey look at this…", "Don't touch with your fingers, it is poisonous. Makes your skin very itchy". Someone pokes the jellyfish with his scouting bamboo pole, turns it over. For a moment their attention is captured by the dead sea-creature, something they do not see very often in everyday life. But the sun is hot and they have been walking for some time. "Someone help me please. My backpack is heavy", a guide pleads. "What's the reward?" a scout responds teasingly. "Nothing!", "Why should I care to do it if it is for nothing?", "Oh come on. You're supposed to be nice to friends". "Absolutely, but carrying an extra backpack for miles under this heat and for nothing…come on". "Okay, okay…a glass of iced tea in Ujung Negara, my treat". Without waiting any further, the scout took the guide's backpack—which obviously did not look heavy at all. Squad One then continued the trek, but the guide and her backpack carrier walked a little distance from the others, side by side, although well within earshot.

In one or another way everybody seemed to enjoy the beach trek. Checkpoint Four was located next to an estuary and the checkpoint master's task was to ensure everybody crossed safely. Seriously, he informed every squad about the depth of the estuary, before leading them to a crossing 20 meters wide, which was waist deep. Being young, instead of crossing the estuary quickly, some scouts seized the moment for a water fight, splashing water among themselves, and then onto the guides. The girls shrieked between worry and joy, yet fought back. Bound by his responsibility the checkpoint master cried from the estuary bank; "Stop it. Stop. Cross quickly. Come on!" Reluctantly the scouts got out from the estuary, followed by the guides, and resumed their walk to Ujung Negara, a half-kilometer away. In Ujung Negara, participants who had arrived earlier gathered at a rocky spot. Some sat on the rocks, while some played on the beach.

By 13:30 all of the troop had arrived. They sat together under a large tree to take lunch, which was followed by a free session. The young people broke up into several groups and chatted happily. In one group, a guide commented that she was missing the Sunday morning television program and the talk steered to popular cartoon movies. In another group the talk was about the homework they had to submit on Monday. Yet another group was busy looking at and commenting on photographs taken along the trek with a digital camera. At 14:30 Rani closed the program, and ordered the troop to climb the truck to bring them back to the troop base. During the trip home the troop sang all kinds of songs, from Pramuka songs to cartoon movie songs. Between songs they proudly cried out their troop yell:

Satu dua tiga empat
Ambalan kita memang hebat
Berfikir cermat
Bersikap hemat
Bertindak cepat

One, two, three, four
Ours is a troop of honor
Shrewd, thrift, swift

As the above description shows, just like in the joint-training day, the PHS 1 Pramuka troop gained productive knowledge from the beach trek program. Working committee members learnt about the proper way to organize a program to maintain troop order, from systematically preparing food and drink provision to protecting safety. The whole trek was carried out in an atmosphere of fun and was free from the intervention and surveillance of the older generation. Seen from the perspective of parents and teachers it might appear that many worrying things could take place among the youth, either physically or morally. *Pramuka*, however, seem to be exempted from this automatic concern on the part of the older generation. This is not because they never do anything which potentially might cause concern, but because they have proven time after time that because of peer group surveillance, as well as their resourcefulness and organizational and physical skills, the Pramuka troop provides a safe environment for youth. Scouts and guides are believed to be trustworthy enough to be left alone to take care of their own programs.

Concluding Remarks

Some might perceive Pramuka as an old fashioned youth institution, heavy with rites and games, squeezed between state intervention and Baden-Powell moral codes. Seen from the scouts' and guides' own perspective however, we must form a different view. For many Indonesian young people joining the Pramuka troop is still attractive because here they find a social space with an ample degree of independence to organize enjoyable activities. Pramuka troops follow an egalitarian credo of "from youth, by youth, for youth". There is an unusual degree of gender equality and girls often take leadership roles. The space for action is indeed tight. Pramuka have to don uniforms, are morally bound to behave in ways appropriate to the ideal of the good citizen, and—since the 1960s—have been politically subdued. Yet the space for independent action is still wide enough for them to learn leadership, teamwork, management and other organizational skills. It can be argued that in the practice of scouting and guiding they engage in the reproduction of the power structures of their society. They learn in practical terms, for example, how to acquire power by taking responsibility on a working committee and how to execute their mandate from the troop—their peers. The practical knowledge they acquire will be very useful for them in pursuing their lives in the modern, highly structured society of contemporary Indonesia, characterized by power relations that favor organizational hierarchy and devolved responsibility. Equipped with the skills for navigating the powerful structures of organizations and institutions, *pramuka* have the potential to be not merely passengers but crew and officers in the ship of life. Moreover, they can have an enjoyable time while acquiring this knowledge and confidence, blessed by the good will of their families. Pramuka learning is not school learning. It is carried out in an atmosphere of fun while enjoying the trust of parents and the society. In the tight social space of the Indonesian Pramuka movement, scouts and guides protect their interest in having fun in the present while undertaking proper preparation for the future. Conducting themselves within the expected boundaries of moral rectitude, they reciprocate the trust placed in them by scoutmasters, guide leaders, and parents by maintaining their social and moral reputation as trustworthy and responsible youth.

References

Abbas, M.A., et al. 1990. *Pedoman Lengkap Gerakan Pramuka*. Semarang: Beringin Jaya
Anderson, Benjamin. 1961. *Some Aspects of Indonesian Politics Under the Japanese Occupation: 1944–1945*. Ithaca: Modern Indonesia Project.
Baden-Powell, R.S.S. 2004. *Scouting for Boys*. Oxford: Oxford University Press.
ENI. 1927. *Encyclopaedia van Nederlandsch Indie*. 1(6).
Gerbang, 2005. "Rencana Strategik Gerakan Pramuka 2004–2009." Vol. 4: 69–72.
Gugus Depan Bandung. 2006. *Sejarah Gerakan Pramuka Gugus Depan (Gudep) 07019–07020 Kodya Bandung*. 2006, accessed May 2006 www.bandung19.or.id
Kwartir Besar SIAP. 1938. *Gedenkboek SIAP-PMI. 1928–1938, 10 Tahoen Oesianja Pemoeda PSII*. Djokjakarta: Persatoean,.
Kwartir Nasional Pramuka [National Scouting Organization]. 1981. *Petunjuk Pelaksanaan Jambore Nasional 1981*: Jakarta.
Kwartir Nasional Pramuka [National Scouting Organization]. 1987. *Patah Tumbuh Hilang Berganti. 75 Tahun Kepanduan dan Kepramukaan*: Jakarta.
Kincir. 1973. "Taruna Bumi dan Pengembangannya," *Majalah Kwartir Nasional Pramuka* 7, July 1973.
Marr, David, and Stanley Rosen. 1998. "Chinese and Vietnamese Youth in the 1990s." *The China Journal* 40:145–72.
Mertoprawiro, H.S. 1992. *Pembinaan Gerakan Pramuka Dalam Membangun Watak dan Bangsa Indonesia*. Jakarta: Balai Pustaka.
Muecke, Marjorie A. 1980. "The Village Scouts of Thailand." *Asian Survey* 20:407–427.
Pandu Rakjat Indonesia. 1951. *5 Tahun Pandu Rakjat Indonesia*. Djakarta: Pengurus Besar PRI.
Politiek-Politioneele Overzichten van Nederlandsch-Indie. 1982. *Politiek-Politioneele Overzichten van Nederlandsch-Indie. Deel I, 1927—1928*. The Hague: Martinus Nijhoff.
Pramuka. 1969. *Pramuka. Indonesian Boy Scout & Girl Guide Movement*. Jakarta: Japenpa.
Pryke, Sam. 1998. "The Popularity of Nationalism in the Early British Boy Scout Movement." *Social History* 23:309–24.
Raharjendra, Surti. 1990. *Perkembangan dan Peran Hizbul Wathan Yogyakarta dalam Bidang Kepanduan (1918–1961)*. BA thesis, Gadjah Mada University.
Rosenthal, Michael. 1986. *The Character Factory. Baden-Powell and the Origins of the Boy Scout Movement*. New York: Pantheon Books.

Sedia, Madjallah Kepandoean KBI Surabaja. 1938. "Berita dari Kwartier Daerah Djawa Timoer." No. 9.

Semedi, Pujo. 2006. "Petungkriyono: Mitos Wilayah Terisolir." In *Esei-esei Antropologi*, edited by Heddy Shri Ahimsa, 127–143. Jogjakarta: Kepel Press.

Suharini, Theresia Sri. 2000. *Javaansche Padvinders Organisatie: Awal Munculnya Kepanduan Indonesia, 1916–1942*. BA thesis, Gadjah Mada University.

Takijoeddin, Mh. 1968. *Petundjuk Pembina Pasukan Gerakan Pramuka*. Bandung: Pelita Masa.

Tsing, Anna. 2005. *Friction*. Princeton: Princeton University Press.

PART 4

Performing Youth in Space and Time

Introduction to Part 4

Social space is both restrictive and enabling in regard to young peoples' activities and autonomy. The papers in this section address two different kinds of social space. Guinness discusses the changing designation of social spaces and places in urban and rural Yogjakarta over several decades and the ways this impacts on youth activities, while Nilan explores youth socializing in what she terms the "public-private" spaces of a shopping mall and an internet café, as well as in the expanded social space enabled by ICTs. Both authors also deal with time. Guinness explores one peri-urban location over four decades, showing the different constraints and opportunities for each generation that has moved through the youth "slot" while Nilan explores the time dimensions of social experience in the fixed locations of the mall and cyber-cafe. These social spaces change in character and are used for different kinds of socializing throughout the day and night. Both authors highlight gender differences in the uses of space, with boys allowed more freedom than girls, but the spaces of the mall and café do allow young, middle-class girls to socialize in groups, including in mixed sex groups.

Malls are important sites for middle-class youth experience, as they are zones of parent-free interaction. They provide places of employment as well as spaces of leisure. Picking up on themes explored in other papers in this volume (such as Parker, Bennett), the young girls studied by Nilan feel protected in these modern leisure spaces by their religious values and pious practices, as well as by peer surveillance.

Nilan's paper presents the much-discussed youth "lifestyle", which is identified with consumption and the growing middle-class. This theme is addressed in other papers in this volume that focus on the leisure activities of high-school aged young people (such as the chapters by Wright Webster, and Parker).

An important theme in Guinness's chapter is the class-based character of youth experience that impacts on opportunities such as education and employment, as well as on outlook and lifestyle. The young people of Yogyakarta that he discusses are divided by class, and they engage in conflict across class lines. Interestingly, one of the foci of class conflict is cross-sex mixing (especially middle-class males in sexual relationships with lower-class girls), and the peer surveillance discussed in the papers in the previous section, involving the exercise of moral authority and guardianship, does not operate across class hierarchies in Yogyakarta.

For the youth in the communities he studies, class is expressed in spatial terms (*kampung* versus *gedhongan*), which in fact refer to the differences between poor lower class-and urban middle-class neighborhoods and, by metaphoric extension, lifestyle and opportunities in life. The core of his chapter is a story that takes place over 40 years in a particular lower-class urban neighborhood, and the way that the youth "space" has been transformed through the impact of regime change at the center, and as people move into and out of this space.

CHAPTER 7

Dwindling Space and Expanding Worlds for Youth in Rural and Urban Yogyakarta

Patrick Guinness

In the rapidly changing worlds of urban and rural Java, youth are constantly challenged by the tensions between their home communities' expectations and the alternate attractions of contemporary society. They are both the creations of existing structures and the creators and renewers of culture. White (this volume) refers to tensions between "being young" and "growing up". In the pleas of their parents and their home communities there is often an espousal of tradition, and indeed in the parents' appeal to the sanctity of certain ways of thinking and acting such traditions are constantly being processed into the social consciousness of the next generation. Yet, as Siegel points out in his portrayal of student youth in Solo, Central Java, "it is still the case that students are seen to bear a special responsibility for the transformation of society" (1986, 139). There is, therefore, a tension for many of them between forging new paths oriented to global trends and continuing in the old ways espoused by their parents and familiar to home communities.

Yet I will indicate in this chapter that the home spaces so significant in youth choices in earlier generations are much less so in the 2000s. The dwindling spaces and opportunities of their home communities are set against the exploding possibilities of the worlds beyond. I will suggest that this has not always been a smooth process and was, at least during one decade, marked by a distinct "morbidity" of proliferating violence and drug use (White, this volume). The historical perspective offered in this study indicates that tensions, morbidity, and exploding opportunities are not the experience of all youth of all generations but are reflective of particular social, political, and economic environments in the wider society.

In this Chapter I compare the fortunes of youth, students and otherwise, in both urban and rural societies in Yogyakarta. I have followed these changes through four decades, and here I designate three "periods": the early New Order of the 1970s and early 1980s; the New Order swansong of the late 1980s and 1990s; and the first decade of the Reformasi period. This period of over forty years has impacted hugely on youth through global trends in secular education, religious revival, expanding communications networks, and the consumer revolution. Youth have largely been the consumers of new fashions and ideas, watched at a distance by parents whose education and experiences keep such novelties at a distance. As White (this volume) puts it, "new generations of young men and women grow up behaving in different ways than the previous generations". Yet many of these youth do return to the homes of their parents and renew home ways rather than invent radically different worlds. Such a choice may be the only one they see as viable in poor economic circumstances, or it may be seen as an opportunity to renew the world of their parents.

There are three general categories of youth discussed in this chapter: firstly, youth from the urban off-street neighborhoods (*kampung*) of Yogyakarta city who represent the poor proletariat and underclass of the city; secondly, middle-class and elite youth who came to the city in their thousands from provinces all over Indonesia to take advantage of the fifty or so tertiary institutions in this *Kota Pendidikan* (Education City); and thirdly village youth from the mountains of Kulon Progo Regency within the Province of Yogyakarta. Data was gathered by myself, mostly in the urban ward (*kampung*) that I call Ledok, and by myself and students during field schools supervised by myself and Dr. Paulus Bawole of Universitas Kristen Duta Wacana in 2009 and 2010 in various Yogyakarta *kampung* (Bawole and Guinness 2009; 2011) and in 2011 and 2012 in the rural village of Banjaroyo in Kulon Progo (Bawole and Guinness 2014). These teams of Australian and Indonesian students worked and lived in twelve *kampung* in Yogyakarta city over a period of four weeks in each year of field research (2009–2010), and for a similar period each year (2011–2012) in twelve rural hamlets of Banjaroyo (Bawole and Guinness 2009; 2011; 2014).

The Indonesian Central Agency of Statistics estimates that between 1971 and 2000 the proportion of the 15–24 year old Indonesian population living in urban areas increased from 21.5 per cent to 47.1 per cent (Soeprobo 2002). This urban youth population also increased exponentially in that time from 19 million to over 38 million. The impact of modern urban society and culture linked to both secular and religious education and to consumerist lifestyles has come to dominate youth expectations in both rural and urban areas.

Youth as *Pemuda* and *Remaja*

In Indonesian history *pemuda* "young people" hold a special place: university and high school students are seen to have led the revolution, challenging Dutch rule and pressuring Sukarno to declare Independence. As the new nation-state crystallized through those first decades students, through their *Dewan Mahasiswa* (Student Councils) on each campus, led calls for reform, demonstrating first against the ineffectiveness of the Old Order and then later against the repressive military machine of President Suharto as it privileged the elite and deserted the goals of the revolution (Anderson 1988). *Pemuda* became a political category with a celebrated history in Indonesia (see White, this volume; Hasan, this volume; Spyer, this volume)

As the New Order progressively curbed the political voice of youth another term for youth became more prominent. *Remaja* (adolescent) is a less politically-loaded term and is the more popular referent for young people once they move to high school age and explore the opportunities available in wider society (Nilan 2004). They are, the Javanese say, *durung wong* (not yet become adult) but on the cusp of being adult (*mula dewasa*). Male *remaja* are expected to try things out, to stray from the strict etiquette of Javanese communal ways, before they return as adults to marry and take on the responsibility of fatherhood. Javanese elders expect *remaja* to gain an education and to explore new forms of self-expression such as new music styles and modes of dress, but it is a time of anxiety for parents as their children stray from the ways of their home communities. There is an energy and freedom in young males that Javanese find both attractive and dangerous. The same did not apply to female *remaja*, at least before the 1980s, as they were more closely disciplined before their marriage (Geertz 1961; Guinness 2009). However, education and the consumer revolution after the 1980s have brought new freedoms for young women as well as young men, and these began to create very different *remaja* patterns in the new century (see for example Parker, this volume; Nilan, this volume).

My argument from the analysis of these three groups in Yogyakarta is that, at the beginning of the New Order, youth (*pemuda*) continued to hold a special status as the result of the crucial role they played in winning Independence. That political role was increasingly curbed by the military authoritarianism of the New Order, and in response youth political energies were channeled into consumer and religious interests heavily impacted by global trends. This led to considerable frustrations and disorder ("morbidity") among youth (*remaja*) which has been somewhat resolved through the recent decade of the Reformasi era. White (this volume) remarks on the tensions between the generations that fuel this morbidity, as youth are both "romanticized by the adult world as the nation's future , but at the same time pathologized and feared when they behave in ways that adults do not like". I describe these frustrations as arising from a realization of the dwindling "space" of their home communities and the exploding possibilities of worlds outside those spaces.

Widening horizons have brought radical changes to the way youth perceive and promote themselves within their respective origin societies of rural village, urban *kampong*, and urban streetside (see below), and this has led to questions about their commitment to the social orders of *kampung*, palace, and agricultural hamlet promoted by their parents. At this time moment of global incorporation through the internet and international commerce, youth in Yogyakarta are seeking to forge a new place for themselves that has little connection with their home worlds.

1970s—Student Elite and Their Poorer Counterparts—The Development Divide

The era of *pembangunan* (development) under the New Order of President Suharto through the 1970s witnessed the flooding of middle-class and elite youth into the city of Yogyakarta from the cities and rural centers of Java and the outer islands. Yogyakarta, the home of the first Indonesian university post-Independence, consolidated its position as the education hub of Indonesia. Prestigious state and private universities attracted inter-provincial migrant students who sought accommodation in neighborhoods close to campus, including the cheaper off-street neighborhoods. These students were the vanguard of a new mobility of population that marked the New Order. They were primed in their education to succeed to the new opportunities in government and corporate business afforded by *pembangunan* (development).

Despite their location often at the geographical center of Yogyakarta city, *kampong*, or "off-street neighborhoods", in the 1970s were largely isolated from the society and economy of the streetside[1] and remained locations for the urban marginalized, landless villagers who had drifted into the city and those surviving on irregular wage work in the informal sector. A few youth continued on to high school but most completed primary school and then looked for work. While the New Order had established free (or rather cheaper, if ancillary expenses of school uniforms and other fees are included) primary schooling, high schools charged a range of fees that made this level of schooling prohibitive. A few *kampung* residents had jobs as lower-level public servants (*pegawai*) of the Province or Municipality and were able to obtain similar positions for their children through nepotistic connections, but most residents worked in the informal sector, providing services (transport, foodstalls, construction work) to the wider city. Their children found work as shop assistants and laborers with the expectation they too would spend the rest of their lives in informal work.

---

1 *Kampung* residents distinguish themselves from *gedhongan* or 'streetside', referring to the *omah gedhong* 'mansions' that line the main streets of the city.

One of these *kampung* which I call Ledok is situated on the Code River that runs through the center of Yogyakarta city (Guinness 1986; 1991). It is hidden behind large commercial properties located on the main arteries of the city, and was—for long periods of colonial and national administration—irrelevant to city planning as its sloping riverbank, roughly fifty meters wide, was considered too difficult to develop commercially. It became home to poorer citizens prepared to live in a settlement accessed only by narrow, maze-like pathways and steep steps. It therefore attracted short- and long-term migrants from the rural hinterland who had not the land to support their families (White and Margiyantin, this volume)

However, many *kampung* homes opened spare rooms to student boarders. These students were a privileged group, who largely lived apart from their *kampung* neighbors, though they paid good money for lodgings and meals at *kampung* food-stalls. They owned motorcycles which they brought down the steep ramps and parked in alleyways; they dressed well in cosmopolitan fashion; and built friendship and study circles among themselves and with their peers at university and high school rather than with *kampung* youth. *Kampung* alleyways thus exhibited quite dramatically the radical divide between urban students and underclass youth.

Interestingly, *kampung* youth (*remaja*) played a key role in socializing the student boarder population. Some of the latter were active in *pemuda* political roles increasingly critical of the New Order government but were largely absent from neighborhood affairs. While only a few boarders participated in local activities, the young people impressed upon them the essence of local codes of morality, the need to show formal respect to elders, and the importance of contributing at least occasionally to neighborhood working bees constructing *kampung* infrastructure. They thus played a crucial role in enforcing the cultural standards of their home/parents' community. *Kampung remaja* ensured student boarders conformed in one further aspect, in the relationships that the predominantly male student boarders formed with young local women. There was strong disapproval of any such relationships, built on a suspicion of the boarder's intentions. A few misadventures where young women had fallen pregnant by student boarders had resulted in enforced marriages, but such unions proved unstable and in several cases the student husband escaped the marriage and *kampung* as soon as his studies were over. *Kampung* male *remaja* were adamant about preventing such partnerships, to the extent of terminating late night conversations between local girls and male boarders and evicting non-resident male student visitors from the *kampung*. Through these years *kampung* youth were thus recruited into the wider male cohort that policed the security of the *kampung* at night, focusing in their activities on the *pos ronda* "security post" erected in every alley neighborhood (Guinness 2009).

Kampung remaja interactions with the student boarders reflected their views of the urban middle classes who occupied the streetside just beyond the *kampung*. They saw streetside youth as prone to arrogance and snobbery, and were inclined to tell them so if they entered the *kampung*. As a result the adjacent streetside youth preferred to stay away. This further emphasized the isolation of *kampung* youth from the wider city in the early New Order era.

Thus, in contrast to the cosmopolitan students, *kampung* youth were restricted to their residential communities where they directed their energies. The kilometer-length stretch of Ledok riverbank was recognized in the city administration as a single *Rukun Kampung* (RK), divided into thirty or so *Rukun Tetangga* (RT), each originally consisting of about thirty households but expanding well beyond that figure as migrants moved into the settlement. Each RT unit designated responsibility for key tasks to specific residents, such as the development of infrastructure, finance, religious activities, women, and youth (Sullivan 1992). Youth "sections" at both RT and RK levels ensured that the annual Independence Day was marked by sporting and cooking contests among the RT and an RK concert featuring *kampung* youth bands. They also organized other activities during the year, such as outings by bus to beachside resorts, and youth attendance as waiters at *kampung* rites-of-passage events (such as weddings and funeral wakes).

Kampung families encouraged youth to contribute to the community through running educational activities, such as English language classes; a wall journal; a library; sporting contests such as table tennis, badminton and volleyball; cooking competitions; and music bands. For *kampung remaja* in the 1970s the neighborhood was the boundary of their everyday domain. Primary schools were situated all around the *kampung* within walking distance, as were junior secondary schools. Community obligations provided regular activities for youth, and they also formed a neighborhood (*lingkungan*) choir for the Catholic church, or attended Quranic reading classes, which integrated them within the religious societies of their parents. Marriage came early, with the expectation that young men, especially, find employment, usually in the city's informal sector. Any new opportunities tended to be within the geographical confines of the *kampung*.

Open space is very important for *kampung* social life. Where adults largely congregate in the narrow alleyways, youth require wider spaces (Bawole 2009, 18, 20–1; Campbell et al 2009; Winarna 2009). In the 1970s the river flat below the riverbank where they lived provided space for residents to grow fruit trees, develop commercial fishponds, keep goats and sheep, and for youth to play volleyball and badminton. Some used the river flat area to pursue extraordinary powers (*ngelmu*) such as in the ORHIBA (Olahraga Hidup Baru) "New Life Sport" group or snake handling or meditation. Such activities appealed to a Javanese spiritualism that sought an experience beyond the formalities of mosque or church but within the space of the *kampung* and the ambit of their parents' spiritual traditions.

However, during the 1970s the river flat was settled, first by a few vagrants (*gelandangan*) desperate for a spot to sleep and put their few belongings while they sifted through the municipal rubbish tip beside the river or begged on city streets. They were followed by others who earned incomes through sex work and theft. As a result, the river flat areas throughout the city became associated with criminality and thus targets for police raids. There was considerable anxiety among adult residents about the growing associations of *remaja* with the river flat occupants, who rather overtly had a different set of moral norms to their riverbank neighbors—they dressed scantily, gambled, ate dog meat, brewed their own alcohol, applied tattoos, "borrowed" equipment, begged for food from their neighbors, and conversed only in the (low) *Ngoko* register of the Javanese language (Guinness 1986). For all these reasons, riverbank residents sought to prevent their youth from associating with river flat occupants, but this was difficult, given that the vacant recreational spaces were mostly at river flat. The social and cultural explorations of youth in those years had their boundaries on river flat rather than the wider social and cultural expanses of the expanding city.

Mondal et al. (2011) describe the settling of the river flat in Sidomulyo *kampung* in the northwest of Yogyakarta city in similar terms. This *kampung*'s leaders allowed the settlement of former urban vagrants (*gelandangan*) in 1976. Reputed as a home to marginals and criminals, in the 1980s the *kampung* attracted transgendered youth *waria* from Java and beyond. They recognized it as a place where they could be accepted and from where they could carry out their occupations as street-buskers, hairdressers, and sex-workers. They made use of the open spaces along the river to foster a volleyball team that played against other youth, and to construct their own group activities. The *waria* provided artistic contributions to the *kampung* through their singing and dancing, performing regularly at *kampung* ceremonies and festivals. They passed on these and related skills, such as make-up, to children in the *kampung*, which parents saw as a positive inspiration for their children to be involved in the arts. (Interestingly *waria* claimed to still be youth into their 30s, because they counted their age from the age they were "born again" [Mondal et al 2011]).

Rural village youth were also largely isolated in their communities through these years. An isolated rural village such as Banjaroyo in Kulon Progo provided few opportunities for its youth to engage in wider society. In the 1970s, to attend high school young rural people faced the prospect of moving to urban centers where they would need to board in *kampung* lodgings. Indeed, village students were rare boarders in the city. Few village youth could afford the luxury of high school education and so primary school was followed by a return to farming, trading within the village, and early marriage and progression to "adulthood". White and Margiyatin (this volume) report from another village in Kulon Progo that a majority of youth progressed to junior high school, but that both girls and boys were contributing significant hours each day to their household economies (girls 10 hours, boys 5.5 hours). Most were engaged in wage-work, often to provide school fees and clothes.

In parts of Central Java in the early 1980s Collier reports that girls could find employment in factories that were being built in rural and peri-urban areas:

> The labor of girls in agriculture, handicraft and home industries has been important in the rural household economy. In such a context, girls function as unpaid family workers...they are rewarded with no more than a small amount of pocket money... Now, increasing numbers of factories in rural and periurban areas in Java offer employment opportunities for these girls. As wage earners they can earn more than just a little pocket money.
> COLLIER 1982, 32

The 1970s in Indonesia was a time of momentous change as the New Order development brought the commercialization of all aspects of life, including village agriculture and urban education. The three categories of youth I have identified in this period remained socially distinct, although not necessarily geographically so. Their major points of reference were the social and cultural worlds of their parents. Only the urban middle class youths enjoyed, to any extent, the mobility enhanced through economic development, and only they realized the potential social mobility that education offered.

1980–1990s Global Impact on Local Youth

We now recognize the 1990s as the last years of the New Order (Anderson 2001). Among streetside students, political activity was curbed by the authoritarian state, and student interests diverted to consumer spending and religious activities. Shifting government attitudes to Islam provided a climate in which university mosque and Islamic prayer room activities were revitalized and intensified, and there was a corresponding focus on intimate prayer and study groups among Protestant students (Guinness 2009; Dhewayani 2005). There was increasing recognition of the polarization of wealth and opportunity through development, and some attempt by universities to cultivate a concern for the poor through student community development (KKN) programs. Generally, however, these reflected a paternalistic attitude among students and their supervisors to reform *kampung* and village populations, including their youth. One exception to this trend, Yayasan Pondok Rakyat, a youth NGO, bridged the cultural divide, setting itself up as an advocate for *kampung* lifeways, living in *kampung* homes, and publishing accounts of *kampung* culture in popular magazines (Guinness 2009).

Increasing numbers of shopping malls and entertainment venues provided a mix of Western-style contemporary dress and music fashions that emphasized individualism, pejoratively proclaimed as 'hedonism' in the local press. The character of *kampung* in the north of the city changed as they became known as dormitory suburbs and lost their poverty label. Samirono, for example, witnessed the conversion of homes and open spaces to student dormitories and the multiplication of laundry services, internet cafes, food stalls, street vendors, computer, printing and stationery services, and mobile phone outlets to service the youth needs (Naylor et al. 2011). Both streetside and *kampung* youth took up 'Western' fashion in both music and dress. In Ledok, grunge music became popular. *Remaja* from the *kampung* frequented shopping malls and adopted what they saw there. But there were distinct Indonesian versions of these trends. Siegel commented of Solo youth in the 1980s that in contrast to the traditional Javanese music of their parents the western-style music the *remaja* listened to 'seems to pass through them; it matters to them that it does so' (1986, 229). Siegel commented that their dress symbolized the energy and freedom and personal indulgence of their aspirations, yet raised feelings of ambivalence as they tried to simultaneously address their parents' norm of self-restraint. Such ambivalent feelings provided for Siegel the explanation for youth attacks on the perceived origin of this hedonism, the Chinese shops in Solo and the widespread riots that fueled these attacks (Siegel 1986, 247). In his account, streetside and *kampung* youth in Solo had begun to exhibit similar inclinations.

At the same time, the government increasingly sought to integrate local communities in the nation-state and undermine vestiges of local autonomy. The RK (*kampung*-wide neighbourhood), which most *kampung* residents identified as their home community, were abolished as administrative units, divided instead into *Rukun Warga* (RW), smaller groupings of about five RT. As a result many youth activities, such as the Independence Day sport and music celebrations, were lost. The state imposed itself by constructing *kampung* infrastructure, previously the domain of *kampung* males. The Municipality spent the 1990s constructing a flood wall along the Code River, including Ledok. This was welcomed by residents as a means to avoid the once-in-a-decade floods that devastated the increasingly crowded riverflat areas. However, in the construction process *kampung* labor, skills, and knowledge were marginalized. Outside contractors were employed to oversee construction, the army provided labor, and residents were largely left to provide refreshments for the workers. *Kampung* leaders pointed out that although they welcomed the construction it represented a lost opportunity: unemployed youth were not engaged in waged employment and skilled artisans in the *kampung* were not consulted. The wall radically altered the status of the river flat by formally demarcating it as residential. Residents were quick to occupy it and as a result recreational space was greatly diminished and youth lost their space to play football, table tennis, badminton, volleyball, and music. *Kampung* social organization lost the means and space to channel youth energies into activities that promoted community harmony (*rukun*). Sporting activities were confined to tiny housing lots awaiting development within the *kampung* alleyways, and even these were under threat. Just as the commercial appeals of the wider city were beginning to draw *kampung* youth away from their home territory, the loss of space within the *kampung* was also forcing them away. In *kampung* Jetisharjo, also on the Code River, residents competed to privatize open space by planting of green shrubs, with consequent loss of recreational space (Garner et al. 2009). On the city outskirts Campbell et al. (2009) reported that in one neighborhood with no open space youth activities were non-existent, whereas in an adjacent RT with open space there was a wide selection of sporting and social activities. Such was the impact on youth of this loss of recreational space.

With their *kampung* links diminished *kampung remaja* were increasingly sucked into the excitements of the larger city and global culture. More of them were able to attend junior and senior secondary schooling as their aspirations changed and their parents were willing to make large sacrifices for their children's education, even to tertiary level. White and Margiyatin (this volume) indicate that in rural Kulon Progo during the 1980s-90s four-fifths of youth entered senior secondary school, and as a consequence their childhood was prolonged and their contribution of labor to the household economy declined.

In the main this improved education did not better the youths' chances of gaining employment in the desired formal government sector, as huge numbers of educated youth competed for a small number of places. Those *kampung* youth with parents in the formal sector were the lucky ones, as their parents could use 'connections' to gain their children's entry, but most had to resort to poorly paid wage work in the city's commercial, construction, and industrial businesses or discover their own niche in the urban informal sector. Even many tertiary educated youth spent their days on city streets, busking or selling cakes, other foodstuffs, or greeting cards they or others had made in the *kampung*. Young men and women alike were caught between their aspirations raised through education and the limited opportunities they had in the city's formal economy. As a result there was considerable disenchantment with the New Order government which continued to trumpet the success of development but failed to deliver jobs, or empowerment, to *kampung remaja*.

The consumer revolution impacted both *kampung* and rural youth. Increasing numbers of youth—including high school students—were able to access credit packages to purchase motorcycles during the 1980s and 1990s. Every *remaja* aspired to purchase a motorcycle, and there were ramps constructed throughout the *kampung* to allow these new symbols of wealth and sophistication to be ridden to the house and parked outside. *Remaja* thus become much more mobile, riding to school, visiting their school friends scattered about the city, visiting the main shopping malls, and other recreational spots.

As university campuses multiplied on the outskirts of the city student boarders deserted the inner-city *kampung* and moved into custom-built private student dormitories situated on streetside where they could pursue a life-style unburdened by 'conservative' *kampung* expectations. City authorities and social observers, including the Governor of the Province Sultan Hamengku Bowono X, expressed concern about the growing moral laxity of the student boarder populations, and their indulgence in pre-marital sexual activity and drug consumption (Kedaulatan Rakyat 31/10/2000). They were a vanguard for global trends at extreme variance with the moral code of the Sultan's palace or that of the many local communities. *Seks bebas* ('free sex') became a characterization of the student population among many of the *kampung* and village populations who decried this abandonment of local moral codes. White (this volume) refers to Robison and Hadiz (2004) in characterizing these as 'morbid symptoms', 'the old is dying and the new cannot be born'. Student boarders experimented not only with freer sexual mores and drug use but the opposite extreme of 'fundamentalist' identity politics and religious exclusivism. It was a period marked by heightened moral concerns for the youth among the wider society.

For *kampung* youth in Ledok during the late 1980s and 1990s the issue that caused most concern was consumption of alcohol. Nearby *kampung* more closely integrated into the city's tourist and streetside youth scenes had brewed and sold their own alcohol from the 1970s (Sullivan 1980). In Ledok alcohol consumption only became an issue during this later period, and it was particularly evident among youth. Backpacker tourism had developed in *kampung* surrounding the nearby train station and several Ledok *remaja* became successful in befriending overseas backpackers and guiding them to accommodation, art galleries, tourist attractions, and food outlets. These tourists reciprocated by sharing alcoholic drinks. At the same time a new *kampung* economic activity developed, brewing alcohol using imported ginseng root. Alcohol could be brewed at home in plastic drums and then sold on to vendors on streetside who sold it in concoctions of egg, milk, and coffee.

Ledok *remaja* began to frequent these drinking spots and often became inebriated, and so drunken behavior in the *kampung* alleyways became a regular occurrence late at night, and even during the day. Some *remaja* became producers and vendors of the home brew, and those with less cash experimented with their own intoxicating mixes of sleeping pills, mosquito repellent, soft drinks and the like, that they could buy locally from *kampung warung* (grocery stores). Fights occurred among inebriated *kampung* youth. On two occasions youth in Ledok were fatally stabbed, and on other occasions youth were found unconscious from these toxic mixes and rushed to hospital—on one occasion too late to prevent a fatality.

Many drinkers acquired tattoos (seen by their elders as signs of youth deviance), and the river wall became the favored location for drinking parties, with a few night drinking stalls established by enterprising residents. Alcohol parties replaced earlier pastimes of sport, music, and study groups. Many *kampung* leaders, elders, and parents were at a loss at what to do about this delinquent behavior. The *remaja* showed them little respect and were disinclined to change their habits. Their behavior in such gatherings became an open challenge to the moral economy of the *kampung* with its emphasis on self-restraint (*pamrih*), cooperation (*gotong royong*), and harmony (*kerukunan*) (Guinness 1986)

This behavior reflected *remaja* feelings of being marginalized and excluded from opportunities to participate in the trumpeted successes of the New Order. Where *kampung* leaders were able to counter this disaffection and violent behavior among the youth it was by creating meaningful employment. One neighborhood in Ledok commissioned *remaja* to take over delivering their neighbors' household electricity and rates payments to the sub-district and Kelurahan office. A neighboring *kampung* sponsored youth to set up repair businesses. A major change in Ledok occurred in the mid-1990s, when a local casino employed young local men as security guards and young women as croupiers on the gambling tables. Other solutions were informal sector activities outside government control or planning, but these did little to relieve the disaffection youth felt.

This period thus offered youth an abundance of delights through the growth of the wider city commercial sector. Lack of space within the *kampung* forced youth to spend more of their time on the streets and spaces of the streetside where they sought a living and got acquainted with other cultural norms, such as those of the Western tourist. At the same time, the privileged middle class youth of the city were cultivating new life ways largely independent of parental control.

2000s—Global Horizons

The financial crisis of 1998 impacted heavily on urban and rural life. In the city tourism declined, construction faltered, government employment was curtailed, and shops cut back on their work force. The government and private business established relief packages in the years that followed; food and grocery packages were distributed and temporary employment programs instituted, but these efforts largely continued the state-centric modeling of earlier years. A World Bank support intervention led to the establishment of the Urban Poverty Program and the Kecamatan (Sub-district) Development Program in rural communities. Neighborhood leaders were charged with identifying acute and moderately poor households who received aid in the form of basic commodities, such as rice, sugar, and soap. For the next decade those identified as 'poor' gained relief from school and health expenses through a government-issued 'poor card'.

The government financed work programs in the *kampung*, especially for unemployed youth who were recruited on a daily basis to construct and repair infrastructure. The wages were welcome and the jobs provided some sense of pride, but *kampung* leaders were critical because they did not provide youth with any skills or training that would ease them into permanent work in the urban formal sector. On the other hand, schooling was criticized as largely responding to state aims of nation-building rather than local concerns with employment, and so was increasingly regarded as an imposition on cash-strapped households. Many parents could not afford school fees and as a consequence some *remaja* dropped out.

However, the fall of the New Order heralded the opening of an era when citizens again felt responsibility for their affairs. There was much talk in the *kampung* about ensuring those in official positions would be held accountable and corruption would be eliminated. In Yogyakarta villages new leaders were elected from among village traders, craftsmen, and farmers rather than from civil servants, military, police, or government appointees, and RT and RW communities focused on organizational efficiency, financial management, and improving the self-sufficiency and political participation of citizens (Hudayana 2009, 90–1). In urban Ledok the new leadership supported *remaja* to gain long-term income by providing funds for them to buy guitars and other musical instruments for busking on city streets. The drinking of alcohol declined. Our research in various communities, however, indicated that youth largely remained outside decision-making in the local communities of *kampung* and village. Ten years after the establishment of the Community Funding System as part of the Urban Poverty Program, youth remained unaware of the opportunities and resources this could offer them to establish business enterprises (Wilson et al. 2009).

During this decade education opportunities continued to improve. In rural Banjaroyo village, youth disappeared during term to attend high schools and universities in urban centers. Dewi et al. (2011) noted their absence was particularly acute in the Banjaroyo hamlet of Promasan, where a large Catholic school and church youth center had long promoted the importance of higher education. With the almost complete absence of high school and university youth parents began to be anxious that their children would not return to take over the family farms:

> In Promasan there are only two youths (17–35 years old) left in the hamlet of 230 people. The rest have moved to other villages once they have married or have moved to the city in search of a high school, university or a job. The youth are attracted to the urban areas not just for economic reasons but also to pursue a life that is more modern.
>
> They do not want to work as farmers like the majority of their parents because it requires an extensive amount of physical energy and a low economic return. The youth now 'look down on this sort of work' as it is manual labour.
>
> DEWI et al. 2011

White (this volume) refers to the expansion of secondary education in rural areas as contributing 'to a process of de-skilling rural youth, in which both farming skills are neglected and farming is downgraded as an occupation'. Many parents encouraged their children to seek education and employment outside the village. However, although most youth seemed to be moving to the cities this should not be taken for granted. In the Banjaroyo hamlet of Slanden, leaders promoted youth involvement in the packaging and marketing of cassava chips (*slondok*) as a way to retain the youth in the village despite their disinterest in agricultural labor (Tri et al. 2014) but this scheme gained little traction. Hamlet leaders criticized youth for their laziness, and yet when a fishpond project was begun with a grant from the sub-district government youth were not invited to take part, demonstrating the growing alienation of youth from village life.

In Banjaroyo village hamlet leaders actively promoted the performance of dance and music to inculcate a knowledge of traditional arts into the young generation. (Cooper et al. 2014; Foote-Short et al. 2014). They saw transmission of such knowledge as the introduction of youth into the spiritual world of the hamlet and a counter to city-ward migration. During our research, several highly successful performances of *ketoprak* (dance form) and other arts were held in Banjaroya, and hamlet leaders were envisaging their regular performance as tourist attractions. However, these activities did not appear to carry much hope of stemming youth disengagement from the home community.

In the city, RT and RW leaders in Samirono constructed an impressive meeting hall (*pendopo*) and established an annual street festival to encourage youth participation, and persuaded some of the students living in dormitories to perform ethnic dances and songs from their home regions. However despite these efforts, student participation in *kampung* affairs remained minimal and leaders despaired of the boarders' disregard for the norms of behavior, community values, and social activities that characterized accepted *kampung* culture (Byrnes et al. 2009; Naylor et al. 2011). From the youth viewpoint Naylor et al. (2011) report that student boarders complained that they were frequently not informed of *kampung* activities and their ignorance of local etiquette was construed as rejection. However, they responded positively when their dormitory owner/manager insisted on their engagement in *kampung* activities.

Our research in the *kampung* of Pandeyan, Suryowijayan, and Samirono indicated that community leaders were aware of the demise of youth interest in traditional arts and crafts (Elmir et al. 2009). Their efforts to establish cultural performance spaces and institute festivals to make use of them had little impact on this loss of interest among youth, who were drawn away from *kampung* performances towards the attractions of the wider city. McLennan et al. (2011) described the dilemma faced by Pandeyan leaders in this way:

> The older residents of Pandeyan suggested that youth disengagement from the traditional arts was due to globalization, preference for Western styles of music and culture, and the perception that Javanese traditional art was only an activity for older members of the community. The young people from Pandeyan that we talked to expressed a preference for 'modern' music, saying that *gamelan* and other traditional art was difficult to learn and they did not have time to do so.... Not only is learning the

> *gamelan* or traditional dance time-consuming, but it is also technically difficult. Furthermore, they said, changing lifestyles and a quickening of the pace of life in Java contributes to a potential lack of time of the youth in Pandeyan. …Indonesian pop and rock music is heavily influenced by Western styles, and American bands, such as Greenday, are well known among the younger generation. Luvas (2009) reports that many Indonesian pop bands remove any overt ethnic or cultural signifiers to 'align themselves with international music "movements" reflecting the globalized world in which they grew up (2009:249). It is this increasing desire for globalized Indonesian pop and rock music which stifles interest in traditional Indonesian art forms, such as *gamelan* or *wayang kulit*'.
> MACLENNAN et al. 2011

In this 'Reform' era religious activity has grown in the *kampung*, and to an extent has engaged the youth. Over the years a number of mosques and prayer houses have been built, usually with outside financial assistance. While, in the 1990s, religious study and prayer groups multiplied in the larger streetside mosques, by the 2000s this religious enthusiasm spread to *kampung* mosques and neighborhood prayer houses (*musolah*). Mosque leaders were encouraged to host students from Islamic colleges and universities, and it was these students from outside the *kampung* who proceeded to preach and teach a more fervent practice of prayer and study. Sermons were broadcast over loudspeakers from the mosque, drowning out any conversation in the immediate locality. Although not all youth were attracted to the new fervor displayed in the mosques, and mirrored somewhat in the churches, these activities indirectly challenged local cultural norms when these student outsiders recruited the youth to the priorities of global religious movements.

As the national economy recovered through the 2000s *kampung* and village youth alike migrated elsewhere for work, for example to Jakarta, Batam Island, and Singapore, where both women and men could find industrial and domestic employment. Some of them married work colleagues and settled in these industrial locations. There was increasing acceptance that successful engagement with the wider economy would mean the loss of youth from within *kampung* and village communities and economies. In the rural village of Banjaroyo, education of the population continued to improve, although access to high school and university was restricted to the better-off. In one hamlet, Rodgers et al. (2014) report a growing polarization of opportunities:

> As a consequence higher levels of education are, for many of the poor, simply not affordable. Pre-existing levels of wealth…enable many affluent

members of the hamlet to advance their education, and, in turn, the education of their children. Of those individuals who have a tertiary level of education, the majority enjoyed financial support from family members, often in the form of a loan....[C]hildren of more affluent families have continued their education with the help from their parents. Poverty thus leads to a situation in which the poor are unable to escape their disadvantaged situation.... A cycle of inherited disadvantage can thus be observed in education.

The importance of education cannot be underestimated when considering the ability of individuals to advance and improve current circumstances and future life chances (Cameron, 2000; Ferreria, 2001). Greater education levels lead to more employment opportunities, and the prospect of better-paid and higher status occupations (Rodgers et al. 2011). In Bumen *kampung* on the city outskirts, where *kampung* bakeries had established a successful brand of bread:

...increasing urbanization and globalization has encouraged young adults to aim for salary work or entrepreneurship in order to avoid the older generations' experience of instability and sometimes poverty in small-scale, ephemeral home industries or labour work. Certain members of 'the youth' that were interviewed indicated they thought the market for Kembang Waru bread was unsustainable, the working conditions were poor (bakers spend hours crouching before extremely hot ovens, and the mixing process is straining on the arms), and the equipment difficult and in some cases expensive to obtain.
AMELIA et al. 2011

In urban Ledok *kampung* children who succeeded in the city formal sector found housing in the rapidly expanding housing estates and came back only rarely. With their absence, leaders expressed a concern for the continuation of the *kampung* moral economy and informal sector trades. Similar concerns were raised, as we have seen, in the hamlets of Banjaroyo. Kathage et al. (2011) provide a counter to such pessimism, describing a young man who established a successful multi-media advertising firm in Bumen *kampung*. However, such success was rare.

The years since the fall of the New Order have witnessed increasing opportunities for youth in the wider cosmopolitan society of Yogyakarta, and further afield. Having only peripherally tasted this world during the 1990s, youth find themselves engaged more in this wider world than within the rural villages and *kampung* societies of their parents. Their networks are formed in the schools, universities, dormitories, home-stays, churches, and mosques where they spend much of their time and where the culture of their parents has been put on hold. If they return to the home community to raise a family they re-engage with that culture, but many are not returning and are seeking a cultural identity with wider cosmopolitan society. It is now the spaces of the shopping mall and fast food halls that design their activities in place of the wide open spaces of the *kampung* and village in earlier eras. In urban *kampung* such spaces have disappeared, in rural hamlets they no longer satisfy the aspirations of youth.

Conclusion

The years of the New Order and subsequent Reform periods extended the horizons of *kampung* and village populations alike, and their youth increasingly embraced the lifestyles and dreams of their streetside youth counterparts. These widening horizons brought youth into the high schools and universities of the urban centers, and opened their aspirations to the formal sector employment promoted by such education. Their recreational choices moved from activities centered on the locality to those driven by national and global media. Tourists from overseas further widened their vision, as did the religious reformists who encouraged them to question or reject the religious traditions of their home communities and 'return' to a global orthodoxy. At the same time that the wider horizons beckoned, local spaces were shrinking not just in the physical sense as in the *kampung* but in their offerings of local home knowledge, skills, and performances. For youth this was no longer enough. In 2014 youth from Ledok households were spending time not with fellow *kampung* youth but with friends from mosque, church, and school. Parents had even less oversight over their children's recreational activities.

Over this period of forty plus years, student, *kampung*, and village youth were increasingly drawn away from the lifeways of their home communities and absorbed into global social and cultural trends. In the 1970s, while middle-class students were expressing their freedom from parental norms, *kampung* and village *remaja* built self-sufficiency around employment and community services located in the home community. As youth worlds expanded in the 1980s and 1990s, through international and domestic tourism and commercial and educational expansion, *remaja* were drawn into an exciting world of consumerism that challenged their political idealism. However, they were disappointed and frustrated by the huge wealth differentials that they experienced there. Distinctions between middle-class students and *kampung* youth grew as development polarized wealth. The consumer revolution of the 1980s, the Islamic revolution of the 1980s and 1990s and the political revolution of the late 1990s and early 2000s were energized by largely middle-class youth and university students. *Kampung remaja* participated from a distance, adopting dress and music styles where they could afford them, participating in political rallies—particularly if they were paid to do so—and observing the increased religious activity in their neighborhood.

Yet there was for many youth a sense of failed hopes, giving rise to what Robison and Hadiz (2004) referred to as 'morbid symptoms'. The moral elite of Yogyakarta condemned the loose morality of the student population, while the parents of *kampung* youth struggled to mitigate the self-destructiveness through alcohol abuse of some youth. There was a sense of crisis among local leaders and elders who felt the moral economy of the local community was under dire threat from the consequences of these expanding horizons.

However, more recent years have brought to all youth a new sense of being part of the wider city. *Remaja* are looking beyond the *kampung* and the village for employment and marriage, and with their improved educational levels are looking more critically at the way of life that sustains the local community. It is now common for both village and *kampung* youth to have a university education and to seek parity with their more elite counterparts. Yet their parents remain in the informal sector and agricultural employment that their children reject. Many youth will not return to their parental community to marry and settle. It is clear that urban and rural *remaja* alike have responded, both in enthusiasm and frustration, as Yogyakarta and Indonesian society have absorbed new, global ideas and fashions, and grown in prosperity.

This offers great cause for optimism. The youth of the 21st century have embraced the educational and technological opportunities that development has offered. Yet that development's focus on the attractions of modernity, employment in government or capitalist enterprise, large streetside homes, "hedonistic" self-interested consumer styles, and national and global concerns hide the importance that the local space must continue to play in guaranteeing the welfare of Indonesia's people. *Kampung* continue to provide a hefty proportion of urban housing and informal services, villages continue to grow the nation's food. The future requires the youth of tomorrow to re-engage with local space and bring their new-found skills to reforming that local space for the comfort of their own and their parents' generations. It is a challenge once more to engage as *pemuda*, not just as *remaja*, in Indonesia's ongoing change.

References

Amelia, Katharina, Cynthia Johnson, and Lauren Harvey. 2011. "Small business and Community – The Bread and Butter of Development? The *Kembang Waru* Bread Making Industry in Kampung Buymen, Yogyakarta." In *Strengthening the Environmental Quality of Urban Kampung*, edited by P. Bawole and P. Guinness, 93–114. Yogyakarta: Duta Wacana University Press.

Anderson, Benedict. 1988. *Revolusi Pemoeda*. Jakarta: Pustaka Sinar Harapan.

Anderson, Benedict. 2001. *Violence and the State in Suharto's New Order*. Ithaca: Cornell University Southeast Asian Publications Program.

Tri, Ana, I. Damanik, A. Permana, R. Sigalingging, R. Susanto, L. Synnott, E. Willemse, and S. Yuwono. 2014. "Youth Empowerment through Economic Activities: Lessons Learnt from Dusun Slanden." In *Agricultural Empowerment and Tourism Potentials in Banjaroya Village Kulon Progo*, edited by P. Bawole and P. Guinness. Yogyakarta: Duta Wacana University.

Bawole, P. 2009. "An Introduction to Urban Kampong in the City of Yogyakarta-Indonesia." In *Experiencing the Dynamics of Kampong Life*, edited by Bawole, P., and P. Guinness, 7–25. Yogyakarta: Duta Wacana University Press.

Bawole, P., and P. Guinness, eds. 2009. *Experiencing the Dynamics of Kampong Life*. Yogyakarta: Duta Wacana University Press.

Bawole, P., and P. Guinness eds. 2011. *Strengthening the Environmental Quality of Urban Kampung*. Yogyakarta: Duta Wacana University Press.

Bawole, P., and P. Guinness, eds. 2014. Agricultural Empowerment and Tourism Potentials in Banjaroya Village Kulon Progo. Yogyakarta: Duta Wacana University.

Byrnes, E., V. Conliffe, L. Hogan, D. Melinda, T. Resirawan, R. Suryaningsih, and R. Anindita. 2009. "The Impact of Anak Kos (Boarding Students) in Samirono, Yogyakarta." In *Experiencing the Dynamics of Kampong Life*, edited by P. Bawole and P. Guinness, 183–91. Yogyakarta: Duta Wacana University Press.

Cameron, L. 2000. "Poverty and Inequality in Java: Examining the Impact of the Changing Age, Educational and Industrial Structure." *Journal of Development Economics* 62: 149–80.

Campbell, A., I. Wati, M. Motombrie, N. Sentoko, and N. Woods. 2009. "Room to Be Young: The Relationship Between Space, Youth, Activities and Community in Kampong Minggiran." In *Experiencing the Dynamics of Kampong Life*, edited by P. Bawole and P. Guinness, 154–63. Yogyakarta: Duta Wacana University Press.

Collier, William L. 1982. "*Accelerating Rural Development in Java: From Village Studies to a Macro Perspective of Rural Java. Occasional Paper no 6, Rural Dynamics Study of Agro- Economic Survey*. Bogor, Indonesia.

Cooper, C., M. Wright, W. Raharjo, A. Nindya, B. Yolanda, D. Gunawan, and O. Kharisman. 2014. "The Acquisition and Integration of Knowledge: Exploring Urban

Influence in the Creation of Knowledge Systems in Rural Java." In *Agricultural Empowerment and Tourism Potentials in Banjaroya Village Kulon Progo*, edited by P. Bawole and P. Guinness, 347–380. Yogyakarta: Duta Wacana University.

Dewi, L., V. Larkin, D. Mathews-Hunter, Z.V. Nicolaus, A. Pertiwi, E. Pingga, P. Sabudi, and E. Swesy. 2011. "The Effect and Impact of Youth Migration on a Rural Javanese Village. Focusing on the Decline of Village Structure and Agriculture." Australian National University 2011 Field School Reports. Australian National University: unpublished.

Dhewayani, Jeanny. 2005. "In Pursuit of the Spirit: Student Prayer Groups in Yogyakarta, Indonesia." PhD diss., Australian National University.

Elmir, R., Y. Uenishi, K. Asmoro, D. Pranasiwi, B. Silitonga, and D. Kurniawati. 2009. "Survival of the Fittest: Kampong Dolahan's Struggle to Maintain its Livelihood." In *Experiencing the Dynamics of Kampong Life*, edited by P. Bawole and P. Guinness, 105–10. Yogyakarta: Duta Wacana University Press.

Ferreria, F. 2001. "Education for the Masses: The Interactions Between Wealth, Educational and Political Inequality." *Economics of Transition* 9:533–52.

Foote-Short, L., M. Kristianingti, I. Minar, C. Mullavey, E. Pangarian, M. Purnama, and Y. Septian. 2014. "Spirits, Religion and Human Welfare in Plengan." In *Agriculture Empowerment and Tourism Potentials in Banjaroya Village Kulon Progo*, edited by P. Bawole and P. Guinness, 141–170. Yogyakarta: Duta Wacana University.

Garner, D., M. Roberts, Y. Probosusetyo, B. Buinei, K. Praptiwi, and E. Wulan. 2009. "Incorporating Greenery: The Social and Spatial Dimension of Green Space in Jetisharjo RW07, Yogyakarta." In *Experiencing the Dynamics of Kampong Life*, edited by P. Bawole and P. Guinness, 124–33. Yogyakarta: Duta Wacana University Press.

Geertz, H. 1961. *The Javanese Family: A Study of Kinship and Socialization*. New York: Free Press of Glencoe.

Guinness, Patrick. 1986. *Harmony and Hierarchy in a Javanese Kampung*. Singapore: Oxford University Press.

Guinness, Patrick. 1991. "Kampung and Streetside: Yogyakarta Under the New Order." *Prisma* 51: 86–98.

Guinness, Patrick. 2009. *Kampung, Islam and State in Urban Java*. Singapore: NUS Press.

Hudayana, B. 2009. "Revitalizing Neighbourhood Association." In *Experiencing the Dynamics of Kampong Life*, edited by P. Bawole and P. Guinness, 87–104. Yogyakarta: Duta Wacana University Press.

Kathage, Angus, A.A. Sulistio, and L.L. Tobing "Life after Silver: Small bBusiness Tradi in Kampung Dolahan, Yogyakarta." In *Stgrengthening the Environment Quality of Urbana Kampung*, edited by P. Bawole and P. Guinness, 45–62. Yogyakarta: Duta Wacana University Press.

Luvas, Brent. 2009. "Dislocating Sounds: The Deterritorialization of Indonesian Indie Pop." *Cultural Anthropology* 24: 246–79.

McLennan, Kate, Maria Sri Hartanti, Danica Browne, and Anggi Rudyanto. 2011. "Guitar or Gamelan? Traditional Javanese Art in Pandeyan, Yogyakarta." In *Strengthening the Environmental Quality of Urban Kampung*, edited by P. Bawole and P. Guinness, 127–40. Yogyakarta: Duta Wacana University Press.

Mondal, Ipshita, Suci Senanti, Nishadh Rego, and Erren Mehidyastuti. 2011. "'Be a Man': Waria Identity in Sidomulyo". In *Strengthening the Environmental Quality of Urban Kampung*, edited by P. Bawole and P. Guinness, 141–58. Yogyakarta: Duta Wacana University Press.

Naylor, Mary Anne, John Kennedy, and Maria Devita. 2011. "Outsiders as Kampung Guests: Student Boarders in Samirono, Yogyakarta." In *Strengthening the Environmental Quality of Urban Kampung*, edited by P. Bawole and P. Guinness, 31–44. Yogyakarta: Duta Wacana University Press.

Nilan, P. 2004. "The Risky Future of Youth Politics in Indonesia." *Review of Indonesian and Malaysian Affairs* 38:173–94.

Robison, R. and Vedi Hadiz, 2004. *Reorganising Power in Indonesia: The Politics of Oligarchy in an Age of Markets.* London: Routledge Curzon.

Rodgers, M., J-P Glavimans, K. Yohanes, M. Nataniel, W. Kartika, S. Septian, and F. Natalia. 2011. "The Relationship between Affluence and Access to Resources in Dlingseng Hamlet, Kulon Progo." In *Agriculture Empowerment and Tourism Potentials in Banjaroya Village Kulon Progo*, edited by P. Bawole and P. Guinness, 45–68. Yogyakarta: Duta Wacana University.

Siegel, James. 1986. *Solo in the New Order: Language and Hierarchy in an Indonesian City.* Princeton: Princeton University Press.

Soeprobo, T. 2002. *Indonesia Youth Employment.* Jakarta: Demographic Institute of Indonesia.

Sullivan, John. 1980. *Back Alley Neighbourhood: Kampung as Urban Community in Yogyakarta.* Melbourne: Monash University Centre of Southeast Asian Studies.

Sullivan, John. 1992. *Local Government and Community in Java: An Urban Case-study.* Singapore: Oxford University Press.

Wilson, S., T. Kennedy, A. Wardhani, S. Gulo, R. Wijayanti, and M. Sugesti. 2009. "The Role of the BKM in the Funding of Public Facilities: Ledhok Tukangan." In *Experiencing the Dynamics of Kampong Life*, edited by P. Bawole and P. Guinness, pp.134-44. Yogyakarta: Duta Wacana University Press.

Winarna. 2009. "Harmony in the Use of Public Space in Kampong Kauman Yogyakarta." In *Experiencing the Dynamics of Kampong Life*, edited by P. Bawole and P. Guinness, 234–42. Yogyakarta: Duta Wacana University Press.

CHAPTER 8

Local Modernities: Young Women Socializing Together

Pam Nilan

Introduction

This chapter reports on teenage girls socializing in Solo, Central Java in 2007. The locations are an internet café and a shopping mall. Although since then the internet has become widely available through cellular phones, it is gendered social interactions within these two spaces that remain of interest in 2014. The girls are part of the new youth generation in Indonesia that participates in a prolonged and somewhat fractured transition to adulthood (see Naafs 2012; White, this volume; Robinson, this volume). It is probable that most will not complete their education or marry until they are in their mid-twenties (see White, this volume; Nilan et al., this volume). The data on socializing below shows young Indonesian women using information and communication technology to enrich and diversify modes of mixed-sex social interaction in urban spaces some seven years ago. They were, as Barendregt argues, "making themselves modern" (2008) through the use of communication technology. At the same time, they were socializing successfully within the constraints of religious and traditional discourses about girls' moral behavior that still prevail today (see Parker, this volume). To achieve this socializing as a "safe" moral practice within the internet café and the shopping mall, the girls socialized in daylight hours surrounded by other people. They also relied on the dynamics of their friendship group to achieve both fun and propriety. I observed that while friends exercised moral surveillance over each other, the group itself seemed to facilitate confidence and playfulness for its members. Lyn Parker's chapter in this book offers a detailed discussion of girls' friendship groups in West Sumatra, finding them close and supportive.

Mixed-sex teen socializing is a source of a pervasive moral panic in Muslim-majority Indonesia (see Parker, this volume; Wright Webster, this volume). Regulatory discourses of behavior are different for Indonesian male and female youth. Boys are permitted far greater freedom in socializing than girls. For example, Parker and Nilan (2013, 107) point out high anxiety in West Sumatra about young women being involved in pre-marital intimate relations. The moral panic centers on the fear that girls will engage in "free" sex (Smith-Hefner

2005 and 2009; Robinson 2009; Parker 2008 and 2009; Rinaldo 2011; Setyawati 2008; Hatley 2008) and thereby not only commit a sin but also bring about "social disintegration" through their immoral transgressions (Parker and Nilan 2013, 206). Muslim discourse is adamant on this topic and provides a wealth of warnings on the dangers of mixed-sex socializing, for girls in particular. Yet girls are rightly concerned about making an appropriate choice of who to marry, and some socializing in mixed company is useful in this regard. For example, in West Kalimantan, Minza (2014, 209) found her young informants of both sexes considered that "involvement in romantic relationships serves the purpose of finding a future spouse and is not just for the sake of exploration". The term romantic relationship here does not necessarily connote intimacy (Minza 2014, 2). The prelude to establishing a romantic relationship is noticing and flirting, which requires some degree of informal mixed-sex socializing.

In Solo there is a strong local cultural tradition of informal socializing (*nongkrong*) (Crosby 2013) in Javanese villages (*desa*) and neighborhoods (*kampung*). Small children are encouraged to be sociable, playing with other children of both sexes, while unrelated men and women mix freely at work and in public places. This positive discourse of Javanese socializing seems to provide some legitimate framing for social practice when young women are in contact with male peers during their teens and early twenties, despite the moral panic. Notably, young people of both sexes socialize informally in groups, usually same-sex groups, in public spaces, maintaining both separation and contact at the same time.

I propose that for the individual girl, engaging in some measure of mixed-sex youth socializing constitutes a cautious yet necessary choice that helps maps a successful pathway to the future (see Threadgold and Nilan 2009), including a well-informed choice of future marriage partner. It has been noted elsewhere that as a result of expanded choice options in late modernity, contemporary youth have an increased perception of the risk of personal failure (Wall and Olofsson 2008); of making the wrong choices. They are thus encouraged to be entrepreneurial in carving out a viable future for themselves (Kelly 2006). The framing of the new entrepreneurial self as theorized in Western youth studies is far from incompatible with contemporary discourses of Indonesian Islam, as a number of writers have pointed out (Ansori 2009; Rudnyckyj 2009; Barendregt 2008; Gerke 2000). I argue that for young Indonesian women, the sense of themselves as "modern" and "autonomous" may translate as confidence in safely handling mixed-sex situations without straying beyond the bounds of morally legitimate behavior. Perceptions of risk and the hazards of socializing are countered by the context of the female peer group, and by judicious control over time and space.

Methodology

In 2007 I conducted four months of fieldwork in the city of Solo in Central Java. The research was part of the four-year project, *Ambivalent Adolescents in Indonesia*. This chapter uses data from interviews and ethnographic observations collected by the author in the meeting places favored by young people in Solo. Of the range of sites visited, two types seemed particularly popular with secondary school pupils and university students in 2007: the internet café and the shopping mall. I translated data in Indonesian with assistance from Indonesian colleagues.

Young Muslim Women in Indonesia

The Islamic resurgence in Indonesia began in the 1960s (Brenner 1996; Howell 2001). Female university students donned the headscarf (Dhume 2008), and from that time on there began vigorous attacks on "new freedoms of sexual expression in media and society, explicitly targeting women" (Hatley 2008, 2). Muslim discourse about public piety in the behavior of women has certainly not disappeared in the new century. Muslim clothing prescription now operates to ontologically separate "good" women from women who might be morally suspect (Parker 2008). So girls wearing the headscarf and modest dress can operate independently in public while preserving their respectability. Yet, in reality, Indonesian Muslim women enjoy more social and personal freedom than women in Middle Eastern countries (Bennett 2005). Over the past two decades, the extension of post-compulsory education (Naafs 2012; Naafs and White 2012), the expansion of the urban middle class, delay in the age of marriage, and growth in consumerism, has driven some marked transformations in the transition of young women to adulthood. A girl's life was once mapped out for her according to the traditional female role in the family, but this no longer applies to most young women. Middle-class girls can expect to complete secondary education, engage in paid work, set up their own bank accounts, choose who they will marry (Jones 2010), practice contraception, and move around independently. The double-income nuclear family with a mortgage is now the urban norm, and this favors the autonomy of women (Nilan 2008).

It has been argued that taken together, "the Islamic revival and transnational feminism" determine the contemporary gender order for Indonesian Muslim women (Rinaldo 2011, 48). Both discourses invite autonomous reflection on submission and emancipation and both claim to advance female rights and equality. Notably, most feminist discourse in Indonesia at present is coming from Muslim women's groups that advance claims for female equity and public representation. Platforms of representation are "built around the reform of Islam along gender sensitive terms, incorporating women's rights, such as those contained in the UN Women's Charter, CEDAW and the Beijing Platform of Action" (Wieringa 2009, 17). At the same time, trends of modern Muslim "cool" have flourished among the young. Trendy Muslim modernity "relates Islam to a modern world of lifestyle, talk shows and fashion", while still "challenging the notion that the only way to be modern is through a Western model" (Barendregt 2008, 161). Heryanto (2011) identifies a rich synthesis of piety and pleasure in the popular culture of Indonesian Islam. It would seem that creativity and self-expression are generated through this kind of modern Muslim representation, which also favors the autonomous practices of young women growing up.

Young Indonesian Muslim women access such discourses and representations through the media, including the internet, as they are techno-savvy. The virtual spaces made available through mobile phone and internet technology enable communication, information, sharing, and networking. Yet worldwide most ICT communication among youth is not in unknown territory, but extends existing relationships and interests (Geser 2007). The technology may be global but the practices and interpretations are local. In Indonesia the dangers of ICT technologies for young women form part of the moral panic about female sexual behavior described above. However, in reality, while discourses of sexualized femininity circulate in the global mass media primarily in English, arguments for Muslim female modesty, segregation, and containment of sexuality are everywhere on Indonesian websites. So, in the online world as elsewhere, the lives of Muslim girls in Indonesia revolve around balancing piety, propriety, and fun (Parker 2009) in the choices they make.

Situated Practice: Space and Time

The phenomenon of young Solonese socializing in the internet café and the mall is examined below as "situated practice" in space and time, taking up the argument that "all social activity is conjoined in three moments of difference: temporally, structurally and spatially" (Giddens 1995, 30). In other words, there are spatial and temporal dimensions in social practice, opening up the "possibilities of immanent and emergent orders" (Crang 2001, 206), including a moral order of legitimacy in young women's socializing. Modern places like internet cafés and shopping malls in Indonesia offer unique opportunities for safe socializing within daylight hours. I term these public-private places, differing markedly from their semantic predecessors: the *warung* and the traditional open-air market. As commercial spaces they are enclosed, clean, air-conditioned, and privately owned, yet patrons pay no fee to enter the premises. In the internet café there is someone near the door taking payment for access to terminals, but others can enter with them to look on while they browse. In theory anyone can enter an Indonesian shopping mall, but in fact there are security guards at every entrance to keep out undesirables (Van Leeuwen 2011). Malls operate for commercial gain, but profit depends on the freely-moving customer who must be left alone to make choices, to browse and discuss. Accordingly, young visitors to these privately-owned but "open" premises treat them like public places for free entertainment (Van Leeuwen 2011; Valentine 1996). An Indonesian teenager can visit a shopping mall with friends to display individual and group style, browse goods on offer, check out the opposite sex, and even listen to live music, for no cost. In the case of the internet café, in 2007 teenagers with no cash to spend could accompany friends to an internet café, read emails, surf the net, play games and so on, through a collectively-used terminal paid for by a friend.

There is, however, a complex moral dimension, with good and bad on offer. Both safe and dangerous material was available online at the internet café. Similarly, the biggest shopping mall in Solo in 2007 offered everything from a dingy male-dominated billiard room on the top floor to a gleaming fluorescent-lit family supermarket in the basement. In either case a young woman is presented with a moral or an immoral choice in situated practice. Digging deeper, the moral dimension is not pre-determined by the setting itself for the spaces described here, but by the time of day and the company the girl keeps (see Hey 1997). Solvang (2002, 88) makes the point that in Indonesian cities, women who are on the street after 21.00 are likely to be "seen as bad women (*perempuan nakal*)". The same point is made by Nilan and Utari (2008) about the work of Indonesian women journalists and media workers. In other words, day-time activities of girls are morally safer by definition, especially if they are with friends.

Accordingly, directly after prayers on Friday afternoon it might be assumed that a young woman strolling in Solo Grand Mall will stick with her girlfriends and go home early. Later on Saturday night another young woman—especially if she enters the mall alone—will probably be suspected of meeting a boyfriend. She might head upstairs with him to the dimly-lit mezzanine eating area to kiss and cuddle, then join him in the male space of the billiard hall where few women venture. As the two hypothetical examples suggest, there is not a single paradigm for the social practice of a young woman walking in the

Solo shopping mall. The moral dimension is constituted not only in what she does and where, but when (time) and with whom she does it (female friendship group). Western ethnographies of teenage girls' friendship groups have revealed "a female policing of girls" sexual reputations among "nice" girls (Chambers, Tincknell, and Van Loon 2004, 408; Hey 1997). In this respect the Indonesian girl's friendship group seems similar. For example, Parker (2009) describes Minangkabau Muslim girls closely monitoring each other's pious practices and moral reputations.

Late modern cultural conditions and discourses impact on Indonesian young women just as they do on youth elsewhere in the world (Förnas 1995). Indonesia has an enthusiastic consumer culture, and access to lifestyle products and entertainment options (Ziv 2002). Yet there has been an avid resacralization of Indonesian cultural life through revitalized Islam (Rudnyckyj 2009; Nilan 2008). These distinctive, late modern conditions drive the enhanced salience of the friendship group for young women. Matters of status and morality are no longer just family concerns, but collective peer concerns, reiterated and defended in the places and times where same-sex peer socializing occurs.

Indonesian Youth Culture and Technology

For the necessary adjustments and negotiations in mixed-sex socializing, the significance of modern communication technologies for young Indonesian women cannot be under-estimated, especially the ubiquitous practice of texting (see Goggin 2006). Elsewhere, Lim (2004, 274) proposes that the "convivial medium" of the internet facilitates informal communication in Indonesia. Slama's (2010) study in Central Java found online social networking to be the favored means of expressing ideas and emotions, with young women frequent users. Anonymity in the virtual space allowed them to do this. The need for privacy—away from the eyes of family—online meant that many young women in 2007 used internet cafés. For teenage schoolgirls, visiting the local internet café on the way home from school with a group of friends appeared to provide a safe opportunity for online engagement.

The Internet Café

In 2007 an internet café near a number of Solo high schools offered teenage girls access to email communication, blogs, celebrity gossip, music downloads, and so on after lessons had finished for the day. Still wearing school uniforms, they would chat, laugh, call out to other users, and send text messages back and forth as they browsed in small groups. The internet café at this time of day was somewhere to socialize and be entertained. It was rare for a single user to access a terminal. It seemed that not only was it cost effective for two, three or even four girls to share a terminal, but the activity itself was a peer social practice. Boys of the same age also crowded around terminals, but in separate groups.

I made the following field-notes in an air-conditioned internet café in Jalan Slamet Riyadi, the main street.

15.00: Junior high students aged 13–15 from nearby Muslim, Christian, and public schools arrive quickly in single sex groups of three to six, buying snacks and drinks as they crowd in. Latecomers chatter outside, waiting for terminals to become free. As the teenagers fill the room, noise and body heat level instantly increases in the small space packed with terminals in tiny booths. Stools are whisked out of booths and tussled over as groups of three, four, and even five try to crowd into the same terminal. Although a few are looking for information relevant to their schoolwork, most take turns to check their emails or Friendster[1] postings. They play online games as friends look on and wait their turn. While waiting, they send and receive texts on their mobile phones, showing their friends and talking and laughing as they do so. Should an email or posting of interest be found by someone, there is a shout and his or her friends all gather to look at the email and comment, even contributing ideas for a possible reply. The sound of many music clips on YouTube being played at once raises the noise level even further. I ask one girl (Juli, 17) what she is doing. She laughs with her friends, "*saya akui, saya senang main game di internet*" [I admit it, I love to play games on the internet]. A girl at another booth (Ayu, 16) explains, "*kalau ada video yang bagus di YouTube, saya akan mencari informasi tentang isi video itu*" [If there is a good video on YouTube, I look for information about the video content].[2] Both of these are straightforward answers suggesting light-hearted leisure practice.

A group of four boys has accessed a celebrity website for the sexy girl band *Dewi Dewi*. Their hit song *Dokter Cinta* (Doctor Love) is the mobile phone ring tone for one of the boys and he tests it out as they examine photos on the site together, whispering and laughing. Along the other wall, a group of schoolgirls

---

[1] Friendster was the most popular social networking site in Solo in 2007. Facebook is the most popular at the time of writing in 2014.

[2] My simple questions were answered in Indonesian, but between themselves the girls spoke very rapid colloquial Javanese mixed with slang—*Bahasa Gaul*—which was extremely difficult to understand.

wearing headscarves is searching for websites and music clips of Ustad Jefri Al Buchori—the singing Muslim preacher. Soon the strains of his hit song *Yaa Rasulullah* (Hail our Prophet) can be heard. A boy nearby joins in the catchy chorus. As time goes on it becomes clear that certain boys and girls in the space are emailing and texting each other. There are covert looks, loud whispers, and syncopated giggling within the single sex groups as interactions flow back and forth in physical space, phone space, and online space. Over the next hour the space progressively clears and the high school students head home.

17.00: An older age group of young people trickles in. They are mostly workers, and some students from senior high school and university. There is far less talking and laughing and the booths are not so crowded. There is less use of mobile phones. Some are preparing job applications and curriculum vitae. Unlike the earlier cohort, there are several couples and mixed groups, including four young activists who are organizing a local protest action in support of the Global Day of Action for Climate Change on 12 December 2007. Frida (21) tells me that she and her friends, who are university students, want to organize a small demonstration in Solo as part of protests on climate change taking place across the world. Although two of them have access to the internet at home, they do not want their parents to know what they are planning, so they meet at the internet café to log onto the global campaign site and devise strategies. Over the next two hours this second cohort of young people progressively leaves the space.

21.00: By now the crowd is predominantly male; an older age group. The room is quiet except for the low murmur of voices and muffled video combat sounds. Customers use hired ear-phones to listen to music downloads. A few couples who appear to be in their late twenties are holding hands and necking as they browse. Some terminals are occupied by older men, usually alone. There are groups of two or three young men who smoke surreptitiously and talk non-stop in whispers, often playing extreme combat games. There is no doubt that some of the sites being accessed at this time of night are pornographic. Online gambling is also taking place.

Discussion

I observed the same physical space of the internet café transform into a very different moral space between the daylight hour of 15.00 and 21.00. It changed from a gender-inclusive teenage space for socializing and entertainment after school (a morally safe place) to a male-dominated adult space for sex, violence, and gambling (a morally dangerous place). These observations in Solo match findings on internet cafés in the nearby city of Yogyakarta, where Furuholt and Kristiansen (2007) studied 270 users. Three-quarters were students and a third were female. While younger students engaged in chatting, games, and so on, use altered with age. Older users had different purposes and accessed the internet at a different time of day. Similarly, Rathore and Alhabshi (2005) studied Malaysian cyber-cafés. Students—one third female—went to the cyber-café mainly during the day. The researchers found multi-purpose use: emailing, chatting, and surfing, playing online games, and listening to music. It was common to spend 1–2 hours every weekday afternoon online with friends, pursuing low-cost entertainment. A reported social benefit was the strengthening of social bonds.

Young Indonesian women care a great deal about what their friends think. For example, devout Muslim girls remind each other to pray and give each other instructions relevant to immoral thoughts and actions (Parker and Nilan 2013). Approximately two-thirds of the girls observed in the Solo internet café were wearing the Muslim headscarf. While remaining physically separate from the boys in the same room, they were socializing with them to some extent, as highlighted. In short, they were having a lot of fun in a non-supervised mixed-sex setting. The fun included mild flirting, made possible by technologically-mediated interaction and the reassuring ambience of the friendship group.

Despite the moral panic about mixed-sex socializing, even quite devout girls in Solo have asked me, in relation to mild flirting "how am I ever to meet a *pacar* (boyfriend) otherwise?" In other words, they intend on scoping out a possible marriage partner. Smith-Hefner (2005, 451) points out that most Indonesian young women today "begin to have boyfriends sometime in mid-secondary school". Early relationships are typically described as *belum serius* "not (yet) serious". Muslim popular culture often addresses the vexed issue of mixed-sex socializing and boyfriends for girls. For example, Ustad Jefri Al Buchoria—"handsome ex-film star and reformed drug addict"—dispenses advice through his sermons and songs on how to be both "socially active and pious" (Fealy 2008, 25–26).

A key activity for the teenagers in the internet café seemed to be accessing celebrity sites and downloading songs. The headscarf-wearing girls along the wall did this too, but in their choice of celebrity: Ustad Jefri Al Buchori—the trendy singing Muslim preacher—they accessed the repertoire of Muslim "cool" discussed previously. Rathore and Alhabshi (2005) express a moral concern that an internet café allows young Malaysian teens access to pornography and gambling. Among the girls there was no sign of such usage in the internet café in Solo. This was collective situated practice, with all the accountability and surveillance that accompanies girls' peer interaction. In my view they were not there to test the limits or risk their reputation; they were there to socialize, have fun, and be entertained after school, while remaining within the limits of propriety.

The Mall

Just as the social and leisure practices of Indonesian young people are facilitated by new communication technologies, so they are also shaped by the expansion of choice in consumer goods (see Chua 2003; Van Leeuwen 2011). Nowhere is this more evident than the Indonesian shopping mall. Socializing with friends in the mall is now an extremely common practice for young Indonesians (Pratiwo 2003; Atmodwirjo 2008). Although shopping does take place, window-shopping while strolling in groups is the most popular activity (Rustan 2010). Malls make the world "safe for life-as-strolling" (Bauman 1996, 27). They offer "a different spatiality more exciting than that offered by the impoverished landscapes of the neighborhood" Toon (2000, 144). Cool, exotically tiled, and ostentatious, malls resemble the houses of rich people (Van Leeuwen 2011), yet are open to any respectably-dressed person. Mall culture has expanded significantly in the cities of Indonesia (Ansori 2009), incorporating ever more facilities, diversions, displays, services, and entertainment to attract the consuming middle-class. They showcase not only "modern commodities", but the successful self (Ansori 2009, 92).

Urban teenagers in the West like spending time in malls (Matthews et al. 2000; Vanderbeck and Johnson 2000). The same preference was found for 11 to 16 year olds in Jakarta. For junior high school students the three top identified mall activities were talking, eating, and hanging out. Ansori (2009) found that young people visited the mall for *mejeng* (hanging out).

> In the mall, they hang around different areas and go from one place to another. They do not really need to buy something because that is not their main purpose. Instead, the cultural meaning of visiting the mall is to articulate and demonstrate their identity and share that interest .
> ANSORI 2009, 93

In other words, the point is to be with your friends as a definitive group for interesting encounters.

Although malls only appeared in Solo after 2004, by 2007, and still today, they are key places for youth to browse and socialize, to see and be seen. In 2007, young people of both sexes—aged approximately from 14 to 22—would congregate in Solo Grand Mall after Friday afternoon prayers and early on

Saturday evening. Small single-sex groups strolled about between the five levels. Time was spent sitting at tables chatting and texting. Lines of youth leaned on the railings that line each mezzanine floor, looking into the deep void to watch other groups of young people on lower and upper floors. In short, their main social practice in the mall was what the Javanese call *nongkrong* (hanging out). During the fasting month of Ramadan in 2007, mall socializing intensified due to the traditional Javanese custom of *ngabuburit*—spending time with friends and family during late afternoon while waiting to break the daily fast. Abaza (2001, 110) observed a similar phenomenon for Muslim youth in Malaysian city malls during Ramadan. The following field-notes give a sense of young women engaging in *ngabuburit* at Solo Grand Mall.

Waiting to Break the Fast During Ramadan

Friday 5 October 2007—late afternoon Solo Grand Mall is buzzing. A live rock band clad in Muslim clothing is blasting out *nasyid* favorites in the forecourt and a young man dressed as *Ali Baba* in a turban and extravagantly curled shoes greets people at the front entrance. The upstairs food court is full of young people but they are not eating or drinking. I meet state senior secondary school student Hidayat, who is 16. She is wearing the common combination of tight jeans, long-sleeved top and brightly-coloured headscarf. Hidayat says that during the fasting month she often waits with her friends in the mall to *buka puasa bersama* (break the fast together). Hidayat's seventeen-year old cousin Iqbal from Klaten agrees: waiting with friends makes the daily fasting seem shorter. Hidayat and her younger brother nod their assent.

Nearby, Raras is a state senior secondary school student wearing a purple headscarf. She states *"yang penting nggak ngurangi pahala puasa"* (the important thing is not to diminish the religious merit of fasting). She says she usually reads the Koran in the mosque for *ngabuburit,* except on Saturdays, when she goes to the mall with her friends to wait. Hearing this, a boy at a nearby table calls out *"ngabuburit paling asyik kumpul bareng teman-teman ngobrol, bahas pelajaran, dan nyanyi sambil main gitar"* (*ngabuburit* is the most fun when you're together with your friends, talking, discussing school, and singing along with the guitar). Raras' friend Fitria laughs, maintaining that *"wah seru abis tuh! Kalau ngumpul ma teman-teman biasnya lupa waktu, puasa sehari singkat"* (totally far out cool! When I'm together with my friends I forget the time, so the fast is shorter). She says *"suka mendengarkan musik rock sambil nunggu beduk"* (I like to listen to rock music while waiting for the drumbeat that signals the end of fasting).

LOCAL MODERNITIES: YOUNG WOMEN SOCIALIZING TOGETHER

Two girls—Addin and Hesti—are at another table. Addin attends Al Islam secondary school. She states, "*kumpul bareng teman-teman ke tempat-tempat seperti mal sambil menunggu berbuka bersama mempunyai kenikmatan tersendiri. Selain itu juga memupuk rasa kekompakan dan kebersamaan*" (going about with my friends to places like the mall while waiting to break the fast really diverts my attention. It also enriches feelings of togetherness and unity between us). Hesti is from Karanganyar, and is the aunt of Addin (a great joke). She says that, in the outer suburb of Karanganyar, "*suka jalan-jalan sambil nongkrong di taman bersama teman-teman sambil menunggu berbuka*" (I love hanging out with my friends in the park while waiting to break the fast) because "*mempunyai makna tersendiri*" (it has a special meaning).

The above excerpt from fieldnotes gives a sense of how the social event of *ngabuburit* unfolded from the point of view of the girls themselves. Yet it was also informative not just to talk to young women in the mall during *ngabuburit* but to observe their group interactions with groups of boys as they all waited to break the fast. The girls described in the excerpt from fieldnotes below are different from those quoted above.

A group of five girls aged about 16, three wearing the Muslim headscarf, two bare-headed, pass a group of six slightly-older well-groomed boys, wearing t-shirts, runners and low-slung jeans. The young men are examining a range of computers on display. The girls obviously know who the boys are because they laugh and talk more loudly as they move slowly past to take the escalator. The boys pretend to ignore them. The girls stop on the next floor, crowding around a kiosk selling handbags, which offers a view of the ground floor. After about five minutes the group of boys take the escalator. As soon as they move, the girls move too, taking the escalators up two floors to a shop which sells jewelry and knick-knacks. Four of the girls examine the necklaces and bracelets on display while the fifth girl is busy sending text messages, some of which she shows to her friends. After circulating around once or twice on the floors below, the group of boys comes up to the same floor. Two of them are texting as they ride the escalators, although it is not clear who they were texting. They walk slowly past the girls, who are still in the jewelry shop, and go into a trendy young men's clothing shop—a *distro*[3]— on the other side of the mezzanine. Text messages are still being sent and showed around.

After about ten minutes, the group of boys takes the escalator up to the food court and games arcade where they wander slowly around. The girls, now giggling incessantly, leave the jewelry shop and take the escalator to the same

---

3 *Distros* are "independent youth-oriented retail outlets which have spread throughout urban Indonesia" (Martin-Iverson 2012, 384).

floor, where they inspect plush children's toys in a stall opposite the entrance to the games arcade. Two of the boys then engage in a game not far from the entrance where they compete in shooting at targets, noisily cheered on by their friends. The girls drop the pretense of looking at fluffy rabbits and kittens to observe the game from a distance. As it comes to a close, one girl looks at her watch and shepherds her friends over to a table in the food court. They sit down to text or play with their mobile phones, continuing to chat. Some ten or fifteen minutes later, the group of boys saunters over and occupies a table not far away. By that time it is only a few minutes to the end of the daily fast. All the tables outside the food outlets on the top floor of the mall are by then fully occupied by young people.[4] The level of chatter and laughter becomes louder and louder until an amplified drumbeat signals the end of the fast.

The girls break their fast with bottles of iced tea; the boys Coca-Cola. As soon as they are all drinking and eating, some of the boys start to call out to the girls, who seem to ignore them while texting furiously. The boys, like the girls, are showing text messages to each other and laughing. This interaction, with the boys paying attention to the girls who pretend to ignore them, goes on for about thirty minutes more and then the same girl who had led the way to the table gathers her friends and proceeds downstairs. All five girls are picked up outside the mall in a van, probably driven by a family member of the girl who led them down. The boys walk around for fifteen minutes more, then take the exit themselves, driving off in twos on motorbikes.

By 20.00 family groups and teens have left the mall and many shops have closed their doors. The young people still present, predominantly male and older, are sitting in fast food outlets such as Pizza Hut and McDonalds on the first floor, or are congregated outside the cinemas and the billiard hall on the top level which remains open until 23.00, with late access only through the adjacent car-park. The air is thick with smoke up there and the lights are dim.

Discussion

The fieldwork accounts above demonstrate how the same physical space of the shopping mall transforms between late afternoon/early evening and night. It changes from a gender-inclusive, morally safe space for girls to socialize into a male-dominated, adult space for billiards and M-rated films as the night wears on. This mirrors the day-to-night transformation of the internet café,

---

4 Families were sitting mainly in fast food outlets on the lower floors, including Kentucky Fried Chicken, Pizza Hut, McDonalds, Dunkin' Donuts and Wendy's.

demonstrating the significance of how "situated practice" may signal different moral directions in young women's socializing, not in terms of place in the broad sense, but of time.

There is no doubt that the live band was a significant attraction for young people to spend their time waiting to break the fast in the mall, providing a deeper sense of bonding as an appreciative audience with the same tastes. Furthermore, the extent of mobile phone texting in the observed mall interaction was intensive, enhancing and supplementing what was going on in the physical space, similar to the internet café. While there is no definite way of judging the content of texts sent and received, observed reactions indicate that at least some, if not the majority, of text messages were exchanged flirtatiously. This is the gap between public conduct and private interaction that mobile phone technology engages (Garcia-Montes et al. 2006).

It is instructive to consider the legitimacy of the situated practice of young female teens visiting the mall to wait out the daily Ramadan fast with friends according to Javanese tradition. In Indonesia, "public celebrations of Islam" help to build a sense of community and promote social ties; "they are also fun. That is important, especially for young people" (Woodward, Rohmaniyah, Amin, and Coleman 2010). The Ramadan-themed rock band in the mall forecourt links the social experience to youth culture, while the local quasi-religious practice of *ngabuburit* engages Javanese cultural legitimacy. The young women maintain public piety by staying in separate single sex groups, even though in the virtual dimension of technological communication, they are having fun with groups of boys. Thus they negotiated normative moral judgements that might be made of them through judicious timing, through sticking together; and by avoiding both "bad" space and "bad" timing.

Modern and Pious—Peer Surveillance

Over 18 years of studying youth in Indonesia, I have found that a point of contrast to youth in the West is the intense sociability of young people, which follows from the cultures and traditions in which they grow up. For example, there seem to be few if any loners in a junior high school class. It is no surprise that young Indonesians are highly sociable, given that most cultures in the archipelago would appear to value the quality of *ramai* (lively) social settings in which there is a lot of enjoyable action and interaction. Young Indonesians from all kinds of backgrounds often tell me that they would rather do something with others because it is more lively (*lebih ramai*). In Solo, both male and female high school and university students seem to be intensely bonded to their friends. They want to fit in with them and do things together in a harmonious and enjoyable way, whether browsing in the internet café or waiting out *ngabuburit* in the mall.

In the female friendship group, peer surveillance works in two ways. On the one hand, individuals are under close scrutiny and one of their friends is sure to notice if they step out of line, so this is a normalizing tendency. On the other hand, being in a female friendship group permits some behaviors which would not be possible for the individual alone, inviting confidence, creativity, and self-expression. In the two examples from fieldwork above, one of these group-mediated social practices is mild flirtation. It seems that a girl in a group is much better placed in terms of moral legitimacy to do this than a girl on her own. In a group, mild flirtation can seem light-hearted and playful (*main-main*). Furthermore, if a girl shows a text message to a boy to her friends before sending it, one of them can say, "no, don't say that, be careful", and so can make the right choice of words. In this way, the moral surveillance of the group is in itself reassuring, confidence-building, and even permissive, within the tacit agreement on morally legitimate behavior. For example, in Solo in 2007 there was much discussion among young Muslim women of my acquaintance as to what was *zina* (immoral, sinful) and what was not during informal interaction with male peers. For example, debate went on over the moral significance of *tp-tp*—an abbreviation of *tebar-pesona, tebar-pesona*. It literally means "to spread enchantment" and refers to attracting someone in an indirect way, such as making, then ceasing, eye contact as you walk past a boy, while subtly walking in a way to make sure he notices you. Notably, the girls all agreed that it might be *zina* if a girl did it while she was alone, implying that in a group of her friends *tp-tp* was not to be taken so seriously. Logically, the same distinction also applies to whether the boy in question is alone or not. Once *tp-tp* was explained to me, I realized how common it was when same sex groups were strolling adjacent to each other around the mall. However, if the same girl walked anywhere alone, she would keep her head lowered and walk in a quick, slouched fashion so as not to attract attention.

Female–male interaction in the internet café also demonstrated collective friendship group surveillance, with at least two friends looking over any girl's shoulder who might tell someone if she did something morally suspect. The junior high school girls notably kept to a conservative set of entertainment and networking sites. Their piety was maintained in conservative bodily comportment, signaled by their modest school uniforms and headscarves. They kept separate from the boys and deliberately sought out Muslim popular culture sites. Yet they too seemed to be engaging in mild flirting. In both the internet café and the mall, girls were judged to be achieving a balance of fun and propriety through constantly evaluating and adjusting their behavior within the presumption of mutual surveillance.

Conclusion

The data and discussion above indicate how young Indonesian women are engaging autonomy and modernity in technologically-mediated age peer practices. The examples of the internet café and the shopping mall illustrate how mixed-sex socializing in the context of a moral panic is "situated practice" (Giddens 1995) in space and time. The space element refers to the internet café and mall as modern public/private spaces that facilitate interaction and communication in pleasant surroundings. The time element refers to the fact that in daylight hours they are packed with people, constituting safe places where groups of girls can participate in youth popular culture and limited social interaction with groups of boys. At night they change into male-dominated places where the same girls would never go. Giddens (1995) also spoke of a third element, structure, as a differentiating element of modern situated social practice. The primary structural element of the situated practice of mixed-sex socializing is the solid nature of the girls' friendship group that exercises surveillance over the balance of fun and propriety, yet facilitates support, confidence, and playfulness at the same time.

The example above of young women socializing in the mall while waiting to break the daily Ramadan fast makes explicit the complementary entwining of Islamic, traditional—cultural, and late modern discourses of choice and self-regulation. The earlier example of junior high school girls socializing, communicating, and being entertained in the internet café after school does the same and also foregrounds how the constitution of Indonesian modernity inheres in access to communication technology. Finally, the data imply the intensely collective nature of girls' single-sex friendship groups in Indonesia, ones which provide a kind of guarantee, through surveillance and accountability, of the moral legitimacy of situated social practice in contemporary private/public spaces such as those described above.

References

Abaza, Mona. 2001. "Shopping Malls, Consumer Culture and the Reshaping of Public Space in Egypt." *Theory, Culture & Society* 18:97–122.

Ansori, Mohammad Hasan. 2009. "Consumerism and the Emergence of a New Middle Class in Globalizing Indonesia." *Explorations: A Graduate Journal of Southeast Asian Studies* 9:87–97.

Atmodiwirjo, Paramita. 2008. "The Use of Urban Public Places in Jakarta for Adolescents' Hanging Out." *Journal of Asian Architecture and Engineering* 7:339–46.

Barendregt, Bart. 2008. "Sex, Cannibals, and the Language of Cool: Indonesian Tales of the Phone and Modernity." *The Information Society* 24:160–70.

Bauman, Zygmunt. 1996. "From Pilgrim to Tourist—Or a Short History of Identity." In *Questions of Cultural Identity*, edited by Stuart Hall and Paul du Gay, 18–36. London: Sage.

Bennett, Linda. 2005. *Women, Islam and Modernity: Reproductive Sexual Health in Indonesia*. London: Routledge.

Brenner, Suzanne. 1996. "Reconstructing Self and Society: Javanese Muslim Women and 'The Veil.'" *American Ethnologist* 23:673–97.

Chambers, Deborah, Estella Tincknell and Joost Van Loon. 2004. "Peer Regulation of Teenage Sexual Identities." *Gender and Education* 16:397–415.

Chua, Beng-Huat. 2003. *Life is Not Complete Without Shopping*. Singapore: Singapore University Press.

Crang, Mike. 2001. "Rhythms of the City: Temporalized Space and Motion." In *Timespace: Geographies of Temporality*, edited by John May and Nigel Thrift, 187–207. London: Routledge.

Crosby, Alexandra. 2013. "Festivals in Java: Localising Cultural Activism and Environmental Politics, 2005–2010." PhD diss., University of Technology, Sydney, Australia.

Dhume, Sadanand. 2008. *My friend the Fanatic: Travels with an Indonesian Islamist*. Melbourne: The Text Publishing Company.

Fealy, Greg. 2008. "Consuming Islam: Commodified Religion and Aspirational Pietism in Contemporary Indonesia." In *Expressing Islam: Religious Life and Politics in Indonesia*, edited by Greg Fealy and Sally White, 15–39. Singapore: Institute of Southeast Asian Studies.

Fornäs, Johann. 1995. "Youth, Culture and Modernity." In *Youth Culture in Late Modernity*, edited by Johann Fornäs and Göran Bolin, 1–11. London: Sage.

Furuholt, Bjørn and Stein Kristiansen. 2007. "Internet Cafés in Asia and Africa—Venues for Education and Learning." *The Journal of Communication Informatics* 3. Accessed 30 December 2009: http://ci-journal.net/index.php/ciej/article/viewPDFInterstitial/314/352

Garcia-Montes, José M., Domingo Caballero-Muñoz, and Marino Pérez-Álvarez. 2006. "Changes in the Self Resulting From the Use of Mobile Phones." *Media, Culture & Society* 28:67–82.

Gerke, Solvay. 2000. "Global Lifestyles Under Local Conditions: The New Indonesian Middle Class." In *Consumption in Asia*, edited by Beng Huat Chua, 135–58. London and New York: Routledge.

Geser, Hans. 2007. "Patterns of Multi-channel Communication Among Older Teens." Soziologisches Institut der Universität Zürich. Accessed December 31, 2009: http://socio.ch/mobile/t_geser4.pdf

Giddens, Anthony. 1995. *A Contemporary Critique of Historical Materialism,* 2nd edition. Stanford: Stanford University Press.

Goggin, Gerard. 2006. *Cell phone Culture.* London and New York: Routledge.

Hatley, Barbara. 2008. "Hearing Women's Voices, Contesting Women's Bodies in Post-New Order Indonesia." *Intersections: Gender and Sexuality in Asia and the Pacific* 16. Accessed May 20, 2011: http://intersections.anu.edu.au/issue16/hatley.htm

Heryanto, Ariel. 2011. "Upgraded Piety and Pleasure: The New Middle Class and Islam in Indonesian Popular Culture." In *Islam and Popular Culture in Indonesia and Malaysia,* edited by Andrew Weintraub, 60–82. London and New York: Routledge.

Hey, Virginia. 1997. *The Company She Keeps: An Ethnography of Girls' Friendship.* Buckingham: Open University Press.

Howell, Julia. 2001. "Sufism and the Indonesian Islamic Revival." *Journal of Asian Studies* 60:701–29.

Jones, Gavin. 2010. "Changing Marriage Patterns in Asia." *Asia Research Institute Working Paper 131.* Singapore: National University of Singapore. Accessed March 2, 2011 http://www.ari.nus.edu.sg/docs/wps/wps10_131.pdf.

Kelly, Peter. 2006. "The Entrepreneurial Self and 'Youth at-Risk': Exploring the Horizons of Identity in the Twenty-first Century." *Journal of Youth Studies* 9:17–32.

Lim, Merlyna. 2004. "The Internet, Social Networks and Reform in Indonesia." In *MediaContesting Power: Alternative Media in a Networked* World, edited by Nick Couldry and James Curran, 273–88. Lanham, MD: Rowman and Littlefield Publishers.

Martin-Iverson, Sean. 2012. "Autonomous Youth? Independence and Precariousness in the Indonesian Underground Music Scene." *The Asia Pacific Journal of Anthropology* 13:382–97.

Matthews, Hugh, Melanie Limb, and Barry Percy-Smith. 2000. "Changing Worlds: the Microgeographies of Young Teenagers." *Tijdschrift voor Economische en Sociale Geografie* 89:193–202.

Minza, Wenty Marina. 2014. *Growing Up and Being Young in an Indonesian Provincial Town.* Amsterdam: University of Amsterdam Press.

Naafs, Suzanne. 2012. *Youth, Work and Lifestyles in an Indonesian Industrial Town.* Rotterdam: Institute of Social Studies, Netherlands.

Naafs, Suzanne, and Ben White. 2012. "Intermediate Generations: Reflections on Indonesian Youth Studies." *The Asia Pacific Journal of Anthropology* 13:3–20.

Nilan, Pam. 2008. "Youth Transitions to Urban, Middle-class Marriage in Indonesia: Faith, Family and Finances." *Journal of Youth Studies* 11:65–82.

Nilan, Pam and Prahastiwi Utari. 2008. "Meanings of Work for Female Media and Communication Workers." In *Women and Work in Indonesia,* edited by Michele Ford and Lyn Parker, 136–54. London: Routledge.

Parker, Lyn. 2008. "To Cover the Aurat: Veiling, Sexual Morality and Agency Among the Muslim Minangkabau, Indonesia." *Intersections: Gender and Sexuality in Asia and the Pacific* 6. Accessed May 20, 2011: http://intersections.anu.edu.au/issue16/parker.htm

Parker, Lyn. 2009. "Religion, Class and Schooled Sexuality Among Minangkabau Teenage Girls." *Bijdragen tot de Taal-, Land-en Volkenkinde* 165:62–94.

Parker, Lyn, and Pam Nilan. 2013. *Adolescents in Contemporary Indonesia.* London and New York: Routledge.

Pratiwo. 2003. "Markets and Malls in Jakarta." *IIAS Newsletter* 31:12.

Rathore, Animesh Singh, and Sharifah Mariam Alhabshi. 2005. "A Case of Urban Cyber Cafés in Malaysia." *Information Technology in Developing Countries* 15. Accessed December 30, 2009 http://www.iimahd.ernet.in/egov/ifip/apr2005/article3.htm

Rinaldo, R. 2011. "Gender and Moral Visions in Indonesia." *Asia Pacific Perspectives* 10:44–60.

Robinson, Kathryn. 2009. *Gender, Islam and democracy in Indonesia.* London and New York: Routledge.

Rudnyckyj, Daromir. 2009. "Spiritual Economies: Islam and Neoliberalism in Contemporary Indonesia." *Cultural Anthropology* 24:104–41.

Rustan, Mario. 2010. "In Defense of Shopping Malls." *The Jakarta Post.* Accessed July 8, 2010: http://www.thejakartapost.com/news/2010/08/07/in-defense-shopping-malls.html

Setyawati, Lugina. 2008. "Adat, Islam and Womanhood in the Reconstruction of Riau Malay Identity." In *Indonesian Islam in a New Era: How Women Negotiate Their Muslim Identities,* edited by Susan Blackburn, Bianca Smith, and Siti Syamsiyatun, 69–93. Melbourne: Monash University Press.

Slama, Martin. 2010. "The Agency of the Heart: Internet Chatting as Youth Culture in Indonesia." *Social Anthropology* 18:316–30.

Smith-Hefner, Nancy. 2005. "The new Muslim Romance: Changing Patterns of Courtship and Marriage among Educated Javanese Youth." *Journal of Southeast Asian Studies* 36:441–59.

Smith-Hefner, Nancy. 2009. "'Hypersexed' Youth and the New Muslim Sexology in Java, Indonesia." *Review of Indonesian and Malaysian Affairs* 43:209–44.

Solvang, Ingvild. 2002. "'Vagrants cannot have success': Street Youth as Cultural Agents in Yogyakarta, Java." PhD diss., University of Oslo.

Threadgold, Steven, and Pam Nilan. 2009. "How do Young Australians View the Future? Habitus and Reflexivity." *Current Sociology* 57:47–68.

Toon, Ian. 2000. "Finding a Place in the Street: CCTV Surveillance and Young People's Use of Urban Public Space." In *City Visions,* edited by David Bell and Azzadine Haddour, 141–61. Harlow: Pearson Education.

Valentine, Gill. 1996. "Children Should Be Seen and Not Heard: The Production and Transgression of Adults' Public Space." *Urban Geography* 17:205–20.

Van Leeuwen, Lizzy. 2011. *Lost in Mall: An Ethnography of Middle-class Jakarta in the 1990s.* Leiden: KITLV Press.

Vanderbeck, Robert M., and James H. Johnson. 2000. "'That's the Only Place Where You Can Hang Out': Urban Young People and the Space of the Mall." *Urban Geography* 21:5–25.

Wall, Erika, and Anna Olofsson. 2008. "Young People Making Sense of Risk: How Meanings of Risk are Materialized Within the Social Context of Everyday Life." *Young* 16:431–48.

Wieringa, Saskia. 2009. "Women Resisting Creeping Islamic Fundamentalism in Indonesia." *Asian Journal of Women's Studies* 15:30–56.

Woodward, Mark, Inayah Rohmaniyah, Ali Amin and Diana Coleman. 2010. "Muslim Education, Celebrating Islam and Having Fun as Counter-radicalization Strategies in Indonesia." *Perspectives on Terrorism* 4. Accessed July 19, 2013 from http://terrorismanalysts.com/pt/index.php/pot/article/view/114/html

Ziv, Daniel. 2002. *Jakarta Inside Out.* Jakarta: Equinox Publishing.

PART 5

Performing Masculinity, Claiming the Street

Introduction to Part 5

Indonesia's transition to democracy was marked by outbreaks of communal and inter-religious violence, much of it perpetrated by young men who took control of the streets. The papers in this section take two very different groups who have territorialized space in order to express their youth/masculine identities: middle-class students in Jogjakarta who are attracted to the millenarian promise of the radical Islamic group Hizbut Tahrir (HT), and young lower-class men in post-conflict Ambon. Both papers describe the way these groups of young men carve out social spaces for action in the street through the deployment of symbols. In the case of Ambon, described by Spyer, young men paint giant hijacked billboards with religious-themed images that tower over the street and mark a domain of Christianity. The HT activists deploy symbols of Arab-inspired dress, flags, and banners to mark out the space of protest that they occupy in an effort to destabilize the secular state.

While one style of action has been reactive (the Christ billboards) and the other future oriented (towards the millenarian dream of the *khalifat*), both authors write of the broken dreams and difficulties confronting these young people, who are experiencing prolonged periods of youth in modern Indonesia but without receiving the transition to modern adulthood that development rhetoric promised. Hasan argues that the Islamic symbols deployed by the radical Islamic youth are an alternative symbolic identification from the global symbols of consumer culture that are offered to the young. Similarly, the young men in Ambon "occupy" the space of billboards, hitherto used for advertising the promise of consumer culture, to visually mark their space.

Spyer's photo essay can be read as a response to White's claim (in this volume) that young people's voices deserve to be heard. Here we do not have voices that have been solicited through research, but rather voices that have demanded to be heard, albeit through a visual medium.

CHAPTER 9

Streetwise Masculinity and Other Urban Performances of Postwar Ambon: A Photo-Essay

Patricia Spyer

Surprisingly perhaps, a good place to start thinking about some of the more momentous changes that have begun to refigure Indonesia in the wake of President Suharto's step down in May 1998 is from the lifeworld of the streets.[1] Indonesia's history has conventionally been written more grandly in terms of the center's influence and reach, seen as remarkably successful in holding the sprawling archipelago in check, modulating and delimiting the ambitions and concerns of its huge citizenry, and imposing a state-endorsed unity on the country's celebrated diversity. If one striking feature of the post-Suharto era has been the widespread perception of a "loosening at the center" (Kusno 2010), another is the spectacle and pronounced publicity of a panoply of new political, religious, and artistic forms and performative styles which claim the nation's streets as their recurrent stage. Central to this stage are the country's young men and women who marched in the capital Jakarta and other Indonesian cities in 1998 and 1999, bravely stood off the army at often considerable risk to their own lives, occupied the parliament, and celebrated exuberantly under *Reformasi*'s hopeful banner when the downfall of

---

[1] This photo-essay is a spin-off of an Australian-Netherlands Research Collaboration (ANRC) workshop "Growing Up in Indonesia: Experience and Diversity in Youth Transitions", held at The Australian National University in Canberra in September 2009. I would especially like to thank Kathryn Robinson, Pujo Semedi, and Ben White for sharing their insights on youth and, more generally, their suggestions and input on this essay. The essay forms part of research for a larger book project for which I have received support from the Netherlands Organization for Scientific Research (NWO), the Netherlands Royal Academy, and Leiden University's Institute of Cultural Anthropology. I would like to thank all of these institutions for their generous support of my research. Rafael Sánchez's suggestions on an early version of this essay were helpful and I thank him for this. I owe an immense debt to the painters with whom I worked in Ambon and to the motorbike-taxi drivers who support them, also to the many journalists, religious leaders, NGO activists, and ordinary Ambonese who have shared with me their views on the city during the conflict and thereafter and, specifically, commented on the rise of a new religious iconography indebted to the divisions of the war.

the regime actually came to pass after some thirty-two years of hard-handed, authoritarian rule.[2]

This photo-essay is part of a larger project in which I explore the relations between aesthetic-epistemological change and religious and social transformation in the immediate post-Suharto era. Here my aim is more modest—to sketch some of the ways in which a bottom-up visual history might be more attuned to the affective intensities that animate the lifeworld of the street and, as such, offer an intimate take on some of the forces redefining Indonesia today (Pinney 2004, 203). Rising in the midst of religiously inflected violence between Christians and Muslims in Indonesia's Moluccan Islands, the images I discuss here lend themselves especially well to this kind of history. Animated by hostility towards the enemy other, self-love and identification on the part of the young men who produce them, as well as all the anxieties, fears, and desperation brought on by war, these pictures bestow visual shape upon and draw their power from the economy of violence understood in Bataille's general sense of economy as a circulation of energies (Bataille 1988–91; Bahrani 2008, 13). At the same time, if much of war's art reproduced in this essay may be seen as the more manifest dimension of quieter, slow-moving shifts that describe the gradual emergence of a different Indonesia in post-Suharto times so, too, are the energies and affect associated with violence not only dramatic but also, for the most part—although alas, not exclusively—relatively short-lived.

Photographs of and by these young men, often posed in front of the street pictures, "come closest to a direct expression of youth style" (Steedly 2013, 128), and therein to their highly performative, embodied practice, offering another avenue through which to tap the energies and "affective intensities" of the street. Taken together these young men and others, such as the members of the militant Islamist group FPI, known for their spectacular actions and attire (Hassan, this volume), and the huge street pictures that arose in the Moluccan provincial capital of Ambon are all part of a post-*Reformasi* public space that is highly contested and crowded with "a visibility contest" (Paramaditha 2014). In the following pages, I argue that the murals, hijacked billboards, immense Jesus faces and so on, articulate a demand to be seen and, in so doing, give expression to and inflect—in a visual and specifically Christian register— some of the "views and visions" of this particular, youthful part of the city's population (White, this volume). If Indonesia's streets today form privileged arenas for the staging of the myriad "heroic messages" of the country's young men and women (Hasan, this volume), then this is also one site that demonstrates most powerfully the capacity of young people as "creators and renewers

---

2 On the figure of the activist and the iconography of the street see Doreen Lee 2011.

of culture par excellence" (White, this volume). By the same token, neither the oft celebrated "voices" of young people or the visions they articulate through various means in the avenues, alleyways, and public spaces of Indonesia's urban environments are ever unmediated. Apart from the specific media of youth slang, graffiti, paint, physical location, or the sheer materiality of city walls, ultimately, no matter how "youth-centered" we may be, it is also "the ethnographer who in the end assumes an executive, editorial [or for that matter, too, curatorial] position, assigning value and precedence to certain things over others" (Clifford 1988, 51).

Captions of an Unstable Cityscape

The billboards and murals of Jesus Christ depicted here sprung up and proliferated across Ambon City during the conflict—carried out in religion's name—that engulfed the Indonesian provincial capital and the neighboring Moluccan islands in rampant violence from 1999 until 2002, with occasional outbreaks thereafter, most recently in 2012. During the war and in its immediate aftermath, popular Christian painters plastered the city's main thoroughfares and Christian neighborhood gateways with gigantic portraits of Jesus and scenes from his life, Christian symbols, martyrdom, and resurrection. Towering over passers-by in public space, these artifacts perform in several capacities: as visible emblems of Christian territory, as a way of making God manifest, as a pedagogical mode of intervention in everyday Christian behavior, as a material counter to the public visibility of Islam in Muslim majority Indonesia (close to 90 per cent of the total population), as a way of branding Ambonese Christian communal identity, and, one suspects, as a kind of huge amulet meant to ward off the Muslim Other. As I have argued elsewhere, the post-war explosion of Christ pictures is a manifestation of deep uncertainty and crisis (Spyer 2008). Captions of an unstable cityscape,[3] the paintings emerge out of and partake of this uncertainty. As "symptoms and transitional solutions" to crisis, they constitute an effort to secure the solace of home and community and, crucially, too, God's partisan presence in the face of what many Christians understood as their own imminent annihilation (de Certeau 1996, 2). The work of young, largely formally untrained artists and their motorbike-taxi driver supporters, Ambon's new Christ pictures emerged quite literally out of the city's sidewalks and on the ruins of the recent war. [Figures 9.1–9.4]

---

3 This phrase originates with David M. Henkin, cited in Nancy Munn, "Places in Motion: Spacetime and Memory in Antebellum New York" (unpublished manuscript), 29.

FIGURE 9.1–4 *Christian billboards and murals in and around Ambon City, 2003–11*

This Face Wants YOU

This is what the Christian murals say to the pedestrians, motorcycles, cars, and minibuses that pass them by. It is also what they say to the young, often un(der)employed men who in many Christian neighborhoods hang out on raised platforms facing the mega-pictures—passing their time, smoking cigarettes, gossiping, and reviewing passers-by (especially young women) while awaiting motorbike-taxi customers. Grouped into neighborhood-based associations, often with their own names and emblems, these young men are those who sponsor the pictures, supplying the painters with paint, cigarettes, and snacks while they work, assisting them, offering occasional upkeep when the murals are done, and decorating these sites festively on the eve of important Christian holidays. In the mid-2000s, some of the older members of such groups were those who in war's wake were among Ambon's most adrift; their past clouded and often violent, their present precarious, and their future up for grabs. Others were more settled—young men for whom motorbike-taxi driving was both a source of income and a privileged component of masculine style, students aiming to support their studies, or the odd civil servant moonlighting to supplement his salary (cf. Amin 2012).

Due to their predominantly young age and their gender, these men tend to inhabit a place at authority's edge—their creative activities are not sanctioned by the local churches who regard them with a certain ambivalence, praising the public Jesus pictures while often voicing doubts about the religious commitment of the men who make them or cynicism regarding the markedly "unreligious" behavior that they assume takes place in the images' immediate surroundings. Indeed, it is these young men who the painter John has in mind when he describes his murals as pictorial *khotbah* or sermons, and he claims some success—sitting across from Christ's face, these men are less inclined to drink or fool around with women, or so John says.[4] As elsewhere, such men are the recurrent object of suspicion and surveillance and, where possible, mobilized to political ends in decentralized Indonesia's ongoing campaigns and elections (Amin 2012). Although older women from the neighborhood may pause briefly with their parcels from the market in the motorbike-taxi stand before climbing the hills where the majority of Ambon's Christian neighborhoods are found, these locations are decidedly male.

Beyond their explicit wartime and postwar visual identification with Christianity, these men and the neighborhood stands form part of a wider masculine youth culture that draws inspiration, emblems, and sources of style from a common repertoire that is seen across Indonesia. While the specific designation of these locations as motorbike-taxi stands dates from the war, when the bikes flourished as substitutes for public minibuses and cars due to their safer and more malleable mobility, such sites, generally, enjoy a longer history in the archipelago, one that dates to Dutch colonial times, if not earlier, in the form of neighborhood "guardhouses" where young men would customarily hang out (Kusno 2006).

The young men I spent time with in Ambon during the summers of 2005 and 2006, and briefly revisited in 2011, and those I spoke with in April 2006 in North Moluccan Ternate and in 2008 both there and in neighboring Tidore (where the populations are predominantly Muslim) embellish their stands with designs drawn from the CDs and DVDs of loud musical groups like the Sex Pistols, Guns and Roses, Limp Bizkit, and Linkin Park. Faces like those of Che Guevara or the Indonesian *Reformasi* cult singer Iwan Fals, along with slogans like "Punk" and "Rebel", also move indiscriminately across Indonesia's many

---

4   Recorded interview, Ambon, 27 June 2005.

religions and regions and settle into the rich stratigraphy of these sites' (Kadir 2008, 126).[5] Besides such consumer-based sources, a study of these sites' stratigraphy would reveal other groups markers as well, especially those of political parties and soccer teams. Beyond the display of consumer culture and myriad emblems, the Christian billboards—whether free standing or adjacent to murals painted with Christian scenes—often emerge on the same kind of location, along the city's main thoroughfares or at crossroads facing onto major streets, as commercial advertisements—if, indeed, they have not been painted over these. This, for instance, is said to be the case of the alleged first Christ portrait in the city overlaying, as it does, a former *Sempurna* cigarette advertisement. [Figures 9.5–9.8]

FIGURE 9.5 *Motorbike taxi-stand, Ambon City*

FIGURE 9.6 *Motorbike taxi-stand with Megawati Soekarnoputri, Ambon City, 2003*

FIGURE 9.7 *The fading reputation of a former president, Ambon City, 2005*

FIGURE 9.8 *Motorbike emblem and the 'orange' and lion of the Dutch national soccer team, Ambon City*

5   On the history of Che Guevara's image and its vast circulation, see Casey 2009.

With only a few exceptions, the new monumental Christian images rely on the global Christian print capitalism that has long been available in Ambon. Images are culled from Christian calendars previously seen only in homes or stores, or from posters sold during and after the war at *pasar kaget*, "spontaneous (sidewalk) markets" that were literally "shocked" into existence when the city's main markets burned to the ground during the first days of the war. Other design sources include T-shirts, old Dutch- or newer English-language Christmas cards, or even the Israeli flag, since early on in the conflict both sides hijacked the terms of enmity associated with the highly mediated Middle Eastern "hot spot". They did so, I propose elsewhere, to lend importance to the violence in their own city which many Christians and Muslims alike felt had been abandoned by Jakarta and the international community. Along the same lines, designating the main boundary between the warring parties as Ambon's own "Gaza Strip" would have served to further underscore this conflict's alleged equally intractable nature (Spyer 2006). [Figures 9.9–9.10]

While the majority of Ambon's street painters reproduce the works of such renowned artists of popular Christianity as Warner Salman and Heinrich Hoffman faithfully, several spoke of how they used the pictures drawn from Christian print media as a model but supplemented these with their own "imagination".[6] To mention a few examples, this homegrown painterly practice yielded images of Christ overlooking Ambon Bay rather than Jerusalem, hovering Oz-like over the destruction of one of Ambon's landmark churches, gazing mournfully on a globe turned to the Moluccan Islands, and, by way of exception to the predominance of a European Christ, a "native Jesus" overseeing Christian refugees evacuating Seram Island to where the conflict spread from Ambon. [Figures 9.11–9.12]

Figures of Territory and Landscape

Much like gang emblems, the pictures erected at the gateways of Christian neighborhoods and strategic sites in the city throw up strict boundary markers in an already radically divided urban situation. Like some monstrous checkerboard, this city turned rapidly into a patchwork of Christian "red" versus Muslim "white" areas, issuing in a highly segregated everyday with "red market, white market, red and white speedboat quays, red and white pedicabs (*becak*), red and white minibuses, red and white banks, and so forth" (Margawati and

---

6 For a discussion of the popular religiosity and Christian visual culture of which the works of Warner Sallman and Heinrich Hoffman are a part, see Morgan 1998 and Morgan 2005.

FIGURE 9.9   *A spontaneous sidewalk market Ambon City, 2003*

FIGURE 9.10   *Motorbike taxi-stand with text from a Dutch Christmas card, Ambon City, 2011*

FIGURE 9.11
Jesus overlooks Ambon Island on a dismantled billboard, Ambon 2006

FIGURE 9.12   *A 'native Jesus' looks down on refugees fleeing on Seram Island. Soahuku, 2005*

Aryanto 2000, 124). Command and communication posts (*posko*), commonly set up on the same locations that today accommodate the motorbike-taxi stands, were places where prayers were spoken and trumpets sounded before battle, the neighborhood watch was based, and multiple other social and strategic needs were met as, indeed, they continue to be today. Looming over this terrain, Jesus' gigantic, glossy face with its adjacent murals simultaneously "gates" the community and brands it as decidedly Christian. In doing so, these pictures posit a direct relationship between the core symbols of the Ambonese Christian community and physical territory at the same time that they facilitate an identification between the martyred male Jesus and the young men who gather around his image and, in turn, through them, a connection to the suffering of the wider community for which these men and their neighborhood location stand. This is, not incidentally, an identification fully enabled by the teachings of Protestant Christianity.

Born out of conflict and an intimate part of the scene of war, the Christ at large in Ambon's postwar streets is also an emblem of violence where the difference between self-love and directed aggression is hard to discern. Invoked frequently by Christians lamenting their plight during the war, many claimed that "Christ was our only weapon" as they went on to describe the flimsy bows and arrows, makeshift rifles, home-brewed poisons, and occasional black magic (*ilmu*) through which they aimed to protect themselves. A picture of Jesus of the Sacred Heart—a clear expression, incidentally, of the remarkable wartime rapprochement between Ambon's Protestants and Catholics, as the former visually appropriated key symbols of the latter—looked to some like an exploding bomb encased in barbwire (Figure 9.13). Seen in this light, it vividly intimates how easily Christ and violence came to collaborate during the war. Beyond these Christian associations, bullet holes with bloody skin bent back to frame motorbike association emblems or pistols in the place of heads on torsos have long been popular.

If Ambon's Christ images may be said to poetically, if unequivocally, publicize the question of territory in a city rent by violence, the wartime practice of graffiti served to advertise territorial conquests by inscribing the respective losses and gains of the enemies directly onto urban space. On either side competing sound bites sprayed on city walls claimed territory for the self, while defacing the opponent's insults of Jesus or the Prophet Muhammad traded places with references to Muslim Power and Muslim Pigs, stars of David, the names Israel and Mossad, or *allahu akbar* in Arabic writing. All of these markings violently scratched onto the face of the city can be said to bear (with)in them highly charged figures of territory (cf. Jain 2007, 112): they stake claims to homes, public buildings, beaches, and stores, and to strategic loci in and around

FIGURE 9.13   *Entrance to a Christian neighborhood. Ambon, 2005*

the city. They desecrate the ground only recently relinquished by the foe, register the vicious back-and-forth of enmity and contestation, cordon and enclave the community.

Besides territory in the sense of a physical space fought over and (re)mapped through urban warfare, landscape as an imaginary terrain of Christian habitation also receives due attention in the billboards and murals. While Jesus' portrait consistently graces the city's new street pictures, the backdrops to his face vary widely in terms of the scenes into which the Christian God is inserted and which he Christianizes by virtue of his presence. With the telling exception of those instances when the portrait is "cut-out" along the lines of a photo-ID recalling Indonesia's Citizen's Identity Card and producing an authorized landscape in its own right (by Christ rather than the State), the backdrops display a myriad of otherworldly and this-worldly landscapes of possible future Christian habitation (Spyer 2013). (Figures 9.14–9.15) These include familiar topoi like Gethsemane and Jerusalem, Christ portrayed *in situ* in Ambon, and a tiny minority of brown, burly Moluccan Christs (ibid).

FIGURE 9.14   *Jesus portrait. Ambon, 2003*

FIGURE 9.15   *Jesus portrait. Ambon, 2005*

In several different registers, these public, strategically placed pictures themselves depict and perform the larger drama of deterritorialization and social displacement suffered by Ambon's traditionally privileged Protestant Christians. From the early 1990s onwards Ambon's Christians saw themselves overtaken by Indonesia's "greening", or Islamicization, set in motion during Suharto's last decade. This drama of dispossession was further enhanced during the violence by the sense that the community and the very terrain it inhabited were vitally at risk—existentially, socially, physically, and in terms of its futurity. Taken together, the figures of territory and landscape built into and arising at these defensive neighborhood locations fed on and were energized by the symbolically charged, dense sociality that converges on the borders demarcating the city's Christian neighborhoods from the city and country around them.

At these potent sites highly territorial versions of community became articulated at the same time as the very idea of community in relation to territoriality became the site of creative exploration and experimentation. Nowhere more so than through the young men who themselves were already intimately identified with these places, as with the movement between places and therefore, too, with what lies beyond them. What is more, the urge to "territorialize" and claim a space within complex social relations may even be a tendency of youth more generally within as well as beyond situations of war (Hasan, this volume). An image offered by a motorbike-taxi driver to convey the impact of the spectacle his motorbike-taxi group was preparing for the upcoming Christmas holiday speaks volumes to the general mobility characteristic of urban experience (Urry 2007) to the role of youth as "a source of alternative, yet-to-be imagined futures" (Comaroff and Comaroff 2000), but also to the "yearning to be somewhere else in a different time and space", even perhaps "journeying abroad away from the national territory"—something that, incidentally, is found more diffusely within the architectural designs of post-1998 New Towns of the capital Jakarta (Kusno 2004, 2390). Not only were the murals and adjacent Christ billboard due for an annual "refreshening", but cords of multi-colored lanterns were to be strung along the road leading up into the hills "like the lights on the side of an airport runway".[7] It is worth noting that the presence of multiple such groups of young men in the city and the creative dynamism of the street art is, in part, also due to the considerable competition among them, at no time more so than in the weeks preceding Christmas and, to a lesser extent, Easter.

---

7   Notes from an interview, Ambon, 14 July 2006.

Streetwise Masculinity

In his fascinating analysis of the long history of guardhouses (*gardu*), "visible at almost every junction in major cities" in today's Indonesia, Abidin Kusno invokes a photograph of *pemuda* or male youth from the Indonesian revolution waged against Dutch colonizers—young men who might have either belonged to the Indonesian national army and/or to unofficial militias known as *lascar* but whose stylistic formation (in the photo at least) recalls the image of security guards standing at the *gardu* in more contemporary times (Kusno 2006, 96, 142; cf. Frederick 1997). This scene is worth citing at length for the powerful ways the image resonates with the young men grouped across the city at the edge of their neighborhoods in postwar Ambon:

> It is an image Indonesians would expect to confront as they approached the entrance to a guarded neighborhood. These youth represent the city (in ruins) behind them. They consider the city as being under their guard and see themselves as its protectors, as well as the destroyers of things associated with the enemy. Patrolling in self-styled uniforms, they considered themselves to be the vanguard of the newly liberated world of the Indonesian masses (the *rakyat*). They took the urban space as a gigantic canvas on which they inscribed writing, slogans, and flags associated with this new time and new identity. They saw themselves as the embodiment of order and security, even though many of them participated in political violence and acts of destruction.
>
> KUSNO 2006, 142

Importantly, this passage captures not only the *longue durée* of such loci and the young men with whom they are linked but also the masculine style and sense of threat which the latter equally embody. In this respect, Ambon's young men resemble others all over the world where such similarities seem to be founded on a "doubling", or a simultaneous exclusion and inclusion, attributable to the workings of neoliberal capitalism and the larger alterations in the planetary order (Comaroff and Comaroff 2000, 307). Indeed, like young people elsewhere, Indonesian youth have been increasingly marginalized and disenfranchised with neoliberal capitalism's rise, general conditions that have been further exacerbated in Ambon and its surroundings by the war and its devastating social and economic consequences. Following the Comaroffs, the exclusion has to do with the ways young men are denied full, waged citizenship in the nation-state and often, as a result, take to the streets. Pointing to the feminization of post-Fordist labor, disruptive of gender relations and domestic reproduction, they identify a "crisis of masculinity" afflicting young men in particular, though by no means exclusively (ibid; cf. Naafs 2012). At the same time, they note the rise of "assertive, global youth cultures of desire, self-expression, and representation; in some places, too, of potent, if unconventional forms of politicization" (Comaroff and Comaroff 2000, 307). With insight that now appears prescient in light of the youth-driven movements in Tunisia, Egypt, and of Occupy, they conclude that "pre-adults have long been at the frontiers of the transnational" (Comaroff and Comaroff 2000, 309).

Cocky, streetwise, and displaying their own sense of style, youth in Ambon can still only cautiously be said to be at the forefront of anything. Comprising close to 60 per cent of the urban population, there is much un(der)employment among them and, in one way or another, like just about everyone else in Ambon, they bear the scars and experiences of the city's war. An anthropologist who has worked for many years in the region observed how the more open atmosphere initiated with *Reformasi*, along with the unrest of the conflict, offered such young men "an opportunity to express their freedom from authority through acts of violence" (*Manado Pos* 28 August 2000 in Bartels 2003, 139). He also mentions the presence of "Western-style gangs" which at times fought each other in some parts of the city prior to the war, as well as how these gangs morphed during the violence "into freedom fighters defending their neighborhoods against outside attacks and invading those of their enemies to burn them down" (Bartels 2003, 139). Other researchers detail how the specific conditions of postwar Ambon have left many more men than women without sources of employment (Adams and Peilouw 2008). There is also disturbing evidence of quite widespread domestic violence, as well as violence in schools (Margiyatin, Peilouw, Sano, and White n.d.).

War and the city's postwar streets elicit masculine performances in which the male body figures centrally. Add to this a possible "crisis in masculinity" which, whatever its myriad derivations, may provoke further displays of male power in the form of domestic or other physical violence or, through more sublimated if also aggressive forms, like Ambon's Christian street art. Once the Christ murals and billboards emerged during the war men would apparently pose before them to be photographed, weapons in hand, before setting off to battle. A Protestant minister spoke to me of the first Pattimura Day celebration held in the city in mid-May 2005 to commemorate the resistance to Dutch colonial rule on the part of the 19th-century Christian hero and his followers.[8] Part of the ceremony includes a performance of the *cakalele* war dance by Christian men dressed in ancestral wartime attire upon their arrival in Ambon

---

8   Notes from an interview, Ambon, 20 June 2005.

City by boat from Sapurua Island. If always impressive, the first postwar performance took place in the part of the city where the conflict began and in other ways, too, was especially uncanny. Following so closely upon war's conclusion, the spectacle of the bare-chested men brandishing many of the same machetes (*parang*) they had only recently used in war could not but evoke the city's immediate past and, indeed, be infused by some of the same passions and energies that animated its widespread violence. On a somewhat different note, the minister commented how quite a number of the men had clearly prepared themselves beforehand for the performance through some extra body-building.

If style generally is something to be put on display then such display was performed with a vengeance during and following Ambon's war—Christian crosses grew to immense sizes around male necks like some sacred Moluccan *bling*, music, and emblems distinguishing minibuses destined for different parts of the city became demonstrably religious in nature, while, last but not least, the Christian billboards and murals should similarly be understood as the launching of a spectacle with a vengeance. In 2003 I witnessed numerous practice sessions of young men marching in military style (*baris-barisan*) in preparation for the city's first national Independence Day celebration following the war (cf. Kadir 2008, 120). Variations on this style include "beautiful marching" (*baris indah*) which replaces the tight discipline of the military version with graceful flowing movements or another in which the military march alternates with short bouts of break-dancing. At the time people remarked upon the impressive number of groups that had signed up for the Independence Day parade and how fabulous they would look in their different, color-coordinated outfits.

Style among Ambonese young men is an ongoing preoccupation in which the motorbike assumes special importance as a crucial component of masculine performance. In his fine ethnography of local masculinity Hatib Abdul Kadir describes the strutting and cruising that takes place in Ambon's streets and how men critically assess each other's performances. Equally important is the creative work that goes into turning the motorbike into a tool and emblem of masculine display (cf. Kadir 2008, 297–301; Naafs 2012). While taking photographs one day of a motorbike taxi stand, a number of the bikers offered to show me their own *documentasi* or photo albums documenting the "before" and "after" of the embellished motorbike stand and its corresponding wall covered with various designs along with group activities, such as a motorbike excursion to Seram Island during *durian* season.[9] Scenes of male camaraderie

---

9   See Karen Strassler's (2006) "*Reformasi* Through Our Eyes: Children as Witnesses of History in Post-Suharto Indonesia" for a discussion of what she calls Indonesia's "culture of documentation".

and fun, the photographs also register the shifting stylistic, political, and religious identifications of the group and the creativity displayed in their articulation. Most striking, however, were several photographs showing young men performing motorbike stunts in front of the Christ billboard and murals. In these pictures male bodies merge with the Christian landscape behind them as in one remarkable image in which the erect bike supported by its owner attired in his Christmas best aligns perfectly with the crucified Christ behind it. In these carefully preserved photographs, the double import of backdrops in the construction of both Christian identity and youthful masculinity comes dramatically to the fore: bikes, bling, and backdrops work together as prostheses of male bodies in public space, as the props of male performances, or even, following a more expansive definition, as bodily adornment where the backdrop "serves as a kind of adornment of the pictured body, as a fashion that fashions the subject within" (Strassler 2010, 80). This is nowhere more clear than when the bike aligns with the Christ backdrop enabling a "heroic message", a masculine assertion of public Christianity, and "another way of telling" that is not dependent on "voice" in some narrow understanding of human agency but on visual expression and performance (Berger and Mohr 1982). [Figures 9.16–9.17]

Sighting the Street

This photo-essay begs the question of how or what we see or, more specifically, how or what different Ambonese and Indonesians saw when they passed Ambon's motorbike taxi stands, the wartime and postwar images that widely adorned them through and in some instances beyond the mid-2000s, and the young men who identify with these sites. The passage from Abidin Kusno cited above offers an initial orientation by detailing what Indonesians "expect to confront" and, by extension, experience when they approach the secured neighborhood guardhouses that are found in cities and provincial towns across the archipelago. Yet he also notes more generally how such guardhouses tend to disappear from view and be absorbed into their immediate surroundings (Kusno 2006, 98). To a certain extent, Ambon provides an exception to this general rule insofar as the Christian billboards and murals hovered over passers-by in a city that was radically divided along religious lines, generally anxious and tense in the aftermath of war, and where, as a consequence, forms of religious branding continued to be especially charged. On the eve of Christian holidays the Christ pictures and accompanying scenes asserted themselves with an acute force as a result not only of the common awareness of their

FIGURE 9.16   *Dokumentasi of a motorbike taxi-stand, Ambon 2006*

FIGURE 9.17
Motorbiker poses on Christmas morning in front of a Jesus billboard, Ambon 2006

respective religious calendars among Christians and Muslims alike but because at this time of the year the images materially also jumped out of their immediate environment. In the weeks preceding the Christmas holiday the images would receive a fresh coat of paint, be illuminated by colored lanterns, and supplemented by a Christmas tree or Nativity scene. Taken together, all of these distinct elements served to highlight and draw attention to them. At other times of the year, however, these same images faded more easily into the wider visual ecology of the street where they vied for attention with cigarette and cell phone ads, the increasingly predominant shiny vinyl posters and banners boasting the faces and slogans of regional electoral candidates, and other urban distractions. Over time the images also naturally lose color and definition through the wear and tear of Ambon's burning equatorial sun and seasonal downpours. Importantly, at any time, what "Ambonese" see is also inevitably inflected by age, gender, and religion, among other sociological variables, as I have tried to intimate throughout this essay. But although some pictures were still brightly in place when I last visited Ambon in 2011, most of the Christian images had disappeared into the city walls or left only spectral traces along its streets. At the same time, one picture, which I came across at several places, not only in the streets but also inside some churches, stood out due to its novelty: an image of Christ as King or Christ of the Second Coming betraying not only the wartime surge in the popularity of Pentacostalism among the city's Christians but also the steady Pentacostalization of Ambon's Dutch colonial derived Calvinist Protestant Church from within. While by 2011 most of the street pictures had faded from public view, these newer ones stood as silent witnesses to the larger role of images in both refiguring the complex religious composition of the city and prefiguring things to come but also, crucially, as a material tribute to the ongoing contribution of youth as creators and renewers of culture generally.

The photographs collected in this essay also offer some insight into the energies and affective intensities that animated Indonesia's streets in the immediate post-Suharto era. In Ambon specifically, these energies may be gauged from the enormous scale of the Christ faces and murals that interpolated urbanites and visitors to the city in multiple ways—from the more intense if disparate engagements of some Christians and Muslims to the pride of neighborhood inhabitants, notably if not exclusively the young men who sponsored the pictures, or the more muted, even distracted attention of other passers-by. "Affective intensities" come variously to the fore in the photographs that young men took of themselves and "documented" in the archives they maintained of the street, of their male camaraderie, and of their collective endeavors. As such, the photographs provide some perspective onto who these young men "want to be when they pose before the camera", as when male bodies blend into the Christ behind them or the photograph's foreground competes for attention with the Christian backdrop in moments of male bravado caught on camera, or when the creative work of male youth unfolds across a series of photographs that track the emergence of the motorbike stand's new décor (Pinney 1998). If the Indonesia that is currently in the making promises and encompasses much more than the young men who hang out and perform in its many streets, sighting the street and the exacerbated forms of publicity and style emerging there offers one productive take on, especially, the immediate post-Suharto times foregrounded in this essay and the kinds of passions and energies that suffused them.

References

Adam, J. and L. Peilouw. 2008. "Internal Displacement and Household Strategies for Income Generation: A Case Study in Ambon, Indonesia." *Social Development Issues* 30:78–90.

Amin, Basri. 2012. "Youth, *Ojeg,* and Urban Space in Ternate." *The Asia Pacific Journal of Anthropology* 13:36–48.

Bahrani, Zainab. 2008. *Rituals of War: The Body and Violence in Mesopotamia.* New York: Zone Books.

Bataille, Georges. 1988–91. *The Accursed Share: An Essay on General Economy.* New York: Zone Books.

Berger, John, and Jean Mohr. 1982. *Another Way of Telling.* New York: Pantheon Books.

Casey, Michael. 2009. *Che's Afterlife: The Legacy of an Image.* New York: Vintage Books.

Certeau, Michel de. 1996. *The Possession at Loudun.* Translated by Michael B. Smith. Chicago: University of Chicago Press.

Clifford, James. 1988. *The Predicament of Culture.* Cambridge, MA: Harvard University Press.

Comaroff, Jean, and John L. Comaroff. 2000. "Millenial Capitalism: First Thoughts on a Second Coming." *Public Culture* 12:291–343.

Frederick, William H.M. 1997. "The Appearance of Revolution: Cloth, Uniform, and the Pemuda Style in East Java, 1945–1949." In *Outward Appearances: Defining State and Society in Indonesia,* edited by Henk Schulte Nordholt, 181–99. Leiden: KITLV Press.

Jain, Kajri. 2007. *Gods in the Bazaar: The Economies of Indian Calendar Art.* Durham, NC: Duke University Press.

Kadir, Hatib Abdul. 2008. "Biar Punggung Patah, Asal Muka Jangan Pucat" Melacak Gengsi dan Gaya Tubuh Anak Muda Kota Ambon, BA thesis, Gajah Mada University, Yogyakarta.

Kusno, Abidin. 2010. *The Appearances of Memory: Mneumonic Practices of Architecture and Urban Form in Indonesia*. Durham, NC: Duke University Press.

———. 2006. "Guardian of Memories: Gardu in Urban Java." *Indonesia* 81:95–149.

———. 2004. "Whither Nationalist Urbanism? Public Life in Governor Sutiyoso's Jakarta." *Urban Studies* 41:2377–94.

Lee, Doreen. 2011. "Images of Youth: On the Iconography of History and Protest in Indonesia." *History and Anthropology* 22:307–36.

Margawati, Margaretha, and Tony Aryanto. 2000. "Konflik Antaragama atau Politisasi Agama?" *Jurnal Antropologi Budaya Indonesia* 63:123–30.

Morgan, David. 2005. *The Sacred Gaze: Religious Visual Culture in Theory and Practice*. Berkeley, CA: University of California Press.

———. 1998. *Visual Piety: A History and Theory of Popular Religious Images*. Berkeley, CA: University of California Press.

Naafs, Suzanne. 2012. "Youth, Work and Lifestyles in an Indonesian Industrial Town." PhD diss., Institute of Social Studies and Erasmus University, Rotterdam, The Netherlands.

Paramaditha, Intan. 2014. "The Wild Child's Desire: Cinema, Sexual Politics, and the Experimental Nation in Post-Authoritarian Indonesia." PhD diss., New York University.

Pinney, Christopher. 2004. *"Photos of the Gods": The Printed Image and Political Struggle in India*. London: Reaktion Books.

———. 1998. *Camera Indica: The Social Life of Indian Photographs*. Chicago, IL: University of Chicago Press.

Spyer, Patricia. 2013. "Images Without Borders: Violence, Visuality, and Landscape in Postwar Ambon, Indonesia." In *Images That Move*, edited by Patricia Spyer and Mary Margaret Steedly, Santa Fe, NM: SAR Advanced Research Press.

———. 2008. "Blind Faith: Painting Christianity in Postconflict Ambon." *Social Text* 26:11–37.

———. 2006. "Some Notes on Disorder in the Indonesian Postcolony." In *Law and Disorder in the Postcolony*, edited by Jean and John L. Comaroff, 188–218. Chicago, IL: University of Chicago Press.

Steedly, Mary Margaret. 2013. *Rifle Reports: A Story of Indonesian Independence*. Berkeley, CA: University of California Press.

Strassler, Karen. 2006. "*Reformasi* Through Our Eyes: Children as Witnesses of History in Post-Suharto Indonesia." *Visual Anthropology Review* 22: 53–70.

Ugik, Margiyantin, Lusia Peilouw, Atsushi Sano, and Ben White. (n.d.) "Teenagers' Accounts of Insecurity and Violence in Three Indonesian Regions." Unpublished manuscript.

Urry, John. 2007. *Mobilities*. Cambridge: Polity Press.

CHAPTER 10

Violent Activism, Islamist Ideology, and the Conquest of Public Space among Youth in Indonesia

Noorhaidi Hasan

Introduction

The Asian economic crisis of 1997 brought about the dramatic meltdown of the Indonesian currency, inflation, and mass dismissals, which contributed to the collapse of Suharto's authoritarian New Order regime in May 1998 after holding power for over thirty-two years. As the crisis deepened, more and more people were thrown into the harsh reality of joblessness, and youth were the most severely affected group. In 1997 young people constituted 72.5 percent of the total unemployed, the highest proportion in the world. Despite the new government's relentless efforts at economic recovery, ten years later youth still represented 70 percent of the total of unemployed in Indonesia (Hendri 2008). The mounting discontent among Indonesian young people, who channel their frustration by engaging in street politics and collective actions and violent activism, cannot be dissociated from the economic reality.

The emergence, post-New Order, of Muslim paramilitary groups with names like the Front Pembela Islam (FPI, the Front for the Defenders of Islam), the Laskar Jihad (LJ, the Holy War Force), the Laskar Mujahidin Indonesia (LMI, the Indonesian Holy Warriors Force), and other militant Islamic groups, including the Hizbut Tahrir Indonesia (HTI, Indonesian Islamic Liberation Party) and the Kesatuan Aksi Mahasiswa Muslim Indonesia (KAMMI, Indonesian Muslim Students United Action Front) is emblematic of this phenomenon of youth mobilization. These groups achieved notoriety by organizing a variety of radical actions. Not only did they demand the comprehensive implementation of the *shari'a* (Islamic law), but they also raided cafes, discotheques, casinos, brothels and other reputed dens of iniquity. Most importantly, they called for *jihad* in the Indonesian provincial towns of Ambon in the Moluccas and Poso in Central Sulawesi in the turbulent years, beginning in 1999.

Young people aged between 15 and 29 years serve as the backbone of these organizations and constituted the key to the success of the organizations' leadership in promoting collective violence. The best of the youth were recruited to organizational roles, spending much of their time planning events, making predictions about consequences, and organizing actions. Youth provided relentless support to translate the movement's programs into collective actions by participating in *tabligh akbar* (mass religious gatherings) and other mass events organized in numerous cities across Indonesia. They were also at the forefront in risking their lives, venturing to the front lines in conflict areas of post-Suharto Indonesia. The most radical among them were the masterminds and perpetrators of bombings that claimed hundreds of lives in strategic places in Bali and Jakarta.

The involvement of youth in organizing street politics and in violent activism in Indonesia is not new. Youth have played important roles in major social, political, and cultural changes, including the demonstrations that led to the collapse of the Sukarno regime in 1966. Having succeeded in bringing Suharto to power as a replacement for Sukarno, they then apparently took a critical position toward the Suharto regime, especially in the anti-Japanese demonstrations that turned to riots in 1974 (the Malari incident).[1] After the government's grip on political activities tightened during the 1970s, in part by restrictions on campus activism, they turned toward socio-economic and religious activism by pioneering the establishment of NGOs and civil society organizations, and this included *da'wa* (religious proselytizing) activities from the 1980s. Within the framework of *da'wa* they called for the implementation of Islam in all walks of Muslim life, and this has facilitated the wave of Islamic resurgence since the 1980s. The campus movement and the wave of Islamic resurgence since this period has contributed to the growing influence of transnational Islamist ideas and movements, including the Muslim Brotherhood, Hizb ut-Tahrir (the Party of Liberation), and the Salafi *da'wa* movement, in Indonesia.

The definition of youth is fluid and arbitrary in regard to physical and social attributes, and varies across cultures and eras. In general, though, youth as a category is defined as the life stage of adolescence, a period in which young people experience changes in their roles and shifts in social expectations. But they have yet to establish the full legal status and roles of adulthood, and consequently, unlike adults, do not have access to familial, professional, and political rights (Fussell and Greene 2002, 21–60). This paper examines street politics and violent activism as attempts by youth to respond to the discouraging situation of prolonged economic crisis and socio-demographic changes by developing an identity influenced by religious movements and the unique social setting of globalizing Indonesia. I move beyond the narrow perspective of Islamic youth

---

[1] In 1974, occasioned by a state visit to Indonesia by Japanese Prime Minister Kakuei Tanaka, students protested on the streets of Jakarta about corruption, high prices, and inequality in foreign investments. Eleven protestors were killed and hundreds of cars and buildings destroyed.

militancy as an expression of ideology, and provide a broader analysis of the nexus between the structure, ideology, and the cultural identity of youth.

Growing Up in a Risk Society

Recent literature on youth has conceptualized that the main problem facing young people who have experienced critical points in their transition to adulthood is the consequence of sweeping social changes associated with modernization and globalization (White and Wyn 2005; Barry 2005; Weil et al. 2005; Blossfeld et al. 2005). The process of globalization, encompassing the internationalization and importance of markets, intensified competition, and accelerated spread of networks and knowledge via new technologies, has not only obscured geographical borders and nation-state territories but has produced new challenges as youth try to cope with increasing uncertainty about the future. It has negatively impacted on young people's ability to establish themselves as independent adults, to form partnerships, and become parents. Globalization has also brought the world we live in under the domination of global capitalism and neoliberalism in public policy, characterized by the increasing concentration of wealth and power into fewer and fewer hands. Recent years have also seen the fragmentation of communities and the emergence of deep social divisions within society (White and Wyn 2005).

Living in a class-divided society in the critical and turbulent phase of early life means that not all young people have the same resources, experiences and opportunities. There are gradations in material resources available to young people of different classes, and class differences are linked to both family and community contexts, essential parts of how young people negotiate their lives in different social situations. For marginalized working-class youth, "leisure" is shaped by lack of money, a strong sense of neighborhood boundaries, and the stigma attached to geographical and class location. This problem no doubt creates a profound and enduring tension among the youth (White and Wyn 2005, 16). The impact of globalization is experienced differently by youth in different countries due to institutional differences such as employment relations, the education system, welfare regimes, and family systems (Mills and Blossfeld 2005). These institutions can filter rising uncertainty brought about by the forces of globalization. Obviously, locality remains important for young people. Their active engagement in negotiating the local and the global eventually informs the social construction of youth identity (Nilan and Feixa 2006).

Indonesia has strived relentlessly to adjust to global developments and accelerate the process of development, which led the country to be labelled as one of Asia's new tigers in the early 1990s. However, the country still has to solve basic problems of transparency and accountability linked to widespread corruption and bureaucratic incompetence. As a result, the government has failed to balance the supply of and demand for workers, engendering rising competition in job markets. Many citizens were alienated as they were denied entrance to the corridors of power, or were disenchanted by the New Order's arbitrary rule and rampant corruption (Johnston 2005, 178–79; Robison and Hadiz 2004, 120–30).Although the majority of Indonesians achieved a higher standard of living under Suharto's New Order, problems of equity and distribution remain: a greater concentration of "development" in urban areas and the rising expectation of the many young people who benefited from expanded educational opportunities in the Suharto period.

However, the government faces an uphill struggle finding young people jobs. In 1998–99 about 600,000 university graduates could not find employment, and over 60 per cent of the labor force between the ages of 15 and 19 with a high school education were looking for work (Vatikiotis 1998, 57–58). The end of this process was the protracted economic crisis in 1997 that led to the collapse of Suharto's New Order in May 1998.

After the prolonged economic crisis, economic recovery moved slowly. Under the democratic government of Susilo Bambang Yudhoyono (2004–2014) Indonesia's economic performance has improved, for example, GDP growth rose to 6.3 percent in 2008. But two to three million people enter the workforce every year, so unemployment is rising, and this problem will get worse over the next ten years because the bulk of the 11 million unemployed will be aged between 15 and 24 years old. Indonesia's unemployment rate could even increase to 20 per cent of its roughly 150 million workforce by 2015, while the number of poor families, currently estimated at 19.2 million could double (Abdullah 2004; Sijabat 2006).

Since the cost for participation in education has become higher and higher as an impact of the commercialization of education, the rate of participation in education through to the final year of secondary education and beyond remains low, especially when compared to neighboring countries. Many young people are only able to complete six years of schooling and after withdrawal from school many of them end up living on the streets doing odd jobs, or are likely to join the informal labor force as street and market vendors.

Unlike welfare states that can provide active employment-sustaining labor market policies, welfare-sustaining employment exit policies, the scope and generosity of family allowances and services and the share of the public sector in the labor force, developing countries such as Indonesia still have to struggle to set up the fundamental economy to guarantee the sustainability of the system.

The increased economic uncertainty, combined with the lack of public support, will impact on youth's ability to plan for the future (Mills and Blossfeld 2005). The consequence of this is that young people's opportunities for upward mobility will become blocked. For young people, who have to be mobile and ready to reap opportunities, living in uncertain conditions is often frustrating (Leccardi and Ruspini, 2006). In Southeast Asia young people are viewed as the hope for the family's future survival and as the symbol of passion and vitality in society. This perception has multiplied the burden of youth in dealing with globalization, as they do not have the full legal status and roles of adulthood (Maria 2002).

Youth appear to be the sector most vulnerable to the rapid progress in society. Not infrequently have they become the "losers of globalization" (Mills, 2005), experiencing a type of identity crisis. As a source of meaning for social actors, identity organizes meaning by determining how the purpose of certain actions is symbolically identified. Melucci (1989) refers to the "homelessness of personal identity" when describing the sort of alienation people experience when identities are relativized, and he proposes that this condition requires individuals to re-establish their identity, and thus their "home" continually.

Islamist Ideology

Amid mounting uncertainty and growing frustration afflicting Indonesian young people in the face of the profound failures of the democratic political system, conservative Islamist discourse has spread widely among them, articulated by Islamist political forces working within a variety of communication channels. These include direct contact and communal activity around the mosque and neighborhood, as well as print media and the internet. The Islamist ideology shapes the narrative of confrontation with the Other (Ismail 2003): the West is perceived to be the main enemy of Islam, seeking to undermine it and subjugate the *umma* in diverse ways, not only through open war but also through the war of ideas (*ghazw al-fikr*) and cultural, economic, social, and political invasion. Muslim backwardness, their marginal global political position, economic crisis, and military dependency are deemed to be the results of the Western imperialism on the Muslim world.

An earlier Islamic modernist trend responded to the backwardness of the Muslim world in the face of Western imperialism and colonialism by calling for the reform of ideas and adopting Western progress believed to inherently represent Qur'anic messages. The contemporary conservative Islamist discourse tends to portray the West as the foe responsible for all the problems afflicting the Muslim world. Instead of encouraging Muslims to develop science and technology, for instance, the Islamist discourse blames Western progress for the results of its imperialist expansion in the Muslim world. The call for a return to the Qur'an and the Sunna, as well as the exemplary model of the early generation of Muslims (*Salaf al-Salih*), is regarded as the only solution to confront the Western powers and their main collaborator, the Zionists. The ability to resist Islam's enemies is determined by the level of the belief of Muslims in the oneness of God and His absolute authority (*tawhid*). The essence of *tawhid* as total submission to God requires sincere determination to implement all His commands and scrupulously avoid all His prohibitions.

The conservative Islamist discourse that developed among the Egyptian Muslim Brothers in the aftermath of Sayyid Qutb's execution in 1966 and spread to various parts of the Muslim world as a by-product of Saudi Arabia's ambitious campaign for the Wahhabization of the *umma* came to influence followers of the NII movement. NII (Negara Islam Indonesia) is a home-grown Islamist movement, a permutation of the DI/TII rebel movement that erupted in 1949 in West Java, South Sulawesi, and Aceh, demanding the establishment of Indonesia as an Islamic state. This opposition to the secular nationalist model of the Republic of Indonesia was initially set in motion by a feeling of disappointment due to rationalization in the military body and a center-periphery gap in development, and then evolved toward a desire to take control over society on the basis of politics. Some former NII activists, who had taken part in the Afghan War, consolidated into the Jama'ah Islamiyah, a clandestine organization set up by Abdullah Sungkar and Abu Bakar Ba'asyir aimed at establishing a pan-Nusantara Islamic state using terror tactics and other violent means.

Seizing control of society has been an underlying doctrine behind the ideology of Hizb ut-Tahrir. The failure of the Arab nations to counter Israeli aggression raised questions for Islamic activists. For Taqiy al-Din Muhammad al-Nabhani, the founder of Hizb ut-Tahrir, the collapse of the *khilafat* system (Government by Islamic law, the Ottoman empire) in 1924 paved the way for the Western colonial powers to set up a Zionist project on Palestinian soil (Taji-Farouki 1996). Therefore Hizb ut-Tahrir relentlessly called for a revival of the *khilafat* system, whereby Muslims globally came to stand shoulder-to-shoulder against the Western-Zionist conspiracy to destroy the Muslim world. Compared to the Muslim Brotherhood, Hizb ut-Tahrir's ideology is in fact more radical. It has been active in campaigning for the establishment of the *khilafat* system, through violent means if necessary.

The Salafi movement began to gain ground in Indonesia in the mid-1980s. Salafis emphasize the purity of *tawhid* (the oneness of God) and other issues centered on the call for a revival of strict religious practice that would develop and guard the moral integrity of individuals. Its efflorescence across the world was part of Saudi Arabia's success in spreading its Wahhabi (modernist Islamic reform) influence under the banner of the Salafi movement, thus reinforcing Saudi Arabia's prestigious position and legitimacy both at the center of the Muslim world and as the *khadim al-haramayn* (guardians of the two holy sanctuaries). From the Salafi point of view, Islam has lost its vitality because Muslims fell into *bid'a* sins (sins of innovation). Returning to the Qur'an and Sunna, based on the exemplary model and practice of the first generation of Muslims (*Salaf al-Salih*), is the only choice if Muslims want to revive their glory which was lost during the *khilafat* era. Based on the doctrine of *al-wala wa'l-bara* (drawing near what is pleasing to God and moving away from what is not) the Salafi movement sought to cultivate solidarity (*ukhuwwah*) among Muslims and draw a demarcation between various elements of *bid'a* and infidelity (Hasan 2006; Hasan 2007). This doctrine also requires Muslims to stand distinctly apart from the "anything goes" open society around them and organize themselves into small, tight-knit, exclusive communities (the *jama'a*), though not necessarily under the oath of loyalty (*bay'a*).

Despite different emphases and tones in these groups, overall the conservative Islamist discourse serves them as a banner for rebellion against the ruling class who they feel often manipulate Islam as a legitimating ideology and as part of the state mechanism. The opposition against the ruling class often takes symbolic form of blaming the West for the failure of ruling regimes in the Muslim world to address unemployment and poverty. The readiness to venture to the front lines in order to repel Western aggression, thus regaining the glory of Islam, is proclaimed as evidence of one's commitment to the purity of *tawhid*. In the face of uncertainties engendered by the process of globalization, the engagement of deprived young people in street politics and violent actions is not simply an expression of religious fanaticism; it is also an attempt to develop a unique identity and gain circumscribed but effective power and autonomy within their exclusive boundary.

In 2008 I conducted Focus Group Discussions with 17 young activists, members of the Hizb ut-Tahrir Indonesia (HTI) from neighborhoods close to university campuses in Jakarta and Yogyakarta respectively.[2] Most of them were members of the Campus Islamic Proselytizing Board (*Lembaga Dakwah kampus*) which played a crucial role in the dissemination of HTI's ideas across Indonesia after 1998. HTI has been one of the most active Islamist organizations in recruiting young cadres and taking them to the streets, both to voice

---

2 Because of sensitivities of the issues discussed, they refused to reveal their names.

their sympathy for the Palestinians and to condemn the US and Zionists for their foreign policy in the Middle East.

HTI activists represent the discontent felt by many Indonesian young people: they relate problems in Indonesia to the adoption of the political, social, economic, and cultural system of the West, in particular the political form of the nation-state and capitalism. These young Islamist activists' rhetoric reflects their growing frustration. There is a romanticism, imagining the past glory of Islam under the Ottoman Empire. They believe that its collapse was caused by external factors, including Crusades, Christian missionaries, and Western capitalist imperialism, which ultimately divided the Muslim world into a dozen competing weak nation-states.[3] They want to revive the *khilafat* system which is derived from the structure of the Medinan state and the Islamic state during the era of the four great Companions to the Prophet (*khulafa al-rashidin*).[4] This is a world political system based on Islamic law.

They regret the loss of desire among Muslims to revive the *khilafat* system that they deem to be the key factor in the glorious centuries of Islam when the *shari'a* was implemented entirely as a system governing all aspects of human life. From their point of view, the majority of Muslims stand idle in the face of the need to revive the *khilafat* and instead idolize the nation-state system and nationalism. They are critical of the ideas of democracy and human rights, which they see as imposed by the West to undermine the *umma*. In the name of freedom of expression, women are almost naked in the public arena. All this, from their perspective, contributes a great deal to the spread of vices, such as gambling, free sex, and drug use. To them, the only solution to the problem is the *shari'a* and *khilafat*, the application of which would bring prosperity and justice.

The *khilafat* is perceived to be different from any political system we have ever known. It is not a monarchy, nor an empire. It is also not a federal or republican state, let alone the democratic system developed intentionally by the West to undermine Islam. The young Islamists in HTI saw that the root cause of all problems afflicting the *umma* lies in the behavior of Muslim people of their age who they deem to be indifferent to the need to revive the *khilafat*.

---

3   An-Nabhani has explained in some detail the causes of the collapse of the Ottoman caliphate system and his call for Muslims to revive it. See Taqiy al-Din An-Nabhani, *Daulah Islamiyah,* which is an Indonesian translation of its Arabic version, *Al-Daulat al-Islamiyya* 2007.

4   A detailed account on the structure of the caliphate, see Hizb ut-Tahrir, *Ajhizatu al-Daulat al-Khilafa fi al-Hukm wa-l Idara*, which has been translated into Indonesian, *Struktur Negara Khilafah (Pemerintahan dan Administrasi)*. Trans. Yahya A.R. (Jakarta: HTI Press, 2008).

Those of their generation who refuse to share their ideology and concerns are regarded as stupid people who are simply giving up on the unfavorable situation. From their point of view, these people let themselves fall under the hegemonic control of the West, since they have no regrets about showing off luxury consumer goods, which are in fact the result of the Western agenda to compromise the younger generation of Muslims. This perception comes from their jealousy of a segment of more fortunate people, who they consider to live in the shadow of Western imperialism. They talked about the need to develop national independence and *shari'a*-based economic empowerment as solutions to the problems afflicting underprivileged groups in Indonesian society. As is typical of youth culture, the Islamist young activists imagine an instant solution to complex problems faced by Indonesia's Muslims. They propose the *shari'a* as a panacea to resolve any problems, including the prolonged economic crisis that undermined the state's ability to survive, and current issues such as deforestation and global warming.

The articulation of injustice provides Islamist ideology with a mobilizing framework that encourages disobedience and participation in conflict; a framework replacing the former dominant interpretive order, which legitimized the status quo and encouraged submission to the authorities. Imbued with the language of rebellion against the ruling elites and privileged classes, Islamist ideology has proved to be appealing to young people—both educated and uneducated—in many parts of the Muslim world, including Egypt, Iran, Algeria and Turkey. In Egypt, for instance, the key to the Muslim Brotherhood's success in recruiting young cadres has been its campaign for the formalization of *shari'a*, which is considered an undeniable part of Muslim belief. They claim that the roots of the *shari'a* provide a secure basis for the establishment of a civilized, independent, dynamic, and just social system. The struggle for the formalization of *shari'a* gives its proponents an opportunity to clamor against the existing conditions and to load public discourse with notions that change the terms of political struggle (Flores 1997; Wickham 1997).

Another attraction of Islamist ideology for young people lies in its ability to offer a dream of future glory for Muslims, provided they stand shoulder-to-shoulder to fight for the implementation of the *shari'a* and the *khilafat* system. It is utopian in nature and believes in the superiority of Islam over any other systems, as all other ideologies are believed to be weak and self-destructive. To them, the rise of Islam as the world superpower is simply a matter of time. Islamist ideology has also a millenarian character, which often meets the dreams of young people for upward mobility and empowerment, especially for underprivileged groups marginalized in the fast current of economic and social changes. It has something to offer the youth in their dreams of justice, prosperity, and future glory, when they are imagining themselves working and earning good salaries, and enjoying security and a good lifestyle.

Conquest of Public Space

A basic problem for young people in their transition to adulthood has to do with their efforts to territorialize, to claim a space within complex social relations. From a sociological perspective, claiming space is the natural tendency of both individuals and social groups in their attempts to "tame the unutterable complexity of the spatial" by constructing an ordered geographical imagining through which to frame their world. It is a way of cutting across the social relations that construct space, thus gaining some control. Deeply bound up with the social production of identities, claiming space seems to be part of wider strategies to protect and defend particular groups and interests, or even to dominate and define others (Massey 1998, 126–27).

Young people frequently come to reject the spatial ordering of the population in terms of age, a limited space dictated by dominant authorities. But they are not yet eligible to claim a larger space as full members of a social community who bear responsibility for that community. In their attempt to break the social fence constructed to protect them from the complexity of social relations, young people from all social classes, males and females, need to demonstrate that they are no longer "under the thumb" of their parents; that they want to get on with enjoying themselves; that they are street-wise. To be recognized as "somebody" and so have access to adult opportunities, young people need to express themselves and their identities, and youth cultures today are all about making distinctions, signifying differences vis-à-vis other crowds of young people (Roberts 2005, 121–22).

The basis of such distinctions comes from many sources, including from a dominant world culture whose influence has spread widely and dictated global trends and lifestyles. Because of globalization, young people from all social backgrounds can now, for instance, wear T-shirts with slogans in English, drink Coca-Cola, listen to classical or rock music, and play baseball (Massey 1998). Yet accessibility to the advantages offered by global capitalist markets differs from one individual to another. Young people on upper middle-class trajectories may prefer clubbing in prestigious venues, where they can enjoy rap, hip-hop, soul, bass and drums, rhythm and blues, techno, retro, or metal music, in an atmosphere of excitement produced by alcoholic beverages and other substances. The ordinary youth may express their individuality by the mixture of fashion they wear and the kinds of music in their personal collections. Certainly there are individuals who, either because of their limited access to leisure activities and adult opportunities, or for ideological reasons, prefer to express their identity by engaging in street politics and violent activism.

For young people, street politics and violent activism often constitute an important part of their efforts to negotiate identity and claim space. Street actions offer youth a privileged arena for the diffusion of their heroic messages and identity when they take to the streets—complete with knight symbols and loudspeakers—to shout Allah Akbar (God is great) and blame the US for whatever happens in the Muslim world. They seek to show that they are not slaves of a hegemonic global superpower, or even the dominant authorities close to home. They desire to be seen as powerful, and capable of doing something for the whole of society. Their attire and the symbols they deploy show that they belong to a certain group which is devoted to and concerned with the *umma*. Nevertheless, symbols alone are not sufficient in their struggle to negotiate identity and conquer the public sphere; they need to demonstrate their determination and capacity through carrying out extraordinary actions, something risky and dangerous, in defense of their fellow Muslims.

The struggle of youth to claim space and negotiate identities frequently forces them to relate themselves to a broader value system that "requires construction of a world enlivened with personal relevance in such a way that authentic ideals and defensive distortions become complexly interwoven" (Gregg 2007, 23). When many urban young people strive to buy into an international cultural reference system—a T-shirt with a Western logo, rock music, or gadgets—young Islamists in HTI prefer to develop a counter-discourse by calling for the *shari'a* and the *khilafa* system. The *shari'a* and the *khalifat* serve as a transcendental value system that can be used to reconstruct a world which is perceived to be in despair. For young Islamists, the *shari'a* and *khilafat* are related to concerns for authenticity, and symbols of authenticity are visible in the attires they wear—*baju koko* (long sleeved shirt) and long-flowing Arab-style dress—as well as the banners fluttering in their hands and pamphlets blaming imperialism, capitalism, and other symbols of US domination. These items draw a contrast between Islam as an authentic value system and what they perceive as a corrupting American hegemonic culture.

Events over recent years have helped young Islamists find evidence for the American political, economic, and cultural ambition to undermine Islam. The post 9/11 US retaliation in Afghanistan, with the rationale that it was responsible for providing a safe haven for Osama bin Laden, and the US military operation in Iraq that succeeded in toppling Saddam Hussein, are for the Islamists only two of many examples of American anti-Muslim imperialist policy. It is only with the *shari'a* and the *khilafat,* then, that the Muslim world can be saved.

The US is also blamed as the main collaborator with Zionist Israel in perpetrating brutal attacks on Palestinians. Here the US emerges as a master frame that helps young Islamists to construct action that resonates loudly among young militants. It functions "in a manner analogous to linguistic codes in that they provide a grammar that punctuates, and syntactically connects, patterns or happenings in the world" (Snow and Benford 1992, 138).

As a response to Israeli military attacks on Gaza in 2008 and 2009, thousands of young militants took to the streets in Jakarta and other big cities in Indonesia. The involvement of young militants in the demonstrations against Israel not only facilitated their attempt to claim space, but also to build a "heroic identity" (Gregg 2007, 178). By demonstrating that their actions are motivated by empathy with the oppressed, they appear to be heroes struggling to defend Muslims against infidel powers. Though rhetorical in nature, hundreds of them even enlisted to venture to the front lines in Gaza when the militant Islamist organizations opened registration desks for *jihad*. The idea of *jihad* provides a symbol and discourse with an aura of sacredness and righteousness (Hasan 2006). It serves as a vehicle for young militant Islamists to resist feelings of impotence and frustration, and thereby establish identity and claim dignity.

In their attempt to claim space young Islamists sometimes show no hesitation to become involved in confrontations with other Muslim groups they perceive to have created obstacles for their struggle. One important example is the brutal attacks of FPI-linked young militants who, in June 2008, mobilized under the banner of the Command of Islam Force (Komando Laskar Islam) against the masses from the pro-democracy Freedom Alliance for Religious Freedom (AKKBB—Aliansi Kebebasan untuk Kerukunan Beragama dan Berkeyakinan). The latter group staged a demonstration in the area around the National Monument in Jakarta to defend Ahmadiyah, a minority sect in Islam. A dozen members of the AKKBB were injured. This attack was the peak of their brutal campaign against the Islamic sect Ahmadiyah, which involved burning down a number of Ahmadiyah's mosques and calling for the killing of its members.

Conclusion

Amid mounting uncertainty and growing frustration afflicting Indonesian young people in the face of the profound failures of the democratic political system, conservative Islamist discourse has spread widely among Indonesian youth. Articulated by Islamist political forces using a range of communication channels, including direct contact and communal activity around the mosque and neighborhood as well as print Islam and the internet, the Islamist ideology is working to shape a narrative of heroic confrontation with the Other. This ideology contributes to youth mobilization in street politics and violent activism which constitute important aspects of their efforts to negotiate identity and thus claim space. Street actions offer youth a privileged arena for the diffusion of their heroic messages and identity, in which they demonstrate their position as agents involved in the adoption, adaptation, and dissemination of a sacred global value system and culture.

References

Abdullah, Zaky. 2004. "Indonesia, Leading the Way in Tackling the Youth Employment Challenge." Paper presented at JILPT International Labour Information Project Liaison Meeting, Tokyo, 27–28 September.

Barry, Monica, ed. 2005. *Youth Policy and Social Inclusion, Critical Debates with Young People*. London and New York: Routledge.

Blossfeld, Hans-Peter et al. (eds.). 2005. *Globalization, Uncertainty and Youth in Society*. London and New York: Routledge.

Flores, Alexander. 1997. "Secularism, Integralism, and the Egyptian Debate." In *Political Islam: Essays from Middle East Report*, edited by Joel Beinin and Joe Stork, 83–96. London: I.B. Tauris.

Fussell, Elizabeth, and Margareth E. Greene. 2002. "Demographic Trends Affecting Youth Around the World." In *The World's Youth, Adolescence in Eight Regions of the Globe*, edited by B. Bradford Brown, Reed W. Larson and T.S. Saraswathi, 21–60. Cambridge: Cambridge University Press.

Gregg, Garry S. 2007. *Culture and Identity in a Muslim Society*. Oxford: Oxford University Press.

Hasan, Noorhaidi. 2006. *Laskar Jihad: Islam, Militancy, and the Quest for Identity in Post-New Order Indonesia*. Cornell, N.Y.: SEAP Cornell University.

——— 2007. "The Salafi Movement in Indonesia: Transnational Dynamics and Local Development." *Comparative Studies of South Asia, Africa and the Middle East* 27: 83–94.

Hendri, Havy. 2008. "Pemuda dan 'Pro-Youth' Pembangunan." *Media Indonesia*, 12 January.

IMF. 2008. World Economic Outlook Database in April 2008, http://www.imf.org/external/pubs/ft/weo/2008/02/weodata/index.aspx, accessed May 4, 2015.

Ismail, Salwa. 2003. *Rethinking Islamist Politics; Culture, the State and Islamism*. London: I.B. Tauris.

Johnston, Michael. 2005. *Syndromes of Corruption, Wealth, Power, and Democracy*. Cambridge: Cambridge University Press.

Leccardi, Carmen and Elisabetta Ruspini, eds. 2006. *A New Youth? Young People, Generations and Family Life*. Aldershot: Ashgate.

Maria, Madelene Santa. 2002. "Youth in Southeast Asia, Living within the Continuity of Tradition and the Turbulence of Change." In *The World's Youth, Adolescence in Eight Regions of the Globe*, edited by B. Bradford Brown, Reed W. Larson and T.S. Saraswathi, 171–206. Cambridge: Cambridge University Press.

Massey, Doreen. 1998. "The Spatial Construction of Youth Cultures." In *Cool Places, Geographies of Youth Cultures*, edited by Tracey Skelton and Gill Valentine, 121–29. London and New York: Routledge.

Melucci, Alberto. 1989. *Nomads of the Present: Social Movements and Individual Needs in Contemporary Society*. London: Hutchinson.

Mills, Melinda, Blossfeld, Hans-Peter Blossfeld, and Klijzing, Erik Klijzing. 2005. "Introduction," In *Globalization, Uncertainty and Youth in Society*, edited by Hans-Peter Blossfeld et al, 1–23. London and New York: Routledge.

Nilan, Pam, and Carles Feixa. 2006. *Glocal Youth? Hybrid Identities, Plural Worlds*. London: Routledge.

Roberts, Ken. 2005. "Youth, Leisure and Social Inclusion," In *Youth Policy and Social Inclusion. Critical Debates with Young People* edited by Monica Barry, 117–132. London and New York: Routledge.

Robison, Richard, and Vedi R. Hadiz. 2004. *Reorganising Power in Indonesia: The Politics of Oligarchy in an Age of Markets*. London: Routledge.

Sijabat, Ridwan Max. 2006. "Youth Unemployment to Get Worse over Next Decade." *The Jakarta Post*, 7 November.

Snow, David A., and Robert D. Benford. 1992. "Master Frames and Cycles of Protest." In *Frontiers in Social Movement Theory*, edited by A.D. Morris and Carol McClurg Mueller, 133–55. New Haven, CT: Yale University Press.

Taji-Farouki, S. 1996. *A Fundamental Quest: Hizb al-Tahrir and the Search for the Islamic Caliphate*. London: Grey Seal.

Vatikiotis, Michael R.J. 1998. *Indonesian Politics under Suharto, The Rise and Fall of the New Order*. London: Routledge.

Weil, Sunan Warner et al. eds. 2005. *Unemployed Youth and Social Exclusion in Europe, Learning of Inclusion?* Aldershot: Ashgate.

White, Rob, and Johanna Wyn. 2005. *Youth and Society, Exploring the Social Dynamics of Youth Experience*. Oxford: Oxford University Press.

Wickham, C.R. 1997. "Islamic Mobilization and Political Change: The Islamist Trend in Egypt's Professional Associations." In *Political Islam: Essays from Middle East Report*, edited by Joel Beinin and Joe Stork, 120–35. London: I.B. Tauris.

PART 6

"Moral Panics" and the Health of the Nation

Introduction to Part 6

In a common Indonesian nationalist formulation, Indonesia's young people form the *generasi penerus* ("generation taking the nation forward to the future"). But other popular discourses characterize Indonesia's youth as constituting a moral hazard. As the Indonesian economy has grown more affluent and open to the world, a competing view has emerged in public discourses regarding the deleterious impact of "globalization" on young people. In this alternative view, the nation's youth present a risk. In one popular framing, young people (*remaja*) are construed as victims of the cultural and ideological influences of the West, and their presumed transgressive behaviors ("free sex", alcohol and drug use) undermine the health of the nation. Indeed, the young people surveyed by the AII team (reported in Nilan et al in this volume) seemed to collectively echo this concern about the threat of such deviant behavior (*pergaulan bebas* or free social interaction). Yet the survey results indicated that even though they listed this as a social "issue" they did not see themselves or their immediate peers as part of the problem.

This contradiction is explored in greater depth by Wright Webster through focus groups and interviews with young people in Yogyakarta as she followed up on the survey. Rather than feeling that they are responding to, or being influenced by foreign cultural practices, they see themselves as being responsible and exercising individual freedom, even if it is in regard to sexual choices and behavior that apparently transgress the supposed normative standards of their parents' generation. And far from seeing themselves as victims of "The West", they identify problems as arising because the institutions of Indonesian society—such as their families or the state education system—have let them down.

This is not dissimilar to the picture that emerges in Bennett's study of young mothers in Lombok. Young marriage is a phenomenon that causes concern in Indonesia and is often presumed to be linked to excessive youth freedom and *pergaulan bebas*.

The Sasak people of Lombok are one community where young age at marriage, especially for women, is of concern. The discourse of *pergaulan bebas* presumes these young women are victims of their own impulsive and careless sexual behavior, and victims of the Western values permeating and threatening Indonesian social life. However, Bennett's ethnographic analysis shows that most young marriages in Lombok are not a "solution" to pregnancy out of wedlock, a sign of contemporary moral decay. She decouples the issues of early marriage and adolescent pregnancy, as she finds that it is not the norm for these teenagers to marry because they are pregnant. Young Lombok women—like the friendship groups described by authors Parker, Nilan and White and

Margiyantin elsewhere in this volume—monitor each other in peer group mixing and enforce "good behavior" in courting practices, and use same-sex youth chaperones as a bastion against "risky behavior".

Bennett finds these women making positive choices in their own social, cultural and economic context: poverty, poor educational and job opportunities, and social norms concerning transitions to adulthood underscore the active choices these young women make to become young wives and mothers. Young women in Lombok do not regard early pregnancy and childbirth as risky or dangerous, and development interventions directed at preventing early marriage (which draw in an un-reflected way, on Western concerns about teenage mothers) do not address the root causes of the practice.

CHAPTER 11

The Ongoing Culture Debate: Female Youth and *Pergaulan* (*Bebas*) in Yogyakarta, Indonesia

Tracy Wright Webster

> Culture—what is that? What is Indonesian culture? Is it true that "foreign culture" is foreign for Indonesians, or is that not the case? Is it actually not foreign but rather has been concealed? What is our own culture like?
>
> NIKI, 23, FEMALE UNDERGRADUATE IN INTERNATIONAL STUDIES, YOGYAKARTA

This chapter is based on fieldwork conducted in 2007–2008 in urban Yogyakarta, central Java, renowned in Indonesia as both the "city of students" and the "cultural capital of Javanese-ness". The research focused on young people's perspectives on *pergaulan bebas* (see below) in a number of educational institutions where I conducted individual interviews and focus group discussions: a Muhamadijah (Islamic) High School, a public tertiary institution, and among youth volunteers at a non-government organization which focuses on youth sexual and reproductive health. *Pergaulan bebas*[1] refers to transgressive social interactions such as pre-marital sex, other sexual interactions "not bound by the social contract of heterosexual marriage" (*nggak ada ikatan pernikahan suami-istri/seks diluar nikah*), homosexuality, pornography, deviance, and transgressions of gender norms.[2] It also is used in reference to clubbing, drug and alcohol consumption, and gang fighting. *Anak muda* (those aged 17–24 years) who have usually left school for higher studies or employment are the demographic considered most at risk of engaging in such behavior, as suggested by the expression *pergaulan bebas anak muda*. I discuss my research findings in the context of a wider survey conducted by the Australian Research Council-funded *Ambivalent Adolescents in Indonesia* (AAI) research project team, of which I was a member. The survey, described in Chapter 3 (see also Nilan et al 2011), identified *pergaulan bebas* as the issue of greatest concern among high school students. This chapter considers the concern with *pergaulan bebas* in the context of increasing secularization,

---

1 In *Kamus Indonesia Inggris* (Indonesian English Dictionary) Echols and Shadily define *pergaulan* as "1. association, social intercourse. 2. society. 3. sexual intercourse", and *pergaulan bebas* as "free sex, promiscuity". The word *bebas* (free) is the qualifying adjective that differentiates normative *pergaulan* from non-normative *pergaulan bebas*.
2 For a comprehensive analysis of the discourse of *pergaulan bebas*, see Wright Webster 2010.

commodification, and, particularly, the focus on "sexploitation" (the latter particularly of the female body) in the media over recent decades, linked to notions of *gaul* (social/sociability).[3]

Cultural Change and Moral Panic

Pergaulan bebas is a conservative discourse with negative overtones which is intensifying in response to perceived changing values and behaviors of Indonesian youth. State, religious, and popular discourses blame the phenomena on a media perceived as driven by hedonistic western, "sexualized culture" (*budaya barat*) which is presumed to influence youth. The 1974 pop song *Muda-Mudi*,[4] which mentions *pergaulan bebas*, sums up these sentiments:

> *Muda-Mudi*
> *Muda—mudi jaman sekarang* (Young people nowadays),
> *Pergaulan bebas nian* (Interact very freely),
> *Tiada lagi orang yang melarang* (Nobody forbids it anymore),
> *Tapi sayang, banyak salah jalan* (But unfortunately, many choose the wrong path),
>
> *Lah, lah, lah,*
> *Lah, lah, lah, lah, lah, lah,*
>
> *Tapi sayang, banyak salah jalan* (But unfortunately many choose the wrong path),
> *Tiada lagi yang melarang,* (Nobody forbids it anymore)
> *Tapi sayang, banyak salah jalan* (Unfortunately, many choose the wrong path).

---

[3] The word *gaul* is a verb meaning "to associate" or "to mix" socially. In formal Indonesian grammar, *gaul* is prefixed by *ber-* (to associate). In informal Indonesian language use, the lexicon of Indonesian speech is abbreviated and prefixes are dropped. The word *gaul*, when used in the context of youth parlance, *bahasa gaul*, refers to a person. For example, "he/she is a *gaul* youth" (*dia anak gaul*) infers that the person referred to engages proficiently in a variety of social contexts, to the point that others comment on it: *gaul* becomes an adjective.

[4] Young Guys and Girls, written by Raden Koeswoyo for his sons, members of the band *Koes Bersaudara* (the Koes Brothers). It is noteworthy that members of the band were imprisoned in 1965 by Sukarno; their incarceration was described in an article in the Warta Bakti newspaper (14 July 1965) as based on the rationale that the band played "Beatles-type songs while moving their bodies like neo-colonialists". (No page number.)

The discourse of *pergaulan bebas* represents what Farrer refers to as "a slow burning moral panic" (2002, 17) that has evolved over decades. The normative center in Indonesia regards it as in opposition to "social norms" (*norma-norma masyarakat*).

Suryakusuma (2004, 59) suggests that the construction of *pergaulan bebas* as non-traditional "appears to be a way of projecting Indonesia's own permissiveness and immorality on the dominant West". Bellows (2003, 79), writing on Bali, concluded the moral panic over sexuality is a response to perceptions of a "dis-articulation of sex and fertility" by female bodies. As Adamson (2007, 5) explains, "in Java, a moral hierarchy of gender relations, mimetically extended from family to nation, dovetails with religious interpretations to resolve anxieties about social change and security through the control of women".[5] In light of these analyses, I argue that the rhetoric surrounding the discourse of *pergaulan bebas* has intensified in the post-Suharto *reformasi* period of media and market deregulation and rapid social change and that, among teenage youth, *pergaulan bebas* is considered a new phenomenon that positions this generation firmly at the center of the moral debate.

Media *Gaul*

McRobbie and Thornton (1995, 560) stress the need to consider the "labyrinthine web of determining relations which now exist between social groups and the media and between 'reality' and representation in our analysis of moral panics". Appadurai (1996, 56) notes in a similar vein that "ordinary lives today are more often powered not by the given-ness of things but by the possibilities that the media (either directly or indirectly) suggest are available".

> Contemporary mainstream Indonesian media promote notions of *sukses*, derived from the English word "success", and these "modern" conceptions of "*sukses*", associated with urban middle to upper class youth pleasures, are tied to the concept of *gaul*. *Gaul* indicates flexible understanding of, and interactions across, social networks. *Gaul*-ness is a sign

---

5 See also Brenner (1999, 34). Brenner quotes Gusti Kanjeng Ratu Hemas, the current Sultan of Yogyakarta's wife, who in her book *Wanita Indonesia: Suatu Konsepsi dan Obsesi* (*Indonesian Women: A Conception and Obsession*, 1992, 102) stated that "the moral sanctions for men who have sex outside of marriage are less severe than they are for women. In contrast, a woman who believes in free sex, or who becomes a mistress or second wife will be penalized by the norms of society".

that one is cosmopolitan, socially competent, capable of negotiating subtle sub-cultural differences and linguistically adept, particularly in *bahasa gaul* (*gaul* language) and English. More than merely a lexicon of youth slang, *gaul* articulates the desire of Indonesian youth for new types of social identification through the formulation of relationships that are more egalitarian and interactionally fluid, as well as more personally expressive and psychologically individualized.

SMITH-HEFNER 2007, 184

Popular media discourse represents *anak gaul* (*gaul* youth) as having strong self-belief (*percaya diri/pede*) that equips them to traverse youth social worlds and subcultures. To "be" *gaul*, is both an interpellation, in which an individual is "hailed" by this subject identity and embraced as an expression of personal power, and an ascribed identity, in which a person is referred to as *gaul* by others.

Smith-Hefner (2007, 184) remarked that "pop media and popular consumption styles have themselves become carriers of *gaul* culture". They offer complex narratives which present a plethora of possibilities, although not without ambiguity, shaping Indonesian youth consciousnesses, desires, bodies, and subjectivities.

For decades, the state has been working with the consequences of an increasingly secularizing and internationalizing mass consumer culture, often at odds with its own policies and ideology (Robinson 2008). Media targeted towards youth consumers relentlessly promote behaviors associated with the discourse of *pergaulan bebas*, such as smoking (among female youth), romantic pre-marital relationships (*pacaran*), and active youth sexuality. Cigarette companies, for example, are explicit in their agenda to capture the youth market through pop cultural forms, such as music, film, and fashion (see Reynolds 1999; Knight and Chapman 2004; Nichter et al. 2009), and glamorous teen girls in miniskirts and high-heeled long boots sell cigarettes and caffeinated energy drinks in places where youth congregate. Youth events often feature attractive female *seksi* (sexy) dancers who perform a soft pornographic dance routine and often simulate strip tease. On prime-time evening television, advertisements promote products to prolong male erections. Later at night, young females in dialup phone sex advertisements promise satisfaction, and voluptuous young girls in negligée pose before the gaze of the camera. In negotiating what Appadurai (1996) has termed the *ideoscape*—in this instance simultaneously an allowing and disallowing dialectic between media/market driven liberalization and conservative moral backlash—we see possibilities for the expression of more personalized, even postmodern, subjectivities. However, these subjectivities must be also negotiated in relation to the dominant discourse of *pergaulan bebas*.

The Survey Question

One aspect of my research was administering a survey to high school students (13–18 years) in Yogyakarta. This survey was a common tool used by all researchers on the AAI team and was administered in high schools in nine cities throughout Indonesia. Respondents were not a random sample of this cohort but rather the survey was used as a complementary methodology in each of the research sites (Nilan et al 2011). One question asked: "According to you, what problems do young people now face? " (*Menurut Anda, persoalan-persoalan apa yang dihadapi remaja saat ini?*). This was an open-ended question, without prompts, and students were provided space to write a maximum of three different responses to this question in their own words. Responses from my sample of 473 students in the city of Yogyakarta (Table 11.1) revealed that the issue of *pergaulan bebas* was the most frequently mentioned concern for high school aged youth.

In the sample, 205 students (43 percent of male youth and 53 percent of female youth) indicated *pergaulan bebas* as one of their three main concerns. Not surprisingly, *pergaulan bebas* was an issue of greater significance among female senior high school students in the 16–18 year old age range who are moving into the social age demographic of *anak muda* (late teens-early adults).

The responses ranked one to four in the table indicate primary concerns around social relations (especially friendships and love relationships), sexuality, and the use of drugs, alcohol, and smoking. The fifth-ranked response, family problems (often phrased "too little parental attention",[6] and *broken home*), is widely viewed in Indonesia as the principle risk factor or antecedent to engagement in the behaviors of *pergaulan bebas*. In Yogyakarta, Guinness (1986, 136) observed "naughty kids"—*anak nakal*—"are thought to reflect the

---

6   *Kurang diperhatikan orang tua*. In relation to the discourses of lack of parental attention (*kurang diperhatikan orang tua*) and *broken home*, see Brenner (1995, 40), who explains that the counter-discourse to the formal Javanese/Islamic gender discourse of male spiritual potency and self-restraint and female lack of self-control, emphasizes women's primary role in maintaining self-control for the sake of family stability when males have little or none when it comes to their desires. Furthermore, the notion of career woman (*wanita karir*) continues to be framed in the media as "a modern, and potentially risky, alternative to women's default position as housewife" (Brenner 1998, 243).

TABLE 11.1 *Frequency of responses regarding issues confronted by youth in the yogyakarta sample N = 473*

Rank	Issues Youth Confront	Number of Responses
1	*Pergaulan bebas, seks bebas, free sex*	205
2	Drugs, alcohol, smoking	136
3	Interactions with friends	118
4	Love/*cinta*	104
5	Family problems, *broken home*	92
6	Education, school and university	92
7	Lazy, lacking the spirit of struggle	67
8	Negative influences in environment	52
9	Lifestyle not conducive	51
10	Lack of self-restraint	48
11	Expenses / family income	38
12	Moral degradation in attitude and behavior	35
13	Lack of religious commitment	35
14	Criminal involvement	34
15	Time management difficulties	33
16	Identity crisis	32
17	Lack of support in environment	29
18	HIV / AIDS	27
19	Puberty	26
20	Negative impact of globalization	26
21	Sexual discrimination	4
22	No answer	24

lack of *rukun* (harmony) in their families".[7] Respondents' concerns with educational achievement rank equally with parental support. This underlines that these young people embrace the importance of family support structures

---

7 Parents often support and maintain the addictions of their offspring. One local roadside food stall owner told me that before his wife died in the 2006 earthquake, she often succumbed to their son's nagging, and gave him cash for his heroin (*putaw*) addiction. Her reasons were many. Besides feeling compassion her son's "pain", she feared that he would steal from locals, which may have resulted in her son's addiction being exposed and public shame for the family.

(emotional/psychological, material, financial, and social) in future education, employment, and marriage opportunities while they are negotiating their own social relations and interpersonal behavior according to peer group norms and the public discourse of *"pergaulan bebas"*.

To explore the language and meanings of *pergaulan bebas* further, I asked students in an extra-curricular English class (aged 15–17 years) at an Islamic Muhamadiyah high school, "What is *pergaulan bebas*?" The collection of terms they produced is shown in random order below. Their responses, other than *pacaran* (courting; pre-marital relationships), were given in (Americanized) English.

These adolescents' responses (Figure 11.1) show a range of behaviors not immediately evident in the AAI survey responses shown in Table 11.1. Drug use, alcohol consumption, smoking, interactions with friends, and love (*cinta*) (issues 2–4 in Table 11.1) are implicit for these students under the rubric *pergaulan bebas*. The Muhamadiyah student group further discriminated between behaviors that generally fall under the umbrella of *pergaulan bebas*, and a sub group of behaviors more specifically related to sex (*free seks/seks bebas*) including

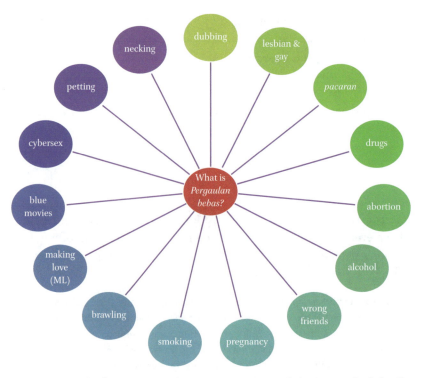

FIGURE 11.1   *Student responses to brainstorming activity on "what is* pergaulan bebas*"?*

either engaging in pre-marital sexual contact or viewing sex acts,[8] making love, cybersex, blue movies, petting, and necking.

While courting or pre-marital relationships (*pacaran*) were seen as *pergaulan bebas*, they were not assumed to involve or connote *free sex*. Interestingly, the students also grouped abortion and pregnancy under *pergaulan bebas* and not *free sex*. They explained that pregnancy and abortion do not constitute *free sex*; rather, these are consequences (*akibat*) of *free sex*. The consequences of *free sex* were therefore included in the overall meaning of *pergaulan bebas*, locating consequences in the wider, hierarchical social networks of accountability. Here we see the concern with premarital sex as *pergaulan bebas*, particularly as it relates to gendered consequences for female youth and others, especially parents and family.

The apparent concern with *pergaulan bebas* as a threat to contemporary youth is consistent with the ways in which the students in the AAI survey responded to the question: "What are your aspirations for the future?" (*Apa cita-cita anda di masa depan?*). Respondents highlighted the value they placed on family and community. The highest aspiration for the future was the entwined notions of *berguna* (to be of use/of purpose), *berbakti* (to be devoted, especially to parents), and *orang sukses* (to be a successful person) at 19 percent, followed by doctor at 13.5 percent.[9] These responses are consistent with the valuing of social and community relations implicit in the notion of *rukun* (harmony). The values of *berguna* and *berbakti* are inculcated from birth through the *syukuran* (gratitude) prayers of family, schools, and religious institutions. The consistency of responses in relation to the question on future aspirations in the survey highlight that parental-generation values received through public discourses, which emphasize adherence to social norms and community values, have a strong hold on the consciousness of Indonesian high school youth and wield greater influence than aspirations for personal (or career) success. In contrast to the pervasive view noted by Suryakusuma (2004) that "tradition" in Indonesia is at serious risk of being lost among the younger

---

8   Bennett (2007, 373) explains that:
    For middle class Indonesian youth who are affluent and have ready access to global media and consumerist lifestyles, the positive association between *seks bebas*, individual freedom and modernity appears to be the strongest. *Seks bebas* is a term now in common usage that functions as an umbrella label for the varied forms of sexual activity that occur outside the bounds of sanctioned heterosexual marriages, and are thus thought to be socially deviant or immoral. It encompasses premarital and extramarital sex, prostitution and homosexual relationships.

9   "To be of purpose" was always expressed in relation to religion and the nation, "to be devoted" was always expressed in relation to parents.

generation, it appears this group of high school students negotiate the choices they make in their rapidly changing social context in relation to parental and community values and to local customs (*adat*) (Buttenheim and Nobles 2009, 277). That is, their expressed aspiration indicated conformity with broader social and parental norms.

"Normal" to "Choice" Biographies?

This chapter will explore how female Indonesian youth narrate their subjective interpretations and negotiations of *pergaulan bebas* discourses. I draw upon Yoon's (2006) methodological concept of "normal" and "choice" biographies[10] in looking at cultural practices in transitions to adulthood in her research among "ordinary" Korean youth. "Normal" biographies represent the predictable move from youth to adulthood, through education, work, and family formation; "choice" biographies represent the opening up of alternative possibilities for self-construction in the modern world. In Korea "local norms of sociality are embedded in the process of becoming adults, while young people's aspiration to academic achievement is also pursued" (Yoon 2006, 385). Education is seen as a means to avert the risk of uncertainty in relation to the future beyond school. Through education, the possibility of "choice" biographies and the transition into adulthood of Korean youth were delayed, because they involved uncertainty and a risky transition into the labor market (ibid, 394).

Indonesian youth are identified as student subjects in government and public discourse. Education has high symbolic value as a mode of mobility in Indonesia and this reflected the government requirement (since 1994) for nine years of education. The familial and social desires of *remaja* (youth of high school age), 82 percent of whom in the Yogyakarta survey sample lived with family members, are articulated in their conservative views on morality as advocated in the discourse of *pergaulan bebas*. Among the *remaja* I interviewed in schools, *pergaulan bebas* was generally defined as social interactions: "that don't respect the rules"; "which forget religious codes"; and "are not monitored closely by parents".[11]

As Yoon (2006, 385) suggests, younger youth generally choose to follow a "normal biography" in attempt to maintain links to the family and ward off the insecurities that the future holds. The AAI survey results found that high school youth articulate "normal" gendered biographies and this was consistent with

---

10 These terms were originated by Ulrich Beck.
11 Students interviewed most often referred to these glosses for *pergaulan bebas*.

their acceptance of the normative prohibitions of the discourse of *pergaulan bebas*. They used terms like "fortress" (*benteng*) and *"filter"* (selective filter) to describe protective moral/personal defenses against the impact of globalization and negative influence of friends, and the role of parents. Many saw parents as moral guardians and protectors of their offspring, especially before their marriage, and their family values were strong. There is a general concern across generations that *remaja* and older youth (*anak muda*) are at risk of cultural and moral weakening from the unfiltered impact of foreign culture, which will lead them to adopt what are constructed as Western values and practices; in particular, liberal attitudes to sexuality.

Feri, 17, Catholic

Feri, from Sulawesi, is in Yogya completing high school at a single sex Catholic boarding school and shares a room with three other girls. Her father is a civil servant and her mother runs a shop at the front of their house. Her sister conceived a child out of wedlock and was disowned by the family after her boyfriend refused to marry her. Feri was upset with her mother over this and cried during our interview. Feri has shortish hair, wears distinctly baggy clothing, and describes herself as a basketball lover (*pecinta basket*) and "not straight" (*belok*). Feri associated the behaviors of *pergaulan bebas* such as "drugs" and "sex" as potentially life changing, as she witnessed with her sister. Similar to the concerns of many youth, she feared what she deemed to be the permanent and irreversible effects of engaging in sex and drugs; of becoming "damaged". She commented

> *Pergaulan bebas* is interactions with people who like drugs and sex. In the beginning they are an ordinary person but after interacting (*bergaul*) with someone who is into it (*rusak*) they too become like that (*rusak*).

Discursive and social practices that posit the behaviors of *pergaulan bebas* as negative and totalizing in their effects, together with notions of the "right" and "wrong" paths, have widespread influence on the attitudes and behaviors of young people and are often uncritically internalized. In expressing "normal" biographies, teenage youth articulate a dependence on others, and articulate the belief that parents, schools, and the government must assume greater responsibility in their lives to minimize the potential risks, particularly from pre-marital sex.

Ika, 17, Muslim

Ika was born in Yogya. Since the death of her father she has lived with her aunt. Her mother lives and works in another city and visits weekly to drop off money. Ika feels she has little opportunity to relate to her mother —"I don't get enough attention from my mother". Ika is studying to be a seamstress and in her spare time plays volleyball, basketball, and guitar. On Saturday nights she hangs out with friends near Gajah Mada University. She loves Indonesian soap operas and Harry Potter books. Many of her friends in high school in Jakarta smoked cannabis, a practice Ika believed would have a negative impact on Indonesia's future generally. A few of her friends fell pregnant in junior high school and although they wanted to terminate their pregnancies, felt this was too sinful and married. This meant their withdrawal from education which Ika judged as "tragic!" "The government does not direct youth so that their social interactions are right (*benar*) and not depraved (*rusak*). That's what I want to see, especially information at school so that youth don't take the wrong path (*salah jalan*)".

The distinctions between *remaja* and *anak muda* in Indonesia mark the transition from high school to tertiary education or work, and often a shift away from family, with greater autonomy, personal responsibility, and self-management. In the interviews I conducted in Yogyakarta with young people from these social age groupings, the older *anak muda* were more likely to express their aspirations as choice biographies and this was reflected in a different response to the discourse of "*pergaulan bebas*". Differences in "normal" and "choice" biographies also reflected differences in religious orthodoxy, educational level, reflexivity, and the level of personal autonomy in managing their daily lives.

The "biographies" of *anak muda* are contingent on greater physical mobility, self-reliance, and independence, and a more personalized belief and religious morality. While they are to a greater extent "choice" biographies, these choices are always negotiated in engagement with the wider social hierarchy and gendered norms. Older than *remaja*, they must assume greater responsibility for their actions. Often living away from the parental home, many manage their educational, work, personal, spiritual, and financial affairs independently. The diversity of their views shows differences in attitudes to changes in youth sociality according to "local context and subcultural identity" (Yoon 2006, 375).

I now turn to four vignettes of female *anak muda* selected to represent the diversity of views in relation to the negotiation of the behaviors of *pergaulan bebas* in the 18–25 age group.

Fatma, 22, Muslim

Fatma, 22, from Medan, Sumatra, lives in a *kos* (student boarding house) with nine others and studies economics. Her parents are retired traders in Medan. Her older sister works thirteen hour days in a clothing export factory in Jakarta to pay for Fatma's education. In her first six months in Yogyakarta, Fatma supported herself selling clothing to friends, making Rp 900,000 (AUD $90) per month (slightly more than her sister now sends). Despite her business acumen, her sister advised her; "if you have already seen money, you won't be happy studying". Fatma agreed to concentrate solely on her undergraduate studies before working to fund her Masters degree.

Fatma's views are orthodox. She wears a *jilbab* (tight veil, covering head and neck) in public and positions herself as sharing a common experience with other female Muslim students living away from home. Her comments emphasize the challenges of living far from family and the difficulties in limiting one's desires:

> *Pergaulan bebas* means we aren't following the rules of religion. For those of us who have a religion, within it, rules were handed down by Allah. We have already contravened them. *Pergaulan bebas* means outside the order of things as they flow from law. The most extreme example is abortion. Among students, while there are those who want to control themselves, in reality, we are far from family and must manage alone. As a result, there are many abortions due to pregnancy outside marriage. In my opinion this occurs because we don't limit our desires (*keinginan*), sometimes we lust (*nafsu*). According to my teachings, *pacaran* (intimacy with the opposite sex) is not permitted because of the risk of sexual sin (*mendekati zina*). If we break the rules by being too close to someone of the opposite sex, over time we may want (*pengen*) a kiss and…all are the temptations of Satan.

Fatma points out the challenges of self-management in a city where so many options are available, and which seem to be normalized. She contrasts life in Sumatra with that in Java as "very different. This is a city of education and students. It is not what I thought it would be like. Here it seems *pergaulan bebas* is a tradition in every boarding house, and among the students. We, who once may have been quite principled, can slacken".

For her, as a devout Muslim, observing one's desires but not acting on them is imperative. Interestingly, she uses the informal word *pengen* (to want/desire) in reference to the desire for a kiss. Despite the official Islamic discourse of her teachings that rules out *pacaran*, and kissing, because of the risk of sinning (*mendekati zina*), Fatma does have a *pacar*, Ari, also from Sumatra, who she met in Yogyakarta. Ari takes her to and from university some days. They eat out together, go to the mall, to town, and further afield on day trips.

Ajeng, 19, Muslim

Ajeng is from Samarinda, East Kalimantan. Her father is a policeman and her mother "just a housewife". She studies makeup artistry (*rias*) and lives in a *kos* with a strict curfew. Male visitors are permitted only on the terrace. She has a *pacar* who has had sex with a previous girlfriend. They share a mutual "commitment" (*komitmen*), though she describes their friendship as "not serious at all"—she does not consent to sex. He is a *"ttm"* (*teman tapi mesra*—romantic friend). She admits that there is sometimes jealousy or possessiveness (*cemburu*) between her and her *pacar* if they are seeing others as well, so they "consider what the jealousy means first" before reacting. Seeing others is part of their search for the most compatible (*cocok*) partner, and as such they try not to limit each other's social lives. Ajeng makes the point that she needs a *pacar*:

> *Pacaran* gives us someone to go out with, 'cos now if we didn't have a *pacar* what would we do? If asked by friends "do you have a *pacar*?" (and you don't), you feel alone. To not have one at this age, what is that? Staying home on Saturday night…if we don't have a boyfriend we can feel envious inside (*iri dalam hati*). How come she's got one and I can't seem to get one? What's so great about her? You know! That makes you feel bad (*buruk di hati*). Saturday night without a boyfriend is no fun and that's all there is to it!

Although Ajeng states that she does not have sex with her current *pacar*, she believes that her views on sex are quite different from those of her female friends. Ajeng says she lives by abstinence, but agrees with the practice of consensual "safe" sex.[12] "*Pergaulan bebas*, I don't have a problem with it if it is safe sex (*aman*)…if we do it and are aware of the health issues. If people mutually agree to it, then why not? The main thing is to guard against (*menjaga*) the negative issues, and that is indeed difficult".

---

12   The expression "free but safe" (*bebas tapi aman*) is used by those practicing safe sex with condoms. Condom use eliminates involuntary disclosure of their behaviors and perhaps infidelities by minimizing the risk of harmful and unwanted consequences such as disease and pregnancy.

"*Aman*" (safe) is often used, in reference to heterosexual relations, to mean sex with condoms in the prevention of conception, or, as Crisovan (2006, 85) found, to refer to sexual practices that do not penetrate the vagina.[13] Sex is made safe from any unwanted consequences such as unplanned or unwanted pregnancy (*Kehamilan tak Dihendaki* or *KTD*),[14] termination of education, and early marriage. The need to be "aware of the health issues" that Ajeng suggests assumes availability of comprehensive sex education yet to be realized in Indonesia (Utomo and McDonald 2009).

Meme (below), who also has a boyfriend, explained her reason for abstinence as explicitly related to the view that a young woman's virginity is the source of her bargaining power, both in terms of procuring a husband and to ensure that within the marriage one is not subject to accusations of pre-martial sexual sinfulness, and of being "used goods" (*barang bekas*). Like many other interviewees, she recalled the trope of blood on the sheets on wedding night as proof of a female's virginity.

> Here many kids are "free styling" (*bebas langgam*) and marrying a guy who is not the one they lost their virginity to. They lose their sense of happiness because their husband does not approve of the fact that they were not virgins at marriage. That is common. So I guard what I have because it is all I have. I can't work yet and have no income. Personally, I feel that my life will be meaningless if I don't have that, because I don't have anything, I have nothing to rely on. My virginity is my only capital.
> MEME, 19, MUSLIM, SOLO

Eka, 21, Muslim

Eka is from Yogyakarta and studies English. She was the only one of the interviewees who openly lived unwed with her boyfriend. She was dubbed a "material girl" (*cewek materi*) by fellow students because of her penchant for European men, her expensive tastes, and desire for international travel. Her peers told me she sold sex on campus (*ayam kampus*).[15] She lived with her English

---

13 Alexander (1986) identified non-coital sex as a common practice amongst Javanese husbands and wives as a form of birth spacing prior to the introduction of modern contraceptives.
14 KTD is an acronym for *Kehamilan yang Tidak Direncanakan/Diinginkan/Dihendaki*.
15 *Ayam kampus* (campus chicken) refers specifically to female students who engage in paid sex work on or off campus.

boyfriend, John, 15 years her senior. Intending to marry in the future, they lived in a large fenced "streetside" house with little interaction with locals. Eka took great pride in cooking his breakfast before he left for work, and in sweeping and mopping the floors and yard. She noted her refusal to hire a maid, a practice quite customary for the well-to-do, as a sign of her devotion to John. Dinner parties, imported alcohol, clubbing, broadband at home, sex, sleeping in, and Sunday brunches at the mall were a part of Eka's everyday life. She was no stranger to sex toys and international porn MMS.[16] She saw *pergaulan bebas* as relating to high school age youth (*remaja*). Reminiscing, she said,

> *Free sex*, really, this is Yogya! Boys come into the girl's room in the boarding house and even stay the night. They hide when the boarding house manager is doing the inspections (*sweeping*).[17] Although at SMA (senior high school) age they are mainly kissing and are still shy (*malu-malu*), they think it is just heaven if they kiss someone their own age.

In these interviews, these young women more often than not associate *pergaulan bebas* with "free sex". Most prioritize virginity in relation to *pergaulan bebas*. Some of them show more evidence of "choice" biographies than the younger school girls as they negotiate networks of power, particularly in relation to heteronormative gender expectations, religion, mobility, and the body, and choose which path to take. Within these networks of power, female mobility is severely restricted by not having a boyfriend. Indeed, Ajeng saw her sense of self bound to her desirability. For Fatma, consistency in religious orthodoxy in the family, coupled with strong familial support and interdependence among family members (not premised on proximity), while consistent with a "normal" biography, also highlights personal "choice" in that she follows a more orthodox Islamic path than many of her friends. There are situations in which a disarticulation of religious belief and practice is revealed. Fatma knows *pacaran* is not acceptable according to conservative interpretations of Islamic doctrine. Given the freedoms of the city, she navigates her own level of religiosity, observing for the most part the religious limitations on her body—she sometimes wants to kiss, but resists. Meme, who believes her virginity to be her only guarantee of future wedded happiness, said she does allow kissing. For Feri, who assumes a more masculine gender subjectivity, pre-marital sex poses less personal risk, while for Eka exploring sexuality is an exciting part of the

---

16   MMS—abbreviation of Media Message Service through mobile phones.
17   *Sweeping* refers to raids, or the practice of eliminating vice, such as pornography, prostitution, music piracy, drugs, alcohol, and pre- or extra-marital sexual relations.

process of growing up in the city. Apart from Eka, who is, for the most part, living a relatively Westernized lifestyle, the developing "choice" biographies of these young women highlight that despite differences in religiosity, ethnicity, education level, and social circumstances, normative gendered religious and social expectations and constraints shape the way they both construct their experience and socially engage.

Normatively gendered religious and social expectations and the constraints these imply were deconstructed in two university student focus group discussions on *pergaulan bebas*. The first group were youth counsellors at the PKBI (Perkumpulan Keluarga Berencana Indonesia—Family Planning Association of Indonesia), aged 20–25, who came from across the archipelago to study in Yogyakarta. They volunteer as telephone and face-to-face counsellors and peer educators in schools, and were well versed in human rights and gender equity discourse. The second group were students of International Relations at a state university. Both student groups were more critical of social norms not relevant to them, and less inclined to subscribe uncritically to normative sex/gender standards. Many saw the discourse around *pergaulan bebas* as hypocritical. Their comments show sensitivity to the gendered nature of the prohibitions associated with the negative views of *pergaulan bebas* (which was perhaps encapsulated in the AAI survey in which girls were more likely than boys to see *pergaulan bebas* as of concern for youth). As one of the female university students put it, "*Pergaulan bebas* is a limit of religion. If I, as a female, have many male friends, that's *pergaulan bebas*" (Nur, 22).

Amidst the rhetoric of human and sexual rights and the prioritization of the sanctity of virginity, marriage and marital fidelity, the normalization of male infidelity in everyday discourse[18] is unsettling to female youth, most of whom aspire to marry and have children. One student argued: "Why are wives getting HIV/AIDS? Because their husbands are having sex with other women. That's a free relationship (*hubungan/pergaulan bebas*)!" (Uni, 21, female, PKBI.)

The hypocrisy of the parent's generation and the rhetoric of *pergaulan bebas anak muda* come under further scrutiny:

> I don't like the term *pergaulan bebas* because usually youth are the scapegoats, (*jadi kambing hitam*, literally "black goat") when in fact it is all people, of all ages, both those who are married and those not yet married

---

18   The expectation of pre-martial sexual experience for males and tolerance of their sexual promiscuity has been documented by anthropologists since the 1960s (see Geertz 1961, 119; Jay 1969, 121).

who do it. It is a poor and misleading (*menyesatkan*) term that forces a specific group into a corner (*memojokan*).

ANI, 23, FEMALE, PKBI

In concluding the comments made in this Focus Group discussion, the senior male counsellor stated unequivocally:

> There is no *pergaulan bebas*. It is constructed by society, by the system. If there are acts that are not in accordance with society, for example one night stands, multiple partners, sex before marriage, and such things, they are considered not socially appropriate, too free and not good. But it is in fact up to the individual. If they want to do it, it's because they take responsibility (*bertanggung jawab*) and they know the risks (*tahu risikonya*), they know the consequences and don't disturb others...it doesn't exist.
>
> LEO, 24, MALE, PKBI

Ideals aside, the reality is that not all youth are equipped with the sexual and reproductive health knowledge to engage in sex such that they take responsibility, or know the risks and the possible future consequences of their behaviors.

These Focus Group discussions revealed a view that *pergaulan bebas* is a discourse that scapegoats youth when in fact people of all ages engage in the behaviors implicated in the discourse—especially sexual behavior. The "moral panic" discourse presumes that *pergaulan bebas* is limited to *anak muda*, and that this risky behavior will come to an end when they arrive at marriage and the social age of "adult"—even if youth engage in behaviors that transcend social norms, they will grow out of it. In framing *pergaulan bebas* as a youth issue, limited to age parameters that will be outgrown (at marriage), the issues of educational deficits in relation to reproductive health and sex education in Indonesia remain insufficiently addressed.

The Focus Group participants expressed their response to the "moral panic" discourse in terms of assertion of the value and necessity of "choice biographies".

> *Anak muda*...live with a million desires, have a million things they want to do. They want change from the norms made by people in the past (*zaman dulu*). They do what they want to do. In my opinion, what they do is not *pergaulan bebas*, they just do what they want to do.
>
> NIKI, 23, FEMALE

> If they are religious or not, if they want to preserve their virginity, take drugs or drink and conceal it, it is personal.
>
> RIRIN, 20, FEMALE

These comments reject the negative and repressive discourse of *pergaulan bebas*. These young people are aware of the prohibitions of the discourse which place particular restrictions on female bodies. They show awareness of the ways in which religion works through gender norms and expectations to control and monitor the behavior of female youth. They problematize preconceived notions of Indonesian social norms, rigid conceptions of culture and religiosity and fears of contamination by the West, as we saw in the quote from Niki that opens this paper. Homogenizing interpretations of culture and subjectivity are countered as antithetical to their realities. Constructions of what is deemed normative are seen as of the past—*jadul* (*jaman dulu*, of a previous era)[19] or *kuno* (old-fashioned). In their choice biographies, values are considered personal rather than being adopted uncritically from those around them, and behavior is a private choice and does not require any explanation to others. They do, however, find social/community harmony critical. Like generations of Indonesians before them, these young adults embrace socio-cultural change itself as normative, as their right. They are agents in the process of cultural change. Rather than viewing their choices as a craving for the West, they embrace all that they perceive to be on offer and express their desires while critically engaging the historical legacies of the nation.

Conclusion

Pergaulan bebas emerged as an issue of concern to the *remaja* surveyed by the AAI project, and their responses echoed the "moral panic" framing of youth constructed as at risk. The consumer market and its central vehicle, the media, perform the paradoxical co-functions of promoting socio-cultural change, advocating active pre-marital youth sexualities and same-sex relationships, reinforcing dominant narratives such as *pergaulan bebas*, and introducing new and more liberal sexual narratives. Active sexuality, particularly for unwed females however, prioritizes pleasure over reproductive fertility and is threatening to the hegemony of hetero-normativity and the patriarchal structures of the family, the village, religion, and the state. In response, state and religious

---

19   The word *jadul* (of the past/old hat) is an amalgam of the two words *jaman* (era) and *dulu* (past).

bodies maintain a reluctance to address the changing sexual mores through significant health educational and reproductive health service policies. Public discourse constructs "traditional" structures and practices for personal and family life in opposition to the increased freedom of interactions among Indonesia's youth. Interviews with young people, however, indicated that *remaja* still express their aspirations in terms of the "normal" biography endorsed by the parental generation and secular and religious leaders, while young adults (*anak muda*) were less concerned about reconciling "choice" biographies in relation to sexuality and relationships with an (selective) endorsement of religious and societal norms. The delayed onset of adulthood, signified by marriage, contributes to the development of this critical facility and makes space for the exercise of individual choice. In the flux and fluidity of the new millennia, the discourse of *pergaulan bebas* holds within it the potentiality for the opening up new forms of resistance to societal norms.

References

Adamson, C. 2007. *Gendered anxieties: Islam, women's rights and moral hierarchy in Java*, MUSE. http://muse.jhu.edu, accessed May 2, 2010.

Alexander, P. 1986. "Labor Expropriation and Fertility: Population Growth in Nineteenth Century Java." In *Culture and Reproduction*, edited by W.P. Handwerker, 249–62. Boulder: Westview Press.

Appadurai, A., 1996. *Modernity at Large*. Minneapolis and London: University of Minnesota Press.

Bellows, L.J. 2003. "Like the West: New Sexual Practices and Modern Threats to Balinese-ness." *Review of Indonesian and Malaysian Affairs* 37:71–105.

Bennett, L.R. 2007. "Zina and the Enigma of Sex Education for Indonesian Muslim Youth." *Sex Education* 7:371–86.

Boellstorff, T. 2007. *A Coincidence of Desires: Anthropology, Queer Studies, Indonesia*. Durham and London: Duke University Press.

Brenner, S. 1999. "On the Public Intimacy of the New Order: Images of Women in the Popular Indonesian Print Media." *Indonesia* 67:13–37.

Brenner, S. 1995. "Why Women Rule the Roost: Rethinking Javanese Ideologies of Gender and Self-control." In *Bewitching Men and Pious Women: Gender and Body Politics in Southeast Asia*, edited by A. Ong and A. Peletz, 19–50. California and London: University of California Press.

Brenner, S. 1998. *The Domestication of Desire: Women, Wealth and Modernity in Java*. New Jersey: Princeton University Press.

Buttenheim A. M., and J. Nobles. 2009. "Ethnic-Based Nuptial Regimes and Marriage Behaviour." *Population Studies* 63:277–294.

Crisovan, P. 2006. "'Risky business': Cultural conceptions of HIV/AIDS in Indonesia." PhD diss., University of Toledo.

Farrer, J. 2002. *Opening up: Youth Sex Culture and Market Reform in Shanghai.* Chicago and London: University of Chicago Press.

Geertz, H. 1961. *The Javanese Family: A Study of Kinship and Socialization.* New York: The Free Press of Glencoe.

Guinness, P. 1986. *Harmony and Hierarchy in a Javanese Kampung.* Oxford and New York: Oxford University Press.

Gusti Kanjeng Ratu Hemas. 1992. *Wanita Indonesia: Suatu Konsepsi dan Obsesi* (Indonesian Women: A Conception and Obsession). Yogyakarta: Liberty.

Jay, R. 1969. *Javanese Villagers: Social Relations in Rural Modjokuto.* Cambridge: The MIT Press.

Knight, J., and S. Chapman. 2004. "'Asian Yuppies…Are Always Looking for Something New and Different': Creating a Tobacco Culture among Young Asians." *Tobacco Control* 13:22–29.

McRobbie, A., and S.L. Thornton. 1995. Rethinking "Moral Panic" for Multi-Mediated Social Worlds. *British Journal of Sociology* 46:559–74.

Nichter, M., S. Padmawati, Y. Prabandari, N. Ng, M. Danardono, and M. Nichter. 2009. "Reading Culture from Tobacco Advertizements in Indonesia." *Tobacco Control* 18:98–107.

Nilan, P, L Parker, L Bennett, and K Robinson. 2011. "Indonesian Youth Looking Towards the Future." *Journal of Youth Studies* 14:709–28.

Reynolds, C. 1999. "Tobacco Advertizing in Indonesia: The Defining Characteristics for Success." *Tobacco Control* 8:85–88.

Robinson, K. 2008. *Gender, Islam and Democracy in Indonesia.* London and New York: Routledge.

Smith-Hefner, N.J. 2007. "Youth Language, Gaul Sociability, and the New Indonesian Middle Class." *Journal of Linguistic Anthropology* 17:184–203.

Suryakusuma, J. 2004. *Sex, Power and Nation: An Anthology of Writings, 1979–2003.* Jakarta: Metafor Publishing.

Utomo, Iwu Dewisetyani and P. McDonald. 2009. "Adolescent Reproductive Health in Indonesia: Contested Values and Policy Inaction." *Studies in Family Planning* 40:133–46.

Wright Webster, T. 2010. "Pergaulan Bebas and Gendered Youth Culture in Yogyakarta, Indonesia." PhD diss., University of Western Australia.

Yoon, K. 2006. "Cultural Practices of 'Ordinary' Youth: Transitions to Adulthood in South Korea." *Asian Studies Review* 30:375–88.

CHAPTER 12

Young Sasak Mothers—"*Tidak Manja Lagi*": Transitioning from Single Daughter to Young Married Mother in Lombok, Eastern Indonesia

Linda Rae Bennett

To date, early marriage and early childbearing in Indonesia have received limited academic attention and the actual experiences and identities of young mothers have attracted even less enquiry.[1] There is a rich and expanding body of work on Indonesian youth, yet those young people who marry while still in adolescence have escaped the attention of researchers seeking to map the experiences, identities, and positions of youth across the archipelago.[2] This chapter seeks to advance the limited ethnographic work on early motherhood by presenting the perspectives of young mothers in Lombok on what it means to be both "young" and a "mother". In doing so it also advances the scope of research on early motherhood in non-western contexts, balancing the predominantly western-based perspectives on the subject. By exploring how young women experience their transitions into motherhood, this work extends our understanding of young people and their social worlds in Indonesia.[3] Young mothers occupy social worlds that are shaped around their parenting roles and identities, which are in turn heavily influenced by family constellations and obligations. These social worlds differ from those inhabited by many Indonesian youth, which include schools and popular sites for the consumption of Indonesian modernity, such as malls, night spots, trendy food outlets, and peer groups (see Nilan, this volume).

---

1 This is with the exception of a few notable works including commentary on historical and political debates over early motherhood in Indonesia by Blackburn (2004), and Blackburn and Bessell (1997), demographic work on age of marriage by Jones and Gubhaju (2008), as well as a comparative study of early marriage and motherhood between Nepal and Indonesia by Choe, Thapa and Achmad (2001).
2 For recent scholarship on Indonesian youth, see the edited works of Manderson and Liamputtong (2002), Robinson and Utomo (2003) and Parker and Bennett (2008).
3 This research was conducted as part a larger project on the experiences of adolescents in Indonesia, the Ambivalent Adolescents Project (henceforth AAI), Chief Investigators Lynette Parker, Linda Rae Bennett, Pamela Nilan and Kathryn Robinson. This larger project involved extensive ethnographic research by collaborators, as well as a school-based survey of 3565 Indonesian youth across nine sites, which I will refer to as the AAI survey.

There is an overarching assumption in research and policy on early motherhood that there is a "right time" and "right framework" in which women should become mothers, and these are culturally and historically specific (Holgate, Evans, and Yuen 2006, 20). This chapter teases out how, in the cultural milieu of Lombok, dominant understandings of womanhood and motherhood support rather than deter young women from marrying and becoming mothers during adolescence. Despite the persistent increases in women's participation in formal education and paid labor, the continuing preference for marriage and motherhood among Indonesian women has also been observed to be stronger than for women in other Southeast Asian nations (Jones 2004).

While this chapter focuses on a case study of early motherhood in the eastern Indonesian province of Nusa Tengara Barat (NTB), and the island of Lombok in particular, the persistence of early marriage and adolescent motherhood is normative among Indonesian women from poor backgrounds throughout the archipelago. Analysis of the 2007 Indonesian Demographic Health Survey (IDHS) confirms that the prevalence of teenage motherhood among women aged 15 to 19 years was 50% in a sample of 845 women, and that the prevalence of teenage motherhood among adult women was 60% in a sample of 29,959 older women (Desriani 2011). This indicated a 10% reduction in the prevalence of teenage motherhood over a decade, but also highlighted that early marriage and adolescent child bearing in Indonesia are not rare. Furthermore, as the IDHS does not include women under 15 years of age, rates of early marriage and adolescent motherhood may well be underrepresented. Analysis of IDHS data also provides insight into the determinants of adolescent motherhood and its strong association with poverty in Indonesia. Low educational attainment among young married women is directly associated with higher levels of adolescent childbearing, with young women who have not completed primary school being three times more likely to become mothers during their teens (Nasril and Samosir 2011). Both young women's and their husband's employment status also had a statistically significant relationship with early motherhood, with young women being three times more likely to become pregnant during adolescence if they were unemployed, and 2.5 times more likely to become pregnant if their husbands were unemployed (ibid). Place of residence is also significant in encouraging early motherhood, with young women living in rural areas being 1.4 times more likely to experience teenage pregnancy than their urban peers (Prasetya and Dasvarma 2011).[4]

---

4 These findings in Indonesia are consistent with previous international studies that have focused on early motherhood in poorly developed settings, and iterate the widely accepted understanding that low formal education for girls, limited employment opportunities, and

The young Indonesian mothers whose experiences feature in this chapter are Sasak and all are Muslim. The Sasak are the indigenous inhabitants of the eastern Indonesian island of Lombok, where they constitute around 90 per cent of the island's population of approximately 3.5 million people, but their socio-economic and political marginalization is well documented (Judd 1980; Grace 1997). Lombok is characterized by a comparatively low level of development relative to elsewhere in Indonesia; in 2009, when this data was collected, the province of NTB had an official human development index (HDI) of 0.641, the second lowest out of 33 provinces (Papua being the lowest at 0.640), while the national HDI was reported as 0.720 (BPS 2010). Among secondary students in Lombok who participated in the AAI survey, a greater percentage than in any other province listed their parents occupation as farmers, while a smaller percentage than all other provinces reported owning a mobile phone or having access to a computer at home. These regional differences point to the relative economic underdevelopment in which Sasak youth negotiate their adolescent years and the constricted opportunities available to them both during and after adolescence in comparison with those of the burgeoning population of middle-class youth in large Indonesian cities.

Comparative international studies have found that levels of development have a measurable impact on age at marriage and childbearing, with women living in more developed areas marrying and commencing reproduction later (Choe, Taupa and Achmand 2001). Indeed, early marriage and child bearing among rural Sasak has persisted for longer than is the case among people from neighboring islands (Government of Indonesia 2007).[5]

While conducting research with young Sasak mothers, I focused on their reproductive health and the health of their children, as well as their social transitions into motherhood. Extensive research into early pregnancy and childbearing has established the considerable health risks for both mothers and babies when women become pregnant under the age of 20, and that these risks are more pronounced for women who conceive before the age of 17 (Population Reports 2005). Elsewhere I have discussed the health implications of early childbearing for Sasak women through a detailed human rights analysis of early marriage and adolescent motherhood in Lombok (Bennett 2014).

---

residence in rural and remote communities all escalate the risk of early marriage and adolescent motherhood (Choe et al. 2001).

5 Recent research into reproductive rights in the province of Nusa Tengarra Barat (NTB) where Lombok is situated, indicated that 40 percent of a sample of 504 women had been married before the age of 18 and that 23 percent of 504 women had given birth to their first child by the age of 18 (MOH 2009).

Here my focus is on explaining how and why young women marry and become mothers early, and on exploring their transitions from single daughters to young married mothers.

Initially I describe my dialogue with young mothers during five months of ethnographic fieldwork, conducted between July 2008 and August 2009. My analysis of this research builds upon 20 years of researching health issues among Sasak women. I explore the nexus between young mothers' identities and their experiences of disadvantage to reveal a distinct synergy between adolescent marriage, early motherhood, and poverty among the Sasak. Having established how and why early motherhood persists for Sasak women, I then explore the divergence between young women's expectations of marriage and motherhood and the realities, and reveal how their transitions from daughters to mothers follows a common pattern of shrinking social worlds. In my analysis of young mothers' experiences I apply the concept of "social age", which refers to "the social meanings and roles ascribed to different stages in the human life cycle" (Clark-Kazak 2014), to highlight how social rather than chronological age is more salient for appreciating the ways in which young Sasak mothers self-identify as distinct from their in-school peers.

Speaking About, and with, Young Mothers

In this chapter, I use the terms "young mothers", "early motherhood", and "adolescent marriage" to describe my respondents and their experiences. I define "young mothers" as those women who gave birth before the age of 20. I have opted not to use popular terms often found in the western literature on young mothers, such as "teen mothers", "school girl mothers", or "children who have children" because they are an uneasy fit in the Indonesian context. When a woman becomes a mother in Lombok (as is the case for much of Indonesia) her primary social status is determined by the fact that she is a mother. Adulthood is predicated on parenthood, so the notion of a "child-mother" or a "child who has a child" is culturally illogical. The label "school girl mother" also has little resonance in Indonesia, as school girls who are known to be pregnant typically drop out of school or are expelled, even though some do manage to pursue their education at a later point. I prefer the terms "young mothers" and "early motherhood" because they are more open to interpretation (Holgate, Evans, and Yuen 2006, 110) and I believe embody less of a sense of moral judgement on young mothers than is the case with other terms.

While "teenage pregnancy" is a popular term in media discourses on the dangers faced by Indonesian youth, and is often over-used in the moral panic surrounding *pergaulan bebas* (free association) and *free seks* (free sex), the term "teenage mother/s" is surprisingly absent.[6] Again, this reflects the incompatibility between the idealized Indonesian notion of the female *remaja* (teenager) as a dependent, chaste, diligent, middle-class school girl[7] and the normative cultural ideal of a mother as an adult who is responsible for her child's welfare. The majority of pregnant adolescents who become mothers are married by the time that they do so, thus rendering the social identity of *remaja* obsolete through marriage. I use the term "adolescent marriage" to refer to marriages that occurred when women were between the ages of 13 and 19 years, considered to be *masih belasan* (still in their teen years).

28 young Sasak mothers from west Lombok shared their perspectives on marriage, motherhood, and maternal and child health.[8] They were aged between 15 and 25, and their ages at first marriage were between 14 and 19 years. 24 out of 28 women resided with their husbands. Four had divorced and returned with their children to live with their own parents. The majority were living with their husbands' families as is customary, and none were living as independent single mothers, as is often the case in western societies. The age at which these young mothers delivered their first child ranged from 14 to 20 years, and they had a total of 31 children, of whom 27 were still living.

All the women in this study were from impoverished families, regardless of whether they resided in urban or rural communities. Their monthly household incomes ranged from zero cash up to 1 million *rupiah* (Indonesian currency), with most between 400,000 and 700,000 *rupiah*.[9] Only two women were able to describe their husband's employment as secure and ongoing. Many described significant periods of economic hardship due to regular cycles of unemployment, resulting from the contract nature of construction work and the seasonal nature of agricultural labor. Seven out of 28 young mothers had participated in paid work since the birth of their children and none of them earned more than 20,000 *rupiah* per day (AU$2.80).

---

6 Harding (2008) provides a thorough critique of the moral panic around teenage sexuality in contemporary Indonesia, including the fear of pre-marital sex and pregnancy for teenage girls.

7 See Handajani's (2008) discussion of the idealized femininity promoted for Indonesian teenagers in teen magazines.

8 Where I have integrated young mothers' voices in my discussion I have their explicit consent to do so. However, the identities of individual women have been obscured by the use of pseudonyms or omission of names when using direct quotes. Permission to publish the photographs include in this chapter was also given by the young women in the images.

9 At the time of fieldwork AU$1 was equal to 7,500 Indonesian *rupiah*.

Their educational attainment was low, although all were literate. Sixteen young mothers had left school at primary level, indicating a serious shortfall in Indonesia's current national education policy of assuring a minimum of nine years schooling, or the completion of junior high school, for all citizens (Jones and Hagul 2001). A further 12 women had begun junior high school, and of these eight had graduated. Out of this eight only four were successful in completing senior high school. Every young mother I spoke with asserted the desire to be more highly educated, and was explicit that they wanted their own children to be more educated than themselves. Their educational aspirations were transferred to their children, as they all perceived education as the key to "*masa depan lebih cerah*" (a brighter future) for the next generation.[10] The educational levels of their husbands tended to be parallel with or slighter higher than their own.

The young mothers who participated in this research were from three communities situated in the municipality of West Lombok; ten resided in the urban environment of Mataram (the capital city of Lombok) and 18 lived in two nearby rural communities. Women who had become mothers by the age of 20 were invited to join the research through advertisements posted at primary health clinics, community birthing huts and a community-based organization (CBO) that conducts literacy and education programs for women.

Our initial contact was at focus group discussions, during which most of the mothers were accompanied by their children. Hence, the discussions were highly informal, punctuated by children's chatter, demands on their mothers, and disputes over toys or snacks (see Figure 12.1). My toddler also attended these group discussions and I believe his antics and periodic disruption of my role as facilitator highlighted the shared roles and experiences between me and young Sasak mothers. I suspect the visibility of our commonalities may have been partly responsible for their surprisingly positive response to my invitation to participate in in-depth interviews. At the end of each group discussion one mother was nominated by the group as a contact person responsible for linking me with anyone who wished to meet again for the purposes of an interview. Using a go-between is culturally familiar in Lombok and allows people to decline invitations without losing face or causing offence to an "outsider". Twenty three out of 28 women chose to participate in in-depth interviews, and many requested multiple interviews. Three focus groups were conducted in Indonesian, and interviews were conducted in a mix of Indonesian and Sasak.

---

10 A significant youth trend in Indonesia observed by Nilan et al. (this volume) is the desire and expectation among Indonesian teenagers to achieve upward socio-economic mobility through their successful participation in secondary and tertiary education.

FIGURE 12.1   *Young mothers and their children relaxing after an informal focus group*

In addition to my dialogue with young mothers, I also spoke with nine expert key informants, including: three *bidan* (midwives); two school counsellors; two members of CBO; and two Indonesian development consultants working in the area of maternal health. Fieldwork also included observations of young mothers in their homes and while attending skills-building classes at a local community based organization. Over the time that this fieldwork was conducted I also resided within one of the rural communities included in the research, and thus had the opportunity to become well acquainted with young mothers and their families in that particular village.

The Synergy of Adolescent Marriage, Early Motherhood and Poverty

Early Marriage Among the Sasak
Research in a variety of cultural settings indicates that premarital pregnancy can be a leading cause of early motherhood in impoverished communities, yet this is not the dominant pattern for young Sasak mothers.[11] Premarital sex and

---

11   See Biddlecom, Richard, and Cynthia (2008) for a recent discussion of pregnancy and early school leaving in four Sub-Saharum African nations. Also see Grant and Hallman's (2008) work on pregnancy-related school drop out in South Africa.

pregnancy do occur in Lombok, as is the case elsewhere in Indonesia[12]; however, unplanned premarital pregnancy is not the primary cause of early motherhood in Lombok. Based on interviews with key informants knowledgeable about early motherhood and marriage from multiple sectors including education, health, and development, I estimate that less than 10 percent of young Sasak mothers become pregnant outside of marriage. This is supported by my discussions with young mothers, who I asked to count the number of women in their immediate social world who had recently become pregnant for the first time or had given birth to their first child in the past year. I then asked them to count the number of women who may have been pregnant prior to marriage. This exercise indicated that less than one in ten women who had recently become pregnant or become a mother for the first time were believed by others to have conceived outside of wedlock. Considering the prevalence of gossip surrounding female sexuality, especially premarital sex in these communities, it was surprising to young women themselves that they could actually identify very few peers who had become pregnant before marriage. It is important, however, to note the impossibility of providing a truly accurate measure of premarital pregnancy in Lombok due to the stigma attached to premarital sex and pregnancy for women, which encourages secrecy and typically ensures that single pregnant women are married by the time their children are born.

Poor Sasak women continue to become mothers early largely because they tend to marry early. When I asked them to reflect on why Sasak women, including themselves, tended to marry early, there were four common responses. Each relates to the entrenched poverty in Sasak society. Their responses as to why they married young, in order of frequency, were:

(1) "*sudah berhenti sekolah*" (had already finished schooling),
(2) "*tidak ada pekerjaan*" (there was no work available),
(3) "*tidak ada kegiatan lain*" (there was nothing else to do),
(4) "*harapan hidup sederhana, nikah dan punya anak sudah cukup*" (simple life aspirations, to marry and have children is enough).

Applying a grounded theory approach,[13] I further investigated individual women's decisions on when to marry in interviews. When I asked if she would have

---

12 See Jennaway (2002), Utomo (2002), and Bennett (2005) for case studies and discussions of young Indonesian women's experiences of premarital pregnancy in Bali, Java, and Lombok.
13 A grounded theory approach involves the ongoing analysis of data in layers, which allows key themes and hypothesis to be developed and explored in response to data as it emerges (see Struass and Corbin 1990).

preferred to continue her education prior to marrying, every woman answered in the affirmative. Lack of financial resources was the reason given, by all women, for ending their schooling before they wished to. Their lack of suitable employment options stems from low levels of formal education and restricted skills, and endemic unemployment on the island. The types of paid employment available to poor young women typically yield very low returns. When there are seemingly insurmountable barriers to continuing participation in education and well-paid work for poor adolescent women their experience is that there is literally "nothing else to do". There are no highly valued alternative social roles available to these women other than becoming a wife and mother. Women adopt a pragmatic attitude towards their life aspirations; they are acutely aware of the constrained options that flow on from poverty, low educational attainment, and limited work skills. Thus, to seek a simple life—*hidup sederhana*—where marriage and motherhood are achievable aspirations is an entirely understandable and realistic response.

Research among poor black women in marginalized communities in the United States highlighted the importance for young women of being able to answer the question; "what do you do?" (Dunn 1988, 173). Dunn's research found that for some adolescent women the most viable and socially rewarding answer was; "I am a mother" (1988, 173). When comparing these findings with my own, I am inclined to agree with Ward (1995, 153), who suggests that for some young women adolescent marriage and early pregnancy may be a solution to their problems, rather than being understood as a problem in itself. Moreover, when we consider the persisting social importance of marriage and motherhood in Sasak society, it is highly evident that these two markers carry greater weight in determining a person's social status than biological age does alone. A teenage girl can be socially considered an adult if she is married and a mother, while a single, childless woman in her mid-twenties or even thirties will not be accorded adult status (regardless of her age) until fulfils the social prerequisites of adulthood.

Another motivation for early marriage that stems from entrenched poverty is the potential economic benefits of a good marriage. Parents may wish a daughter to marry early if she has found a prospective spouse who can support her, as they do not want the possibility of their daughter achieving economic safety to be passed by. Young women are explicit that financial stability is an ideal characteristic in a spouse (Bennett 2005). This concern over their economic future is a pragmatic necessity, often expressed in the rhetorical question: *Jika cowoknya belum mampu, nanti anak saya makan apa?* (If the man cannot provide, later what will my children eat?).

One young mother, Rohun, relayed how her husband proposed to her:

Why don't we marry, I have a house of my own, it's empty. Your mother's house if full, there are too many people for her to feed. Why not help your mother and become my wife?

Rohun and her parents were happy to accept this proposal. She married at 15 and gave birth to her first child at 16. Rohun felt very fortunate to find a husband who could provide her with an independent home, and agreed that it did relieve her mother to have one less mouth to feed as there had been 13 people living in her parents' two-room dwelling before she married. Hence, the financial motivations behind an early marriage are often a desire for basic economic security, rather than imagined fantasies of class advancement.

While endemic poverty is undoubtedly the dominant factor perpetuating early marriage among poor Sasak women, local customs also play a role in normalizing early marriage. Arranged marriages are rare and most Sasak choose their own partners. The two most common ways to marry are by the man asking a woman's parents for permission, or via the indigenous custom *kawin lari* (runaway marriage, or elopement). Nine out of 28 women in this study had participated in *kawin lari*. Elopement can be sudden and difficult for women to resist once it has been initiated (Platt 2009), and women's rights advocates in Lombok have expressed concern that *kawin lari* may be a form of forced marriage for some women. Among the women I spoke with, three stated that they were not ready to be married at the time they were "stolen" by their husbands, and thus felt that their marriages were forced on them. When I asked them to explain what they meant by forced, each said that they were not ready at that time, but did wish to marry the man in question. It was clear that these women felt they had no control over when they married. Hence, it appears that the custom of *kawin lari* can contribute to women becoming married young and before they wish to.

Another factor that can propel women into marriage before they are ready is the dominant cultural construction of female sexuality, which insists on female chastity prior to marriage and the confinement of women's sexuality within marriage (Bennett 2005). When young women are thought to be too close to, or to have spent too much time with a suitor, or to have returned home too late from a date, extremely damaging gossip ensues. This gossip distresses and shames girls and their families, and damages marriage prospects. For two women in this study their marriages were pre-empted by the social censure of their premarital sexual behavior, and their parents hastened the marriages to curb negative gossip. Both of these women did want to marry their boyfriends, but both would have preferred to attempt higher education or to find paid work before marrying. Thus, the strong moral aversion to pre-marital sex for women supports early marriage and motherhood among the Sasak. Age politics, or when women marry and have children, is of far less social significance in these communities than the sexual politics of confining female sexuality to marriage. Thus, understanding social age also requires acknowledgement of how social status is mediated by local sexual morality, and how this is applied differently to young women and men.

Adolescent Marriage and Immediate Motherhood

Having explored why young Sasak women marry early, the next question that requires investigation is: Why do young Sasak women seek to reproduce as soon as they marry? All of the young women who shared their experiences of motherhood asserted that they had expected and wanted to become pregnant immediately after marriage, regardless of whether they had felt completely ready for marriage or not. Their strong maternal desire following marriage was discussed at length in groups and during one-on-one interviews, and was typically related to their, and often their partners', intense emotional craving to become parents. An explicit desire for the wholeness and contentedness that Sasak women believe comes from motherhood was iterated by many women in this study, as highlighted in the popular quote *perempuan tidak lengkap tanpa anak* (a woman is incomplete without a child). Motherhood is understood as fundamental to womanhood and the emotional satisfaction of women; hence, it stands to reason that young women are highly motivated to fulfil one of the most central requisites of femininity in their culture. This quote also emphasizes the importance of relationships in defining social status among the Sasak; a woman is not a woman unless she has a child—completeness is only achieved through the mother-child relationship (see Figure 12.2).

In addition to completing a woman's identity, a child gives a woman a solid emotional anchor and ally in her husband's family where she is initially an outsider due to patrivirilocal residence patterns (see below). Producing a child soon after marriage also fulfils the wider social expectations placed upon newlyweds. It protects women from potential gossip regarding their fertility, demonstrates men's virility, and elevates the couples' social status to that of parents.

Adding a child to the family also consolidates a new marriage and extended family ties. Many Sasak marriages occur before a couple are well acquainted, as both the traditional practice of *kawin-lari* and the often strict social regulation of formal courtship (*midang*),[14] mean that there are limited opportunities for

---

14   See Bennett (2005, Chapters 3 and 4) and Platt (2010, Chapter 3) for details of courtship practices and elopement among the Sasak.

FIGURE 12.2 *Young mother Desi proudly presenting her robust son Fatahila*

couples to spend time alone prior to marriage. Among the women who contributed to this research, seven had married within three weeks of first meeting their spouses and a further ten within three months. In circumstances where relationships are very new at the time of marriage, having a child is thought to be extremely important in deepening marital ties. Young mothers explained that having a baby is desirable *supaya lebih terikat dengan suami* (to be more closely tied to one's husband). From a women's point of view, pregnancy and the arrival of a child is thought to deter men from looking elsewhere and to make it more difficult for a man to divorce. Men also believe that women are less likely to return home to their mothers in response to marital discontent once a couple share a child. Thus, the arrival of a child is a signifier for both women and men that a marriage is less easily dissolved, as a child consolidates them as a family unit.

The arrival of a first child also acts to integrate a new wife much more intimately with her in-laws. As Sasak post-marital residence is patrivirilocal the majority of women in this study relocated to live with their husband's parents upon marriage. At the time of research 17 of the young mothers still resided with their *mertua* (husband's parents), while 23 women had lived with their *mertua* immediately after marriage. A close and mutually supportive relationship with one's *mertua* is a strong determinant of feelings of belonging and domestic harmony for young Sasak mothers. When discussing the arrival of their first child, young mothers frequently described their relationships with *mertua* as *semakin dekat* (closer) and *semakin sayang* (warmer). They also suggested that they felt more secure in extended households as the gift of a grandchild meant that they were no longer merely dependents. Hence, young women's reproductive contribution is understood as a valuable and productive role in the extended family. A final reason occasionally given by young women for wishing to begin their families at an early age is the wish to have adult children before they reach advanced old age themselves. In such instances, children are viewed as an important source of social security. Thus, becoming a mother, and not simply a wife, cements young women's new social identity and completes their public transition from single daughter to married mother.

Shrinking Social Worlds: The Transition from Single Daughter to Married Mother

A key theme raised by these young women was how motherhood changed their lives. For the majority, their lives had become characterized by increasingly shrinking social worlds, which led to feelings of social isolation. In her study of poor, first-time mothers in East Java, Andajani-Sutjahjo (2003) also found social isolation to be a common experience, and one that impacted negatively on women's mental health. A myriad of factors lead to this in Lombok including: young women's withdrawal from education and loosening ties with school friends; more limited opportunities to work outside the home; relocation to live with their husband's kin; and the dramatic increase in domestic responsibilities associated with marriage and motherhood. As all the women in this study were from poor families, their spatial mobility was curbed by a lack of money for public transport or fuel for motor bikes. Women whose husbands were employed often experienced greater social isolation due to their partners' absence at work and their partners' use of the family's only means of private transport for work.

Siti, a 20 year old mother with a two year old son, reflects below on the divergence between her expectations of social freedom and mobility before she was married and her actual experiences once becoming a mother:

> Siti: When I was a teenager I imagined I would be free when married. While still young, a woman must protect her reputation, she cannot go out all the time, you have to be careful here. I imagined that once married, I would often go out with my husband, and would be free to go out alone because people don't pay as much attention once you have a husband. But it turns out that I'm always at home, looking after my child and rarely go out, I'm bored and really miss my old friends.

Linda: Do you ever get the opportunity to go out with your husband?

Siti: Yeh, sometimes, maybe once a month we will go out and eat together. We look for a nice cheap place like the night market. But if I do go out with my husband, my attention must be on him and my child. There is no time to talk with my friends. I'm required to accompany my husband. It's not appropriate to break off and talk alone with my friends. If I was to do that my husband would feel hurt.

Siti's experiences were typical of the other young mothers. Several pointed out the irony that they had expected marriage and motherhood to grant them greater social freedom, only to discover later that they had actually enjoyed more freedom prior to marriage. Before marriage, same-sex friendships are encouraged and opposite-sex friendships are censured, thus teenage girls are not deterred from having active social lives with their girlfriends. In fact, there is a strong preference for adolescent girls to go out in the company of their same-sex friends. The company of same-sex friends functions as a form of chaperoning to protect girls from gossip and supposedly deter them from spending time alone with boyfriends.

The desire to have regular social contact with their former school friends and other close female peers was expressed by all young women in this study. When I asked them what they would most like to do if they had free time, enough money, and their husband's agreement, the most popular responses were *kumpul sama teman* (get together with girlfriends) and *curhat sama sahabat* (talk/share with close friends) (see Parker, this volume). Many young mothers did not see their former girlfriends at all because they had relocated a considerable distance after marriage. Others who lived within reasonable distance of their friends lamented that they rarely met for a variety of reasons, including: lack of time due to domestic duties; lack of money for public transport; or lack of permission from husbands or *mertua* to visit. When young mothers did find opportunities to meet up with peers, it was most often with neighbors or girlfriends who were also married with children. After discovering the commonality of this experience of social isolation among young mothers I suspected that their desire for female company and to *curhat* may have been another factor influencing women's eagerness to be interviewed.

Siti's experiences of socializing in the company of her husband powerfully illustrate how young mother's identities shift to become strongly oriented around their roles as wives. When socializing in public, young mothers are expected to demonstrate their loyalty and attention to family members, by prioritizing interaction with them above interaction with others. A young married mother is required to perform first as a dutiful wife and mother, regardless of how much she may desire the company of her female friends. The notion that one's husband may be hurt or offended if his "need" for attention is not met in public was commonplace among young mothers, as was the fear that interaction with male peers or old male school friends could lead to jealousy and marital disharmony.

Three young mothers also suggested that they would be embarrassed (*malu*) to meet with their unmarried school friends because they were self-conscious about their appearance and lifestyle since marrying, and feared they would no longer fit in (*tidak cocok lagi*) with their single peers (see Figure 12.3).

Nuri (16 years old) explained:

> Now I only have old/bad clothes, I don't wear jeans anymore, I only wear a sarong, I don't have any beautiful clothes like before. Also my life is too boring for others, I am only in the house, no more school, no work, maybe my old friends will think I am stupid.

Young mothers such as Nuri sometimes feel regret at leaving behind their adolescent status, and the freedom and opportunities represented by that status, although not a single woman in this study expressed any remorse over having become a mother. In Lombok, as is the case for elsewhere in Indonesia, ideal notions of femininity place significant value on the loyalty and sacrifice of

FIGURE 12.3 *Nuri dressed in her sarong, which she refers to as her "old/bad clothes"*

mothers to the family.[15] One consequence of this among young mothers is that they tend to spend what little excess income they have on their children's needs and wishes. For instance, it is common among young mothers to ignore their own desire to dress fashionably and instead to spend money on beautiful clothes or toys for their children.

A popular idiom I heard during my time spent with young Sasak mothers articulates how these women position themselves, and their own needs, within their families, and highlights the ethos of maternal self-sacrifice. It is said that *ibu selalu belakan, mandi belakan, makan belakan, dan tidur belakan* (a mother is always behind: last to wash, last to eat, and last to sleep). This ethos of self-sacrifice stands in sharp contrast to the position of the unmarried girl child. As single schoolgirls, the obligations of young women in Lombok are to be dutiful daughters; to guard their modesty and family reputation; to be diligent students; and to assist and obey their parents as required.[16] In return, the unmarried adolescent girl has the freedom of an active social life: at school; with female friends and kin outside of school; and may enjoy courtship with multiple suitors.

When looking back at their premarital and pre-maternal lifestyles, young mothers often describe themselves as being *masih manja*, still spoilt. In doing so, they acknowledge the attention and support they received from parents when they were still positioned within their immediate family as children. They also note the relative absence of responsibility during adolescence compared with the responsibilities of mothers. Young mothers discussed their lack of personal time, lamenting that they rarely found the time for personal grooming (*kecantikan*), a common preoccupation for male and female adolescents. A number of young mothers with newborns felt such time pressure that they often did not manage to bathe themselves on a daily basis, which was frustrating and physically uncomfortable.

Many young mothers experienced the transition from single adolescent to married woman, and then to mother, as quite sudden. They described often feeling confused (*bingung*) and insecure (*gelisah*) in their new lives. Such

---

15 Many scholars of gender relations and identities in modern Indonesia have observed this idealization of feminine self-sacrifice. In particular, the terms "State Maternalism" (Wolf 1992, 68) and "State Ibuism" (Suryakusuma 1996, 98) have been in popular usage to describe how this gender ideology was promoted to sustain the subordination of women's interests to that of the state, of men, and of the ideal Indonesian family during the New Order period.

16 See Parker's (2009) commentary on the constraints placed on adolescent school girls' sexuality among the Minang of Sumatara.

emotions are not surprising during any significant life transition, however, they may be more pronounced for young Sasak women than in other cultural contexts, for a number of reasons. Firstly, when young poor Sasak women marry they are in many cases still very young and have not experienced high degrees of personal autonomy. Many may never have slept away from home or been separated from their families before marriage. Young Sasak mothers do not get to "practice" living with their spouses before marriage, as is often the case for women in more liberal western settings. When they become wives they are also required to negotiate a whole set of new domestic relationships with their husband's family, rather than simply with their spouse as would be the case if they were living in an independent household. The fact that marriage is typically immediately followed by pregnancy and motherhood also puts significant strain on women's bodies and quickly propels them into a new social identity where they are expected to subjugate their personal needs to those of their child and extended family. Typically, these young women characterized their daily existence as *tidak manja lagi* (no longer spoilt).

Young mothers' self-sacrifice for the good of the family is also apparent in their choices with regard to seeking employment. Prior to marriage, four of the young mothers had sporadically worked in waged jobs—as a waitress, a shop assistant, a massage therapist in a hair salon, and an office helper. Each of these women gave up their employment while pregnant and did not return. None of their jobs allowed maternity leave and all agreed that the required travel and time away from home was impossible once they had given birth. Young mothers felt strongly that their primary role was to raise their children. Many felt uneasy about leaving their children with relatives while they undertook paid work. This relates to feelings commonly expressed by Sasak mothers, that they are best equipped to meet the needs of their own children, particularly during the first two years. They also express fears that others may be harsh to their children or discipline them unfairly. Arguments over young children's behavior and the role of elders in disciplining grandchildren were not uncommon.

Seven out of the 28 women who participated in the research had been involved in some form of income-generation after becoming mothers, including: hauling rocks and sand; doing laundry; domestic service for a neighbor; running a small food stall; wrapping snacks; and rolling cigarettes. All of these occupations were undertaken at home, or close by. The food stall in question was attached to the home of the woman who ran it; laundry for neighbors could be washed at home; wrapping snacks and rolling cigarettes was also done at home; domestic service for one woman was virtually next door; and hauling rocks and sand was for the construction of a neighbor's house and business. By choosing work close to or at home, women are able to supervize their children directly, or frequently check on them. Such close proximity alleviates the need for transport, and the irregular nature of these jobs mean that employers are more tolerant of women's absences. Several young mothers pointed out that jobs with regular monthly wages also require regular attendance and thus provide far less flexibility for women to meet parenting responsibilities. This desire for flexibility centers on the mothers' commitment to being available to their children during times of illness, which are frequent in the early years of a child's life.

In addition to the financial benefits of paid work, several young mothers also discussed the social rewards of work. In particular, they viewed home-based businesses such as food stalls or small stores as highly attractive because they could attract other women to their homes for social contact, without them having to leave their children. Thus, young mothers' ideal jobs are those that allow them to expand their social worlds without compromising their valued primary roles as mothers. This involves bridging the boundaries of the public and private spheres by bringing the public world of production into women's private realm of reproduction.[17] This option was also popular among their husbands, some of whom objected to their wives working outside the home. Yet Women's desire for home-based employment was not consistent with the career goals they reported having prior to marriage, as the transition in women's identities to wives and mothers was accompanied by a significant shift in their employment ideals. The lives of young women are dramatically reoriented to their husband's family and more confined to the domestic sphere than they had imagined prior to marriage. While most young mothers appeared to be resigned to their shrinking social worlds, it was evident that the social isolation that characterized the transition out of adolescence and into motherhood was a fraught experience for many, regardless of the joy they derived from their children.

Conclusion

The experiences and identities of the young Sasak mothers represented above offer an important counter-example of early motherhood in a non-western context that does not fit with popular constructions of early motherhood in other societies. The terms "teen moms", "single welfare mothers", and "children

---

[17] This finding with regard to how poor Sasak women often prefer to bring the work of production into their domestic realms and thus manage both reproduction and production side by side, resonates strongly with Suzanne Brenner's work (1998) analysis of Javanese women's work in the 1990's among women engaged in home-based production of *batik* cloth in Solo.

having children" are misleading for this group of young mothers, despite the fact that many of them are still adolescents. In a political critique of the representation of young mothers in youth studies, Irvine (1994) claimed that regardless of the social or geographical location of young mothers, youth pregnancy is viewed as both undesirable, and unwanted, or accidental. While I am wholly sympathetic to Irvine's critique of the moralizing discourses that often shape research and intervention agendas concerned with policing the choices and behavior of young mothers, I believe that this research has revealed that social condemnation of early motherhood and youth pregnancy is not universal. Rather, I concur with Ward (1995), and believe that for impoverished young Sasak women adolescent marriage and early pregnancy are culturally viable solutions that are not understood as problematic within their immediate communities. I also assert that the endemic poverty of Sasak society perpetuates a cycle in which there is a lack of the necessary economic incentives for young women to delay marriage, such as the ability to complete high school, continue on to tertiary education, or find meaningful or secure employment.

I do not suggest that adolescent pregnancy out of wedlock is not a cause of concern in these communities, which are prone to the same moral panic over adolescent sexuality that is found across Indonesia. What this research has established, however, is that premarital pregnancy is not the leading cause of early motherhood among poor, young Sasak women. As outlined above, the concern over confining female sexuality to marriage can lead both to early marriage when women's reputations are at risk, or in some instances can occur to conceal a pre-marital pregnancy. The importance of disciplining public expressions of female sexuality leads to the sexual politics of confining female sexuality to marriage. This is a greater moral concern in Sasak society than the concern over the age when women marry and have children.

Local understandings of womanhood and motherhood converge for the Sasak to create a dominant ideal of femininity that can only be truly fulfilled through motherhood. The lives of young married women change dramatically once they leave behind their status as single daughters and lose the freedom that they describe as being "spoilt". The key differences between the everyday lives of Sasak adolescents who are still school girls and their married peers who are mothers are the shrinking social worlds and the subjugation of personal desires and needs to those of the family. While this shift in status, from being cared for to being a carer of others, is marked, both unmarried school girls and young mothers occupy social positions that are neither marginalized nor stigmatized. Young married Sasak mothers are not viewed as deviant. They are not at risk of identity failure or social exclusion (although social isolation is common) as long as they live up to societies' expectations of good mothers and dutiful wives. Thus, the social positioning of young Sasak women is far safer than female adolescents in other social situations who fail to achieve dominant social expectations of them, such as street children or adolescent sex worker (see Beazley 2002).

Young Sasak mothers do not experience their identities as marginal, but feel successful in terms of realizing dominant constructions of femininity—but this does not mean that they do not struggle to live with poverty and social isolation. The reorientation of young mother's lives to new social spaces and networks is a key part of their transition from single daughters to married mothers that sadly results in shrinking social worlds for many. Young mothers express loneliness and longing for the companionship of female peers and their natal families. Some women's need to work, especially when their husbands are unemployed, can lead to a welcome extension of their social worlds. The strategy of bringing the public domain of work, or production of income, into the private domain of reproduction is a common and effective response that allows women to prioritize the care of their children, seek financial rewards and extend their social worlds.

Utilizing the concept of social age to analyze young Sasak women's transitions from unmarried daughters to married mothers is highly instructive in teasing out how young women interpret and experience changes in their social status and roles. The idiom *"tidak manja lagi"* (no longer spoilt) succinctly sums up the shift from being a person who is primarily under the care of others (a dependent daughter) to being someone whose primary role in life is the care of another (one's child or children). This idiom highlights the centrality of both socially ascribed responsibilities and social relationships in defining one's social status in Sasak society. For young Sasak women marriage and motherhood cement adult social status regardless of biological age. However, this rarely involves a sharp transition into an independent household as can be the case for middle-class and elite Indonesians who can afford to form nuclear families upon marriage. Young Sasak mothers from poor families almost always reside with their in-laws after marriage. For these young women the end of youth and entry into adulthood is not typically characterized by a higher degree of social independence. Rather, it is shifting social alliances, from one's family of origin and same-sex peers to that of their husband's family (who becomes their own) that are of key significance in shaping women's everyday lives after marriage. In this context, social status is far more dependent on relational factors than on chronological age.[18]

---

[18] See Huijsmans et al. (2014) for a detailed explication of the salience of a relational approach to theorizing age.

While it is true that marriage and motherhood can propel young Sasak women into adulthood in their teens, prolonged formal education can also extend the duration of "youth" for those Sasak teenagers with families fortunate enough to finance their study until the end of high school and beyond. The most common reason given for early marriage among my informants was "*sudah berhenti sekolah*" (had already stopped school) and all of them indicated that they would have preferred to undertake further education. This illuminates the social significance of school attendance for defining and extending the category of youth for the Sasak. It also resonates strongly with the finding of the AAI survey with regard to the enormous value placed on education as the perceived gateway to a better life among adolescents across Indonesia (see Nilan et al., this volume).

Clark-Kazak aptly asserts that "in development programming, age is too often equated solely with chronological age and stripped of social meanings" (2014, 1309). By way of conclusion I offer some suggestions on how adolescent marriage and early childbearing should be approached as a health and development issue in Lombok. While key government bodies, along with the health and development sectors, are understandably concerned with ameliorating early childbearing, the very communities that are most likely to be targeted for interventions tend not to see adolescent marriage and early child bearing as problems. Any successful intervention in this area must respect local constructions of social age within poor communities in Lombok, which underpin the fact that Sasak women who marry and have children while still adolescents are not currently stigmatized or viewed as deviant. Thus, it is imperative that community education on the risks of early childbearing should consider how social age is currently constructed among the Sasak in a manner that does not blame or stigmatize these young women. If intervention discourses represent adolescent marriage and early child bearing as a socially irresponsible or unacceptable choice made entirely by individuals, then poor adolescent women will be disproportionately disadvantaged. Sasak teenagers are not responsible for the cycle of poverty they have been born into, which is the key factor determining the absence of viable life trajectories other than marriage and motherhood.

Acknowledgements

I wish to thank all the women who shared their time, opinions and experiences with me. I am also particularly grateful Ibu Kasmiati and Ibu Rahmi for their discussion of my hypotheses on the aetiology of early marriage and motherhood in Lombok. I must also thank Korporasi ANNISA for use of their training room and permission to observe their training, Eni for her diligent transcription of FGDs, and Ani and Desi for providing childcare. I am grateful to the Ambivalent Adolescents team for their collaboration and the Australian Research Council for their financial support of the research.

References

Andajani-Sutjahjo, S. 2003. "Motherhood and Emotional Wellbeing of Women in Indonesia." PhD diss., University of Melbourne.

Badan Pusat Statistik (BPS). 2010. *Human Development Index by Province and National, 1996–2012*. Jakarta: BPS. Accessed May 1, 2009: http://www.bps.go.id/eng/tab_sub/view.php?tabel=1&daftar=1&id_subyek=26&notab=2

Beazley, H. 2002. "'Vagrants Wearing Make-up': Negotiating Spaces on the Streets of Yogyakarta, Indonesia." *Urban Studies* 39:1665–83.

Bennett L.R. 2005. *Women, Islam and Modernity: Single Women, Sexuality and Reproductive Health in Contemporary Indonesia*. London and New York: Routledge.

Bennett, L.R. 2014. "Early Marriage, Adolescent Motherhood and Reproductive Rights for Young Sasak Mothers in Lombok, Eastern Indonesia." *Wacana, Journal of the Humanities of Indonesia* 15:20–42.

Biddlecom, A., G. Richard, and L. Cynthia. 2008. "Associations between Premarital Sex and Leaving School in Four Sub-Saharan African Countries." *Studies in Family Planning* 39:337–49.

Blackburn, S. 2004. *Women and the State in Modern Indonesia*. Cambridge: Cambridge University Press.

Blackburn, S. and S. Bessell. 1997. "Marriageable Age: Political Debates in Early Marriage in Twentieth-century Indonesia." *Indonesia* 63:107–41.

Brenner, S. 1998. *The Domestication of Desire: Women, Wealth, and Modernity in Java*. Princeton: Princeton University Press.

Choe, M, S Thapa and S Achmad. 2001. "Early Marriage and Childbearing in Indonesia and Nepal." *East-West Centre Working Papers*, Nos. 108–15: 1–22. East-West Centre: Honolulu.

Clark-Kazak, C. 2014. "Towards a Working Definition and Application of Social Age in International Development Studies." *The Journal of Development Studies* 45:1307–24.

Desriani, D. 2011. "Determinants of Teenage Motherhood: Evidence from the 2007 Indonesia Demographic and Health Survey." Paper presented at *Claiming Sexual and Reproductive Rights in Asian and Pacific Societies: The 6th Asia Pacific Conference on Reproductive and Sexual Health and Rights*, Gadjah Mada University, Yogyakarta, 19–22 October.

Dunn, S. 1988. "A Model of Fertility Decision-Making Styles among Young Mothers." *Human Organization* 47:166-75.
Government of Indonesia. 2007. *Indonesian Demographic Health Survey—2007*.
Grace, J. 1997. "Health, Development and Sasak Women." PhD diss., Murdoch University.
Grant, M. and K. Hallman. 2008. "Pregnancy-related School Drop Out and Prior School Performance in KwaZulu-Natal, South Africa." *Studies in Family Planning* 39:369–82.
Irvine, J. 1994. "Cultural Differences and Adolescent Sexualities." In *Sexual Cultures and the Construction of Adolescent Identities*, edited by J. Irvine, 3–28. Philadelphia: Temple University Press.
Handajani, S. 2008. "Western Inscriptions on Indonesian Bodies: Representations of Adolescents in Indonesian Female Teen Magazines." *Body, Sexuality and Gender among Contemporary Indonesian Youth. Special Edition of Intersections*. November 10, 2008. Available at: http://intersections.anu.edu.au/issue18_contents.htm
Harding, C. 2008. "The Influence of the 'Decadent West': Discourses of the Mass Media on Youth Sexuality in Indonesia." *Body, Sexuality and Gender among Contemporary Indonesian Youth Special Edition of Intersections*. November 10, 2008. Available at: http://intersections.anu.edu.au/issue18_contents.htm
Huijsmans, R., S. George, R. Gigengack, and S. Evans. 2014. "Theorizing Age and Generation in Development: A Relational Approach." *European Journal of Development Research* 26:163–74.
Holgate, H.S., R. Evans and F. Yuen, eds. 2006. *Teenage Pregnancy and Parenthood: Global Perspectives, Issues and Interventions*. New York: Routledge.
Jennaway, M. 2002. "Inflatable Bodies and the Breath of Life: Courtship and Desire among Young Women in Rural North Bali." In *Coming of Age in South and Southeast Asia: Youth, Sexuality and Courtship*, edited by L. Manderson and P. Liamputtong, 75–95. London: Curzon.
Jones, G. 2004. "Not 'When to Marry' but 'Whether to Marry': The Changing Context of Marriage Decisions in East and Southeast Asia." In *(Un)tying the Knot: Ideal and Reality in Asian Marriage*, edited by G. Jones and K. Ramadas, 3–58. Singapore: Asia Research Institute.
Jones, G., and B. Gubhaju. 2008. "Trends in Age at Marriage in the Provinces of Indonesia." *Asia Research Institute Working Paper Series*, No. 105:1–29. Asia Research Institute, Singapore.
Jones, G., and P. Hagul. 2001. "Schooling in Indonesia: Crisis-Related and Longer-Term Issues." *Bulletin of Indonesian Economic Studies* 37:207–32.
Judd, M. 1980. "The Sociology of Rural Poverty in Lombok, Indonesia." PhD diss., Berkeley, University of California.
Manderson, L. and P. Liamputtong, eds. 2002. *Coming of Age in South and Southeast Asia: Youth, Sexuality and Courtship*. London: Curzon.

Ministry of Health Indonesia. 2009. *Measuring the Fulfillment of Human Rights in Maternal and Neonatal Health: Report on Provincial and District Laws, Regulations, Policies and Standards of Care.* Jakarta: MOH and GTZ.

Nasril, R., and O. Samosir. 2011. "Factors influencing teenage motherhood in Indonesia." Paper presented at *Claiming Sexual and Reproductive rights in Asian and Pacific Societies: The 6th Asia Pacific Conference on Reproductive and Sexual Health and Rights*, Gajdamada University, Yogyakarta, 19–22 October.

Parker, L. 2009. "Religion, class and schooled sexuality among Minangkabau teenage girls." *Bijdragen tot de Taal-, Land- en Volkenkunde* 165:62–94.

Prasetya, L., and G. Dasvarma. 2011. "Factors Influencing Age at Marriage and Ideal Number of Children among the Youth and Adolescents of Indonesia: Evidence from the Indonesia Youth and Young Adult Reproductive Health Survey 2007." Paper presented at *Claiming Sexual and Reproductive rights in Asian and Pacific Societies: The 6th Asia Pacific Conference on Reproductive and Sexual Health and Rights*, Gajdamada University, Yogyakarta, 19–22 October.

Parker, L., and L. Bennett, eds. 2008. *Indonesian Youth Today: Body, Sexuality and Gender. Special Issue of Intersections: Gender and Sexuality in Asian and the Pacific* 18.

Platt, M. 2009. "Sudah Terlanjur: Women and the Transition into Marriage in Teduk, Lombok." Paper presented at *Growing Up in Indonesia: Experience and Diversity in Youth Transitions*, The Australian National University, 28–30 September.

Platt, M. 2010. "Sasak Women Navigating Dynamic Marital Continuums: Patriarchal Institutions and Female Agency in Indonesian Marriages." PhD diss., LaTrobe University.

Population Reports 2005. *Meeting the Needs of Young Adults*, XXIII(3), October. Accessed at: <http:/infoforhealth.org.pr/j41edsum.shtml> August 25, 2009.

Robinson, K. and I. Utomo. 2003. *Youth, Sexuality and Personal Life—Special edition of Review of Indonesian and Malaysian Affairs* 37.

Suyakusuma, J. 1996. "The State and Sexuality in New Order Indonesia." In *Fantasizing the Feminine in Indonesia*, edited by L. Sears, 92–119. Durham: Duke University Press.

Strauss, A. and J. Corbin. 1990. *Basics of Qualitative Research: Grounded Theory Procedures and Techniques.* California: Sage.

Utomo, I. 2002. "Sexual Values and Early Experiences among Young People in Jakarta." In *Coming of Age in South and Southeast Asia: Youth, Sexuality and Courtship*, edited by L. Manderson and P. Liamputtong, 207-27. London: Curzon.

Ward, M. 1995. "Early Childbearing: What Is the Problem and Who Owns It?" In *Conceiving the New World Order: The Global Politics of Reproduction,* edited by F. Ginsberg and R. Rapp, 140–58. Berkley: University of California Press.

Wolf, D. 1992. *Factory Daughters: Gender, Household Dynamics, and Rural Industrialization in Java.* Berkley: University of California Press.

Index

Abdullah, Taufik   11
abortion   225, 229
abuse and exploitation   16
addiction *see* alcohol production/
    consumption; drug abuse and addiction
adolescent marriage   242, 244–50
adolescent motherhood   238–42
    cultural viability   256–7
    Sasak people, Lombok   238–58
    in youth studies   256
adolescents *see* girls; secondary school
    students; teenagers; young people
adulthood
    definitions   6
    markers of   6, 7, 23, 25–8, 35, 42, 241, 246
    postponement of   6–7, 52–4, 67
    transition to *see* transitions (youth)
    see also social age
agriculture *see* de-agrarianization; farming
Ahmadiyah sect   211
AKKBB *see* Freedom Alliance for Religious
    Freedom
akrab see teman akrab
alcohol production/consumption   144–5,
    147, 152, 224
Aliansi Kebebasan untuk Kerukunan
    Beragama dan Berkeyakinan (Freedom
    Alliance for Religious Freedom)   211
Ambivalent Adolescents (AAI) project
    findings   13, 14, 23–4, 28–30, 72
    Lombok   238–58
    Solo   158–71
    Sorowako   72–89
    West Sumatra   94–111
    Yogyakarta   218–36
    youth transition trends   30–42
Ambon   179–98, 200
American opposition to Islam,
    perceived   210–1 *see also* Western
    imperialism
anak   7, 59
anak baru gede   2, 60, 86
anak muda   218, 222, 228–36
anak nakal   222–3
angkatan   8–9

anti-Japanese demonstrations   201
arts *see* traditional arts and crafts
aspirations   24–5
    the "good life"   24, 34–5, 42, 48
    Lombok young mothers   243, 246
    marriage and family   31–2, 41
    teenagers   58–9, 225–6
    value of family and community   225–6
    work and career   32–6, 42, 77–8
Association of Functional Youth Groups
    (IPK)   11, 12
Association of Sorowako Graduates (Ikatan
    Sarjana Sorowako)   78

Ba'asyir, Abu Bakar   205
backpacker tourism   145
Baden-Powell, Robert (Baron Baden-Powell)
    113, 114, 115, 127
Bali   29
Banjarnegara   29
Banjaroyo village   140–1, 147–8, 149–50
boarding houses   84–5, 98, 103–4
Boedi Oetomo   115
books in family home as class indicator   37, 38
boyfriends and girlfriends   106–8, 164,
    229–34 *see also pacaran*
Britain, friendship studies   96–7
Bumen *kampung*, Yogyakarta   150

Campus Islamic Proselytizing Board
    (Lembaga Dakwah kampus)   206
career *see* employment opportunities; work
cellphones *see* mobile phones
character factory   112
childhood
    definitions   5–7, 59–60
    prolongation of   6–7, 49, 52–3, 67,
        69–70, 258
    value of children   49
    see also youth
choice biographies   226, 228, 229–33, 235
Christianity   52, 63, 139
    educational institutions   41
    versus Islam in Ambon   180–1, 185, 188–91,
        195–6

Christian street art 178, 181–98
churhat (sharing intimacies) 92, 99, 100, 105, 106
citizenship 7, 16, 67, 115, 118, 127, 146–7, 192–3, 202–3
claiming space 209–11
class
    class differences 202
    conflict 132
    friendship differences 97–8
    indicators 37–8
    and life dreams/obstacles 38–41
    see also middle-class success
clothing
    boys/young men 167, 192
    dressmaking/makers 109, 126, 127
    girls 102–3, 166, 167, 170
    Muslim women 158
    school uniforms 137, 170
    scouts (Pramuka) uniforms 117, 124, 127
    young mothers views 252–3
Command of Islam Force (Komando Laskar Islam) 211
communications technology 156, 159, 161, 163, 166, 167, 168, 169 *see also* internet use; mobile phones
Communist Party 117
computers in the home 38, 86
comradeship *see* friendship
consumerism 62–3, 87, 134, 135, 141, 144, 151–2, 161, 165, 221, 235 *see also* shopping malls
crafts *see* traditional arts and crafts
crisis, concept of 15
cultural capital 37–8
curhat 93, 98–9, 100, 105, 106, 108, 109–11, 251 *see also* friendship

dance *see* traditional arts and crafts
de-agrarianization 10, 14–5, 48, 71, 147
dependence on parents 9 *see also* parental responsibility for children's education
dewasa 2, 7, 59–60
disorder *see* "morbid symptoms"
drug abuse and addiction 15–6, 65, 144, 218, 222–4, 227
Dutch colonial rule 115, 135, 183, 192, 193, 197

early marriage 244–8 *see also* marriage and family
early motherhood 238–42
    cultural viability 256–7
    Sasak people, Lombok 238–58
    in youth studies 256
economic crisis of 1997–98 146, 200, 203
economy, Indonesian 24–5, 42, 202–4
education 13–5, 24, 41–2
    cost of 41, 203
    enrolments 25–6
    inequality of opportunity 14, 36, 48, 149–50, 203
    Ministry of Education policy on schools and scouting 117
    outmigration for 48, 73–5, 77, 81–3, 147
    parental support of students 70, 78–86, 88–9
    and prolongation of childhood 6–7, 49, 52–3, 67, 69–70, 258
    and proper conduct 86–7
    quality of 14, 41, 48
    in Sorowako *see* Sorowako
    teenagers' views on 57–9
    transition marker 25–6, 34–5, 42, 69–70
    see also secondary education; tertiary education
educational attainment 14, 25–6, 36
    Kali Loro village 52–3
    Lombok young mothers 243, 246
    Sorowako 81–2, 88–9
employment opportunities 13–5, 26, 32–4, 57
    Lombok young mothers 246
    Sorowako 76–8, 80–1
    see also labor market; livelihood; work
England, friendship studies 96–7
ethical protocols of research 16–9
exploitation and abuse 16

Facebook 62, 162
family *see* marriage and family
farming 14–5, 33, 59, 147
female friendships 96–11, 250–2
female sexuality 12–3, 220, 226–36, 245, 247–8, 256
female youth *see* girls; young women
fertility rate 32

INDEX

financial crisis of 1997–98   146, 200, 203
Flores   30
Forum Betawi Rembug   12
FPI *see* Front Pembela Islam
Freedom Alliance for Religious Freedom (Aliansi Kebebasan untuk Kerukunan Beragama dan Berkeyakinan)   211
"free life" of Western youth   65
free sex   65, 144, 156–7, 224–5, 232, 242
  see also pergaulan bebas
friendship   9, 81–2, 83, 87–8, 93
  among girls   96–111
  among men   96–7, 99–100
  at boarding school   103–4
  boyfriends and girlfriends   106–8, 164, 229–34
  gender differences   96–7
  importance of schools   87–8, 97–100, 108
  living away from home   103–4, 108
  in scouts (Pramuka)   122
  significance for young people   95–100, 103–4, 110–1
  studies of   95–8
  terminology (definitions)   98–9, 100, 103–4, 106, 110–1
  in transition from child to adult   92–3, 94, 100, 101, 110–1
  Western ideal of   96
  working girls   108–10
  young mothers from Lombok   250–2
  see also curhat; pacaran; teman akrab
Front Pembela Islam (Front for the Defenders of Islam)   200, 211
frustration and disorder *see* "morbid symptoms"; youth alienation

gaul   219–22
gender   12–3, 27
  differences in AAI survey data   31–2, 35, 42
  equality   66, 93, 123–5, 158–9
  friendship differences   96–7
generation   7–10, 11, 12, 16–7
generational relationships *see* intergenerational relations
geng (gangs)   63, 100–1, 105, 107
girls
  abuse and exploitation   16
  boyfriends   106–8, 164, 229–34

clothing   102–3, 166, 167, 170
friendship   96–111
Muslim discourse on behavior   158–9, 170–1, 229–30, 232–3
questions of identity   60
restrictions on   64–7, 84–5, 98, 124, 156–7, 251
  see also secondary school students' views; teenagers; young people
globalization   24, 95, 148–9, 151, 202–4, 209
Golkar   11, 117–8
"good life" perceptions   24, 34–5, 42, 48
group education, principle of   118–9, 127–8
guides *see* scouts (Pramuka) organization

Habibie, B.J.   ix
"hanging out"   13, 64, 86, 98, 109, 157, 165–7
  see also socializing
harmony (*rukun*)   222–4, 225
"hedonism"   142
high school *see* secondary education
high school students *see* girls; secondary school students' views; teenagers; young people
"hippie" looks   123
Hizb ut-Tahrir (Party of Liberation)   200, 201, 205, 206–8, 210
home ownership   25, 28, 35, 42
housing   27–8

identity   12, 35, 87–8, 204
  expression of, in violent activism   178, 206, 209–11, 212
  questions of   60
  self-identity   105–6, 111, 165
  social identity   97–8, 248–52, 254, 255, 256–8
ideoscape   221
Ikatan Sarjana Sorowako (Association of Sorowako Graduates)   78
independence   81–3, 89, 127, 228
independent living   82, 84–7, 103–4, 108–9
Indonesian economy   24–5, 42, 202–4
Indonesian nationalist movements   115–6
Indonesian National Youth Committee (KNPI)   7, 11, 12
Indonesian Statistics Agency   26, 135
industrial employment   71–2, 74, 77–8, 80, 141

information technology *see* communications technology; internet use; mobile phones
"informed consent" principles   17–9
inter-generational relations   8, 11, 16–7, 66–7, 69–70, 82–5
International Centre for Child and Youth Studies   50
internet cafés   61, 86–7, 132, 142, 156, 159–65, 170–1
internet use   61–2, 86–7, 109, 159
intersectionality   4–6, 12
IPK *see* Association of Functional Youth Groups (IPK)
Iran, youth transitions   27, 28
Islam   52, 63, 139, 149, 151, 152, 157, 158–9
  American opposition to Islam, perceived   210–1 *see also* Western imperialism
  ideology   204–9, 211–2
  militant groups   200–1, 205–7, 211
  Muslim discourse on female behaviour   158–9, 170–1, 229–30, 232–3
  resurgence   25, 141–2, 158, 161, 201
  versus Christianity in Ambon   180–1, 185, 188–91, 195–6
  see also religiosity
Islamic law   200, 205, 207–8, 210
Islamist activism   178, 200–12
Israel   205, 211

Jakarta   30
Jama'ah Islamiyah   205
jamborees   116, 119, 123–4
Java
  AAI project locations   29–30
  "generations of change"   8
  schooling customs   73–4
  see also Banjaroyo; Bumen; Kali Loro; Ledok; Pekalongan; Samirono; Sidomulyo; Solo; Yogyakarta
Javaansche Padvinders Organisatie (JPO)   115
jealousy   107–8
Jesus Christ street pictures   181–98
jihad   200, 211

Kali Loro village   50–2
Kali Loro village teenagers
  intergenerational relations   66–7
  lifestyles and social life   59–66
  stories   54–7
  views on education, work and futures   57–9
KAMMI *see* Kesatuan Aksi Mahasiswa Muslim Indonesia
kampung
  abolished as administrative unit   142
  infrastructure construction   143
  Yogyakarta *kampung see* Yogyakarta
kampung remaja   138–9, 142, 143–52
kawin lari (elopement)   247, 248
Kecamatan (Sub-district) Development Program in rural communities   146
Kepanduan Putra Indonesia   117
Kesatuan Aksi Mahasiswa Muslim Indonesia (Indonesian Muslim Students United Action Front)   200
khilafat system   205, 207–8, 210
KNPI (Indonesian National Youth Committee)   7, 11, 12
Komando Laskar Islam (Command of Islam Force)   211
Kota Sejuk (West Sumatra) high school students
  friends as moral guardians   102–5
  the '*geng*'   100–1
  girlfriends and boyfriends   106–8
  living away from home friendships   103–4, 108
  schools and friendships   97–100, 108
  significance of friendships   97–100, 103–4, 110–1
Kota Sejuk working girls' friendships   108–10

labor market   26, 33, 42, 77–8, 141, 203
  see also employment opportunities
land tenure systems   15
Laskar Jihad (Holy War Force)   200
Laskar Mujahidin Indonesia (Indonesian Holy Warriors Force)   200
Law on Youth 2009   6–7
Ledok *kampung*, Yogyakarta   135, 138–40, 142, 143, 144–6, 147, 150, 151 *see also* Yogyakarta
Lembaga Dakwah Kampus (Campus Islamic Proselytizing Board)   206
life dreams   36–7
  obstacles to   37, 38–41, 42

lifestyles
    Kali Loro village   51–2, 57–9
    Sorowako   71–2, 86–7
    teenagers   2, 5, 30, 59–66, 86–8, 150–1
lifeworld of the street   180–98
livelihood
    Kali Loro village   51–2, 59
    Sorowako   15, 48–9, 71–2, 74–5
    see also work
living away from home   82, 84–7, 103–4, 108–9
LJ *see* Laskar Jihad
LMI *see* Laskar Mujahidin Indonesia
Lombok   30, 240 *see also* young mothers from Lombok

male infidelity   233–4
male youth *see* young men
mampu   27, 246–7
Mangkunegara VII, Prince   115
Mannheim, Karl   7, 8, 11
Manpower Law 2003   26
marriage and family   25, 26–7, 69–70, 88
    AAI survey findings   31–2, 35
    early marriage   244–8
    family formation   27, 41–2, 226, 248–9
    family problems   222–3
    maternal self-sacrifice   253–4
    Sasak young mothers   242–58
marriage partner, choice of   70, 157, 164, 230, 246, 247
masa remaja   60
masculinity   35
    masculine youth culture   183–92
    style and display   192–8
    see also young men
maternal self-sacrifice   253–4
media   219, 220–2, 235
mejeng see "hanging out"
men's friendships   96–7, 99–100
middle-class success   24, 27, 28, 34–5, 87–8, 220–1
Minangkabau young people, West Sumatra   94–111
    friends as moral guardians   102–5
    the '*geng*'   100–1
    girlfriends and boyfriends   106–8
    living away from home friendships   103–4, 108

schools and friendships   97–100, 108
significance of friendships   97–100, 103–4, 110–1
see also friendship; girls; young people
Ministry of Education policy on schools and scouting   117
Minza, Wenty   5, 7, 157
mixed-sex socializing *see* socializing (mixed sex)
mobile phones   24, 54, 61–2, 72, 159, 161, 163, 166, 167, 168, 169
mobility   144, 146, 228, 250–1
moral guardianship   94, 102–3, 104–5, 107–8, 110–1, 156, 164, 216–7, 227
moral panic/moral concerns   126–7, 144, 145, 148, 152, 156–7, 159, 164, 171, 220, 234–5, 256
moral rectitude   86–7, 107, 114, 115, 118, 126–8, 156, 159, 164–5, 170–1 *see also* sexual morality
"morbid symptoms"   15, 134, 136, 144, 152
mosques   141, 149, 204, 212
motherhood *see* early motherhood; young mothers from Lombok
motorbike ownership   24, 62–3, 72, 82, 138, 144, 194–5
motorbike-taxi drivers and stands   181, 182, 183–4, 188, 191, 194–6
Muhammadiyah movement   115
Muslim Brotherhood   201, 205, 208
Muslim discourse on female behavior   158–9, 170–1, 229–30, 232–3 *see also* Islam
Muslim paramilitary groups   200–1

nationalist movements   115–6
Negara Islam Indonesia   205
New Order   57, 92, 116, 117–8, 134, 136–41, 145–6, 151, 200, 203, 253 *see also* Suharto/Suharto regime
Newly Emerging Needs of Children and Youth project   50
NII *see* Negara Islam Indonesia
nongkrong see "hanging out"
normal biographies   226–9
norma-norma   220 *see also* social norms
normative discourses in Indonesia   41–2, 216–7, 226–7, 233–5 *see also* social norms
normative sexuality in Indonesia   216–7, 220, 233–5 *see also* sexuality

occupations *see* work
optimism   24, 26, 152 *see also* aspirations
Ottoman Empire   205, 207

pacaran   99, 106–8, 164, 221, 224–5, 229–32
Palestinians   205, 207, 211
Pandeyan *kampung*   148–9
parental responsibility for children's education   63, 70, 78–86, 88–9
parenthood   26–7, 32, 69–70 *see also* early motherhood; marriage and family
Party of Liberation *see* Hizb ut-Tahrir
Party Task Force (Satgas Partai)   117–8
patrivirilocal residence patterns   248, 249–50
peer pressure   104–6 *see also* moral guardianship
peer relationships *see* friendship
peer surveillance   101–3, 156, 161, 164, 169–70, 216–7 *see also* moral guardianship
Pekalongan scouts   114, 120–7
pemuda   2, 7, 10–2, 59, 135–6, 138, 192–3
Pemuda Pancasila   11, 12
Pemuda Rakjat (Youth of the People) Group   117
pengampu system   75
pergaulan bebas   13, 216, 218–20, 242
  perceived as hypocritical rhetoric   233–5
  range of behaviors   224–6
  students' views   222–6
  young women's views   226–36
  see also free sex
pesantren   98
photo sharing   62
PhotoVoice   51, 54, 60
Plan Netherlands   50
political action *see* youth political action
political renewal   8–9, 10–1
popular culture in Indonesia   96, 142, 148–9, 158–9, 164–5, 170–1, 209, 219, 221
population   135
positional goods   62
poverty   203
Pramuka (Scouts) organization *see* Scouts (Pramuka) organization
premarital pregnancy   65, 138, 225, 228, 241, 242, 244–5
premarital sex   13, 138, 156–7, 224–5, 232–4, 247–8 *see also* free sex

professions   31, 32–3, 36, 37–8, 42, 72, 77–8 *see also* employment opportunities; work
prolongation of youth   6–7, 49, 52–3, 67, 69–70, 258
propriety   86–7, 107, 114, 115, 118, 126–8, 156, 159, 164–5, 170–1 *see also* moral guardianship; sexual morality
public-private spaces   160, 171 *see also* internet cafés; shopping malls

reformasi   15, 64, 76, 134, 151
religiosity   25, 52, 65, 229–30, 232–3 *see also* Christianity; Islam
religious activities   63, 65, 141–2, 149, 151, 201
religious organizations   12, 63 *see also* Islamist activism
remaja   2, 7, 59, 60, 66, 136, 228
  kampung remaja   8, 138–9, 142, 143–52
  masa remaja   60
  views on *pergaulan bebas*   226–33
reputation   55, 107, 161, 164, 250, 253, 256 *see also* moral guardianship; *pergaulan bebas*; propriety
research protocols   16–9
revolutionary forces   8–9
romance   106–8, 157, 221, 230 *see also pacaran*
rukun (harmony)   222–4, 225
rural village youth   140–1, 143, 147–8, 149–50, 152 *see also* Kali Loro village

safe sex   230–1
Salafi movement   201, 205–6
Samirono *kampung*, Yogyakarta   142, 148, 151
Sasak people, Lombok   240 *see also* young mothers from Lombok
Satgas Partai (Party Task Force)   117–8
Saudi Arabian Wahhabi influence on Islam   205, 206
schools *see* education; secondary education; secondary schools
scoutmasters   118, 120, 122, 124
scouts (Pramuka) organization   93–4, 113–28
  fun   114, 123–7
  group education and working committees   119–23
  membership   113
  structure   115–8

INDEX

secondary education   14, 41, 57–9, 72, 73
   enrolments   25–6, 36, 53
   Sorowako   73–9
secondary schools as source of friendships   87–8, 97–100, 108
secondary school students' views
   Ambivalent Adolescents (AAI) project data   28–42
   Kali Loro survey *see* Kali Loro village teenagers
   on friendship *see* Kota Sejuk high school students
   on *pergaulan bebas*   222–8
   Sorowako   81–8
   see also girls; teenagers; young people
seks bebas   144, 224–5 *see also* free sex
self sacrifice (maternal)   253–4
sex education, absence of   101, 231, 234
sexuality   12–3, 216–20, 221, 226–36, 245, 247–8, 256
sexual morality   13, 233–4, 247–8 *see also* premarital sex; propriety
shari'a (Islamic law)   207–8, 210
shopping   101–3
shopping malls   132, 142, 151, 156, 159–61, 165–71
Sidomulyo *kampung*   140
situated practice   159–60, 164–5, 168–9, 171
smartphones *see* mobile phones
smoking   221, 224
social age   234, 241, 248, 257–8 *see also* adulthood; transitions (youth)
social controls   64–7
social identity   97–8, 248–52, 254, 255, 256–8
social isolation   250–2, 256–7
socializing (mixed sex)   63, 106–8, 156–7, 161, 163–71 *see also* gender; *pacaran*
socializing (single sex)   157, 159–62, 164–71, 251
social media   62, 162
social norms   217, 220, 223–6, 233, 234–6
   normal biographies   226–9
social reproduction   9, 32–3, 37–8, 49, 50, 69–70, 74, 78–9, 88–9
social space   123–4, 127–8, 132–3, 178, 257
social transition (from daughter to mother)   250–8
Solo, central Java   30, 142, 157–71

Sorowako   30, 69
   economy and livelihood   15, 48–9, 71–2, 74–5
   education as hope/entitlement   75–8
   employment opportunities   76–8, 80–1
   lifestyle   71–2, 86–7
   parental support of students   78–86
   pursuit of education   78–81, 88
   schooling   73–7, 86–8
South Caucasus, youth transitions   27
South Sulawesi   15 *see also* Sorowako
space (situated practice)   159–60, 164–5, 168–9, 171
space (territory) *see* claiming space
sporting groups/activities   63, 96, 143, 145
street children, friendship among   95
street pictures and artists, Ambon   180–98
street politics   209–12
streetside youth, Yogyakarta   137, 139, 141, 142, 144
student population, Yogyakarta   137, 138–9, 142, 144, 148, 149
student support by parents   63, 70, 78–86, 88–9
student views *see* secondary school students' views; university students' views
style and display   192–8
success, notions of   24, 27, 28, 34–5, 87–8, 220–1, 225
Suharto/Suharto regime   ix, 9, 11, 116–7, 136, 137, 191, 200, 201, 203 *see also* New Order
Sukarno   9, 116, 135, 201, 219
Sungkar, Abdullah   205
Surakarta *see* Solo
surveys   28
   research protocols   16–9
   see also Ambivalent Adolescents (AAI) project

Tanaka, Kakuei, state visit by   201
teamwork   92, 118–27
teenagers
   friendships *see* friendship
   lifestyles and social life   2, 5, 30, 59–66, 86–8, 150–1
   restrictions on   54–7, 64–7, 84–5, 98
   time-use   53–4, 63
   views on education, work and futures   57–9

teenagers (cont.)
    youth trends (survey)   24–5
    see also girls; secondary school students' views; young people
teman akrab   99, 100, 103–4 *see also* friendship
teman curhat   92, 98–9, 100, 105, 106, 108, 109–11, 251 *see also* friendship
terminology and definitions
    for youth   2, 5–7, 59–60, 201
    friendship terms   98–9, 100, 103–4, 106, 110–1, 229–30
    young motherhood   241–2
terror tactics *see* violent activism
tertiary education   14, 41–2, 150, 243
    cost of   41
    enrolments   26, 36
    outmigration for   75
    parental support of students   78–86, 88–9
    views of Sorowako people   72–3, 78, 79–86, 88–9
texting   161, 163, 166, 167, 168, 169 *see also* mobile phones
time (situated practice)   159–60, 164–5, 168–9, 171
time allocation of teenagers   53–4, 63
tourism   145, 151
traditional arts and crafts   148–9
transitions (youth)   23–43, 228
    AAI research project   23–4, 28–30
    in developing versus western countries   23–4, 27–8
    education and *see* education
    facilitated by friendship   93
    housing   27–8
    markers of   6, 7, 23, 25–8, 35, 42, 69, 241, 246
    marriage and family   26–7, 69, 70, 88, 241
    teenagers' views   59–60, 81–2
    work   26
    young mothers in Lombok   250–8
Twitter   62

unemployment   14, 26, 35, 48, 59, 200, 203
uniforms *see* clothing
United Nations definitions of "youth" and "child"   6–7
universities   36, 41, 81, 137, 144, 149 *see also* tertiary education

university students' views
    Ambivalent Adolescents (AAI) project data   28–42
    Kali Loro people   57–67
    on *pergaulan bebas*   233–5
    Sorowako people   78–89
urbanization   10, 14–5, 28, 59, 135, 203
Urban Poverty Program   146, 147
urban youth population   135

victimhood   15–6
violence   15–6, 142, 145, 180–1, 185, 188, 192–3, 201
violent activism   12, 117–8, 178, 200–2, 205, 210–2
virginity   111, 231, 232, 233

waria   140
Western ideal of friendship   96
Western imperialism   204–8, 210
Westernisation   142, 145, 146, 148–9, 208, 209, 216, 219
West Sumatra   30
    Minangkabau people *see* Minangkabau young people, West Sumatra
Wirakarya Community Development Camps   116
women
    control of   220, 235
    roles   222
    women's rights   158–9 *see also* gender
    see also girls; young mothers from Lombok; young women
work   26, 32–7, 42
    aspirations   35–7, 69
    teenagers' involvement in   53–4, 63, 75, 85, 141
    teenagers' views on   57–9
    see also employment opportunities; livelihood
working girls' friendships   108–10
World Bank   5, 26, 146

Yayasan Pondok Rakyat   142
Yogyakarta   30
    1970s New Order   137–41
    1980–1990s global impact   141–6
    2000s global horizons   146–51
    alcohol production/consumption   144–5

INDEX

Bumen *kampung* 150
kampung community and social life 139–40, 143
kampung employment 145, 146, 150
kampung open space 139–40, 143, 151
kampung remaja 138–9, 142, 143–52
kampung residents 137–40
Ledok *kampung* 135, 138–40, 142, 143, 144–6, 147, 150, 151
marginalisation of *kampung* labor and skills 143, 145
Pandeyan *kampung* 148–9
religious activity 149
Samirono *kampung* 142, 148, 151
Sidomulyo *kampong* 140
streetside youth 137, 139, 141, 142, 144
student population 137, 138–9, 142, 144, 148, 149
student views on *pergaulan bebas* 222–36
youth, impact of change 132–7, 151–2
young men 12, 64
activism *see* violent activism; youth political action
adult status 27
freedom 136, 157
friendships 96–7, 99–100
involvement in work 53–4, 200-
streetwise masculinity, Ambon 180–98
young mothers from Lombok 216–7, 241–58
circumstances 242–3
employment 254–5, 257
female friends 250–2
social identity 248–52, 254, 255, 256–8
social isolation 250–2, 256–7
transition from single adolescent 250–8
'young mothers' defined 241–2
young people
aspirations *see* aspirations
claiming space 209–11
concerns 222–6
friendship *see* friendship
in Kali Loro *see* Kali Loro village
in Kota Sejuk *see* Kota Sejuk
in Lombok see young mothers from Lombok

in Sorowako *see* Sorowako
in Yogyakarta *see* Yogyakarta
young women 12–3, 27
aspirations 32–4, 42
control of 220, 235
freedom 136, 158
friendship *see* friendship
involvement in work 53–4
Muslim discourse on behavior 158–9, 170–1, 229–30, 232–3
normal and choice biographies 226–33, 235
obstacles to education 41
sexuality 12–3, 220, 226–36, 245, 247–8, 256
socializing 63, 100–8, 156–7, 159–71
views on *pergaulan bebas* 226–36
see also girls; young mothers
youth
definitions 5–7, 59–60, 201
impact of change over time 134–7, 151–2
prolongation of 6–7, 49, 52–3, 67, 69–70, 258
urban population 135
see also childhood
youth alienation 11–2, 143, 145, 147, 204
youth culture 5, 10, 209–10
masculine, Ambon 180–98
socializing 161–9
Youth of the People (Pemuda Rakjat) Group 117
youth organizations 11–2, 63, 65, 117–8, 123, 200–1 *see also* Muslim paramilitary groups; Scouts (Pramuka) organization
youth political action 8–12, 135–6, 179–80, 192–3, 200–12
youth studies 4–6, 12–3, 50, 157, 256
approaches 19
on friendship 95–8
"generation" concept 7–10
representation of young mothers 256
research protocols 16–9
youth transition *see* transitions (youth)
youth trends (survey) 24–5
youth well-being 35
Yudhoyono, Susilo Bambang 203

Zionism 205, 207, 211